Praxis II

Pennsylvania Grades 4-8 Core Assessment (5152) Exam

Secrets Study Guide

Part 3 of 3

Dear Future Exam Success Story

First of all, **THANK YOU** for purchasing Mometrix study materials!

Second, congratulations! You are one of the few determined test-takers who are committed to doing whatever it takes to excel on your exam. **You have come to the right place.** We developed these study materials with one goal in mind: to deliver you the information you need in a format that's concise and easy to use.

In addition to optimizing your guide for the content of the test, we've outlined our recommended steps for breaking down the preparation process into small, attainable goals so you can make sure you stay on track.

We've also analyzed the entire test-taking process, identifying the most common pitfalls and showing how you can overcome them and be ready for any curveball the test throws you.

Standardized testing is one of the biggest obstacles on your road to success, which only increases the importance of doing well in the high-pressure, high-stakes environment of test day. Your results on this test could have a significant impact on your future, and this guide provides the information and practical advice to help you achieve your full potential on test day.

Your success is our success

We would love to hear from you! If you would like to share the story of your exam success or if you have any questions or comments in regard to our products, please contact us at **800-673-8175** or **support@mometrix.com**.

Thanks again for your business and we wish you continued success!

Sincerely,
The Mometrix Test Preparation Team

Need more help? Check out our flashcards at:
http://MometrixFlashcards.com/PraxisII

Written and edited by the Mometrix Exam Secrets Test Prep Team
Printed in the United States of America

TABLE OF CONTENTS

Science

Earth and Space Science

Plate Tectonics

Main Concepts

Plate tectonics is a geological theory that was developed to explain the process of continental drift. The theoretical separation of the Earth's lithosphere and asthenosphere is based upon the mechanical properties of the materials in the two respective layers and is distinct from the chemical separation of Earth's crust, mantle, and core. According to the theory of plate tectonics, the Earth's lithosphere is divided into **ten major plates**: African, Antarctic, Australian, Eurasian, North American, South American, Pacific, Cocos, Nazca, and Indian; it floats atop the asthenosphere. The plates of the lithosphere abut one another at plate boundaries (divergent, convergent, or transform fault), where the formation of topological features of Earth's surface begins.

Theory

This theory of plate tectonics arose from the fusion of **continental drift** (first proposed in 1915 by Alfred Wegener) and **seafloor spreading** (first observed by Icelandic fishermen in the 1800s and later refined by Harry Hess and Robert Dietz in the early 1960s) in the late 1960s and early 1970s. Prior to this time, the generally accepted explanation for continental drift was that the continents were floating on the Earth's oceans. The discovery that mountains have "roots" (proved by George Airy in the early 1950s) did not categorically disprove the concept of floating continents; scientists were still uncertain as to where those mountainous roots were attached. It was not until the identification and study of the Mid-Atlantic Ridge and magnetic striping in the 1960s that plate tectonics became accepted as a scientific theory. Its conception was a landmark event in the field of Earth sciences—it provided an explanation for the empirical observations of continental drift and seafloor spreading.

Tectonic Plate Motion

The two main sources of **tectonic plate motion** are **gravity** and **friction**. The energy driving tectonic plate motion comes from the dissipation of heat from the mantle in the relatively weak asthenosphere. This energy is converted into gravity or friction to incite the motion of plates. Gravity is subdivided by geologists into ridge-push and slab-pull. In the phenomenon of **ridge-push**, the motion of plates is instigated by the energy that causes low-density material from the mantle to rise at an oceanic ridge. This leads to the situation of certain plates at higher elevations; gravity causes material to slide downhill. In **slab-pull**, plate motion is thought to be caused by cold, heavy plates at oceanic trenches sinking back into the mantle, providing fuel for future convection. Friction is subdivided into mantle drag and trench suction. Mantle drag suggests that plates move due to the friction between the lithosphere and the asthenosphere. Trench suction involves a downward frictional pull on oceanic plates in subduction zones due to convection currents.

Review Video: Plate Tectonic Theory
Visit mometrix.com/academy and enter code: 535013

Convergent Plate Boundaries

A **convergent** (destructive) **plate boundary** occurs when adjacent plats move toward one another. The Earth's diameter remains constant over time. Therefore, the formation of new plate material at diverging plate boundaries necessitates the destruction of plate material elsewhere. This process occurs at convergent (destructive) plate boundaries. One plate slips underneath the other at a subduction zone. The results of converging plates vary, depending on the nature of the lithosphere in said plates. When two oceanic plates converge, they form a deep underwater trench. If each of the converging plates at a destructive boundary carries a continent, the light materials of the continental lithosphere enables both plates to float above the subduction area. They crumple and compress, creating a mid-continent mountain range. When a continental plate converges with an oceanic plate, the denser oceanic lithosphere slides beneath the continental lithosphere. The result of such convergence is an oceanic trench on one side and a mountain range on the other.

Divergent Plate Boundary

A **divergent**, or constructive, **plate boundary** exists when two adjacent plates move away from one another. Observation of activity at diverging boundaries provided unquestionable proof of the seafloor-spreading hypothesis. At this type of plate boundary, kinetic energy generated by asthenospheric convection cells cracks the lithosphere and pushes molten magma through the space left by separating tectonic plates. This magma cools and hardens, creating a new piece of the Earth's crust. In the oceanic lithosphere, diverging plate boundaries form a series of rifts known as the oceanic ridge system. The Mid-Atlantic Ridge is a consequence of undersea diverging boundaries. At divergent boundaries on the continental lithosphere, plate movement results in rift valleys, typified by the East African Rift Valley.

Transform Plate Boundary

A **transform** (conservative) **plate boundary** exists when two tectonic plates slide past each other laterally and in opposite directions. Due to the rocky composition of lithospheric plates, this motion causes the plates to grind against each other. Friction causes stress to build when the plates stick; this potential energy is finally released when the built-up pressure exceeds the slipping point of the rocks on the two plates. This sudden release of energy causes earthquakes. This type of plate boundary is also referred to as a **strike-slip fault**. The San Andreas Fault in California is the most famous example of such a boundary.

Geologic Faults

A **geologic fault** is a fracture in the Earth's surface created by movement of the crust. The majority of faults are found along **tectonic plate boundaries**; however, smaller faults have been identified at locations far from these boundaries. There are three types of geologic faults, which are named for the original direction of movement along the active fault line. The landforms on either side of a fault are called the footwall and the hanging wall, respectively. In a **normal fault**, the hanging wall moves downward relative to the footwall. A **reverse fault** is the opposite of a normal fault: The hanging wall moves upward relative to the footwall. The dip of a reverse fault is usually quite steep; when the dip is less than 45 degrees, the fault is called a thrust fault. In the third type of geologic fault, the **strike-slip fault**, the dip is virtually nonexistent, and the footwall moves vertically left (sinistral) or right (dextral). A transform plate boundary is a specific instance of a strike-slip fault.

Geologic Folding

A **geologic fold** is a region of curved or deformed stratified rocks. Folding is one process by which Earth's crust is deformed. Rock strata are normally formed horizontally; however, geologists have identified areas where these strata arc upwards or downwards. **Anticlines** are upfolded areas of rock; downfolds are called synclines. In anticlines, the rocks are oldest along the axis (a horizontal line drawn through the point of the fold's maximum curvature), and in synclines, the youngest rocks are at the axis. **Monoclines**, or flextures, are rock structures that slope in one direction only, and often pass into geologic fault lines. The process of folding usually occurs underneath the Earth's surface, but surface erosion eventually exposes these formations. Folding is generally thought to be caused by the horizontal compression of the Earth's surface, which is related to the movement of tectonic plates and fault activity.

Orogenesis

Orogenesis refers to mountain-building processes, specifically as they relate to the movement of tectonic plates. An individual orogeny can take millions of years. Generally, mountains are created when compressional forces push surface rock upward, resulting in a landform that is higher than the land around it. There are four broad categories of mountains (which are not mutually exclusive); these categories are based on the mountain's formative origin. **Folded mountains**, formed from the long-term deformation and metamorphosis of sedimentary and igneous rocks, usually occur in chains. This type of mountain often forms at convergent plate boundaries. **Fault-block mountains** occur at normal or reverse faults with high dips. Portions of Earth's crust are vertically displaced along the faults. **Oceanic ridges** are formed at divergent boundaries beneath the ocean. When plates move apart, material from the mantle rises up and creates long mountain chains. **Volcanic mountains** form from the accumulation of products of volcanic eruptions, such as ash and lava. They often occur singularly, unlike other mountain types that usually exist in chains.

Continental Drift

Continental drift is a theory that explains the separation and movement of the continents based on shifts in a plastic layer of Earth's interior caused by the planet's rotation (seafloor spreading). Continental drift is part of the larger theory of plate tectonics. In the early twentieth century, many scientists and scholars noted that the edges of certain continents seemed to look like connecting pieces of a puzzle. Due to this observation, as well as the fact that similar geologic features, fossils, fauna, and flora existed on the Atlantic coasts of continents like South America and Africa, these observers theorized the previous existence of a supercontinent (referred to as Pangaea), in which all of the discrete continents identifiable today were joined together.

Continental Crust

The **continental crust** (sial) is 10–50 kilometers thick. It is more complex and locally variable than the oceanic crust. There is a correlation between the thickness of the sial and the age of the last orogenic (mountain-forming) event recorded at the surface: The thinnest crust occurs in areas of the oldest orogenic activity, and the thickest crust is located near present-day mountain chains. The continental crust consists of two layers separated by a seismic velocity discontinuity located 8–10 kilometers below the surface. The upper layer has an average density of 2,670 $\frac{\text{kg}}{\text{m}^3}$ and is composed mainly of granite. This layer exhibits thermal energy related to the activity of radioactive elements. The lower layer has gabbroic properties and an average density of 3,000 $\frac{\text{kg}}{\text{m}^3}$. The temperature of this layer is thought to be below the melting point of its component rocks and minerals and is extremely variable, depending on the presence of volatiles (elements such as water, carbon dioxide, and sulfur).

Oceanic Crust

The **oceanic crust** (sima) is 5–10 kilometers thick. It is remarkably uniform in composition and thickness and consists of a layer of sediments (fossils of marine life and continental debris) that overlies three distinct layers of igneous rock. The first of these is 1–2.5 kilometers thick and is made up of basaltic lavas. The second, main igneous layer is 5 kilometers thick and is of coarse-grained gabbroic composition. The third layer is very thin (less than half a kilometer thick) and possesses a density of 3,000 $\frac{\text{kg}}{\text{m}^3}$; this layer is made up of basalts. The temperature of the sima is very high along seismically active ridges and lower near oceanic basins. Based on dating of the fossils present in its sediments, scientists estimate that the oceanic crust is only 200 million years old (in comparison, the continental crust is estimated to be several billion years old). The relatively young age of the oceanic crust provides support for theories of the creative/destructive processes of seafloor spreading.

Magnetic Striping

Magnetic striping is a manifestation of the magnetic properties of the oceanic lithosphere. In general, the mineral composition of rocks has one of two magnetic orientations: normal polarity, which roughly corresponds with the polarity of the Earth's magnetic north, or reversed polarity, which is basically the opposite of the Earth's magnetic field. Cooled magma, which makes up the basalt of the ocean floor, aligns itself with Earth's current magnetic orientation during the cooling process. While the Earth's magnetic field normally shifts very slowly, it undergoes radical changes, called magnetic reversals, over long periods of time. Diverging plate boundaries on the ocean floor have been forming new crust material for tens of thousands of years, creating new midocean ridges throughout multiple reversals of Earth's magnetic field. Consequently, the ocean floor displays stripes of rocks with opposing polarities. The discovery of magnetic striping in the oceanic crust contributed to widespread acceptance of the seafloor-spreading hypothesis.

Seafloor Spreading

Seafloor spreading was originally put forth as an explanation for the existence of midocean ridges such as the Mid-Atlantic Ridge. These ridges were identified as features of a vast undersea mountain system that spans the globe. Seafloor spreading postulates that the ocean floor expands outward from these ridges. The process occurs when the upper mantle layer of the Earth (the asthenosphere), just beneath the planet's crust, is heated through convection. The heat causes the asthenosphere to become more elastic and less dense. This heated material causes the crust to bow outward and eventually separate. The lighter material then flows out through the resultant rift and hardens, forming new oceanic crust. If a rift opens completely into an ocean, the basin will be flooded with seawater and create a new sea. Often, the process results in failed rifts, rifts that stopped opening before complete separation is achieved.

Earth's Layers

Chemical Layers

The **crust** is the outermost layer of the Earth. It is located 0–35 kilometers below the surface. Earth's crust is composed mainly of basalt and granite. The crust is less dense, cooler, and more rigid than the planet's internal layers. This layer floats on top of the **mantle**. Located 35–2,890 kilometers below the Earth's surface, the mantle is separated from the crust by the **Mohorovicic discontinuity**, or Moho (which occurs at 30–70 kilometers below the continental crust and at 6–8 kilometers beneath the oceanic crust). The mantle is made up of rocks such as peridotite and eclogite; its temperature varies from 100 to 3,500 degrees Celsius. Material in the mantle cycles due to convection. The innermost layer of the Earth is the core, which consists of a liquid outer layer and a solid inner layer. It is located 2,890–6,378 kilometers below the surface. The core is thought to be composed of iron and nickel and is the densest layer of the Earth.

Sublayers

The **lithosphere** consists of the crust and the uppermost portion of the mantle of the Earth. It is located 0–60 kilometers below the surface. The lithosphere is the cooling layer of the planet's convection cycle and thickens over time. This solid shell is fragmented into pieces called tectonic plates. The oceanic lithosphere is made up of mafic basaltic rocks and is thinner and generally more dense than the continental lithosphere (composed of granite and sedimentary rock); the lithosphere floats atop Earth's mantle. The **asthenosphere** is the soft, topmost layer of the mantle.

It is located 100–700 kilometers below the surface. A combination of heat and pressure keeps the asthenosphere's composite material plastic. The **mesosphere** is located 900–2,800 kilometers below the surface; it therefore spans from the lower part of the mantle to the mantle-core boundary. The liquid **outer core** exists at 2,890–5,100 kilometers below surface level, and the solid inner core exists at depths of 5,100–6,378 kilometers.

Review Video: Earth's Structure
Visit mometrix.com/academy and enter code: 713016

Rock Cycle

The **rock cycle** is the process whereby the materials that make up the Earth transition through the three types of rock: igneous, sedimentary, and metamorphic. Rocks, like all matter, cannot be created or destroyed; rather, they undergo a series of changes and adopt different forms through the functions of the rock cycle. Plate tectonics and the water cycle are the driving forces behind the rock cycle; they force rocks and minerals out of equilibrium and force them to adjust to different external conditions. Viewed in a generalized, cyclical fashion, the rock cycle operates as follows: rocks beneath Earth's surface melt into magma. This **magma** either erupts through volcanoes or remains inside the Earth. Regardless, the magma cools, forming igneous rocks. On the surface, these rocks experience **weathering** and **erosion**, which break them down and distribute the fragments across the surface. These fragments form layers and eventually become **sedimentary rocks**. Sedimentary rocks are then either transformed to **metamorphic rocks** (which will become magma inside the Earth) or melted down into magma.

Rock Formation

Igneous Rocks: Igneous rocks can be formed from sedimentary rocks, metamorphic rocks, or other igneous rocks. Rocks that are pushed under the Earth's surface (usually due to plate subduction) are exposed to high mantle temperatures, which cause the rocks to melt into magma. The magma then rises to the surface through volcanic processes. The lower atmospheric temperature causes the magma to cool, forming grainy, extrusive igneous rocks. The creation of extrusive, or volcanic, rocks is quite rapid. The cooling process can occur so rapidly that crystals do not form; in this case, the result is a glass, such as obsidian. It is also possible for magma to cool down inside the Earth's interior; this type of igneous rock is called intrusive. Intrusive, or plutonic, rocks cool more slowly, resulting in a coarse-grained texture.

Sedimentary Rocks: Sedimentary rocks are formed when rocks at the Earth's surface experience weathering and erosion, which break them down and distribute the fragments across the surface. Fragmented material (small pieces of rock, organic debris, and the chemical products of mineral sublimation) is deposited and accumulates in layers, with top layers burying the materials beneath. The pressure exerted by the topmost layers causes the lower layers to compact, creating solid sedimentary rock in a process called lithification.

Metamorphic Rocks: Metamorphic rocks are igneous or sedimentary rocks that have "morphed" into another kind of rock. In metamorphism, high temperatures and levels of pressure change preexisting rocks physically and/or chemically, which produces different species of rocks. In the rock cycle, this process generally occurs in materials that have been thrust back into the Earth's mantle by plate subduction. Regional metamorphism refers to a large band of metamorphic activity; this often occurs near areas of high orogenic (mountain-building) activity. Contact metamorphism refers to metamorphism that occurs when "country rock" (that is, rock native to an area) comes into contact with high-heat igneous intrusions (magma).

PLATE TECTONICS ROCK CYCLE

The plate tectonics rock cycle expands the concept of the traditional rock cycle to include more specific information about the tectonic processes that propel the rock cycle, as well as an evolutionary component. Earth's materials do not cycle endlessly through the different rock forms; rather, these transitive processes cause, for example, increasing diversification of the rock types found in the crust. Also, the cycling of rock increases the masses of continents by increasing the volume of granite. Thus, the **tectonic rock cycle** is a model of an evolutionary rock cycle. In this model, new oceanic lithosphere is created at divergent plate boundaries. This new crust spreads outward until it reaches a **subduction zone**, where it is pushed back into the mantle, becomes magma, and is thrust out into the **atmosphere**. It experiences erosion and becomes **sedimentary rock**. At convergent continental plate boundaries, this crust is involved in mountain building and the associated metamorphic pressures. It is **eroded** again, and returns to the lithosphere.

ROLE OF WATER

Water plays an important role in the rock cycle through its roles in **erosion** and **weathering**: it wears down rocks; it contributes to the dissolution of rocks and minerals as acidic soil water; and it carries ions and rock fragments (sediments) to basins where they will be compressed into **sedimentary rock**. Water also plays a role in the **metamorphic processes** that occur underwater in newly-formed igneous rock at mid-ocean ridges. The presence of water (and other volatiles) is a vital component in the melting of rocky crust into magma above subduction zones.

Review Video: Igneous, Sedimentary, and Metamorphic Rocks
Visit mometrix.com/academy and enter code: 689294

METAMORPHISM

Metamorphism is the process whereby existing sedimentary, igneous, or metamorphic rocks (protoliths) are transformed due to a change in their original physiochemical environment, where they were mineralogically stable. This generally happens alongside sedimentation, orogenesis, or the movement of tectonic plates. Between the Earth's surface and a depth of 20 kilometers, there exists a wide range of temperatures, pressure levels, and chemical activity. Metamorphism is generally an **isochemical process**, which means that it does not alter the initial chemical composition of a rock. The changes a rock undergoes in metamorphism are usually physical. Neither a metamorphosing rock nor its component minerals are melted during this process—they remain almost exclusively in a solid state. Metamorphism, like the formation of plutonic rock bodies, can be studied only after metamorphic rocks have been exposed by weathering and erosion of the crustal rocks above.

FACTORS

Heat is a primary factor in metamorphism. When extreme heat is applied to existing rocks, their component minerals are able to recrystallize (which entails a reorganization of the grains or molecules of a mineral, resulting in increased density, as well as the possible expulsion of volatiles such as water and carbon dioxide). High levels of thermal energy may also cause rocks to contort and deform. **Pressure** is another factor affecting the metamorphism of rocks. Increased pressure can initiate recrystallization through compression. Pressure forces can also lead to spot-melting at individual grain boundaries. Lithostatic, or confining, pressure is created by the load of rocks above a metamorphosing rock. Pore-fluid pressure results from the release of volatiles due to thermal energy. Directed pressure is enforced in a certain direction due to orogenesis: This type of pressure is responsible for foliation, or layering, which entails parallel alignment of mineral particles in a rock, characteristic of metamorphism. **Chemical activity** affects metamorphism due to the presence of volatiles in pore fluids.

Biogeochemical Cycle

The term biogeochemical cycle refers to one of several chemical processes in which chemical elements are (re)cycled among **biotic** (living) and **abiotic** (nonliving) constituents of an ecosystem. The theory of relativity necessitates the presence of such cycles in nature by virtue of its supposition that energy and matter are not created or destroyed in a closed system such as Earth's ecosystem. Generally, a **biogeochemical cycle** operates as follows: inorganic compounds, such as carbon, are converted from water, air, and soil to organic molecules by organisms called **autotrophs**. **Heterotrophs** (organisms that cannot independently produce their own food) consume the autotrophs; some of the newly formed organic molecules are transferred. Finally, the organic molecules are broken down and processed once again into inorganic compounds by secondary and tertiary consumers and replaced within water, air, and soil. Carbon, nitrogen, and phosphorus provide examples of nutrients that are recycled in the Earth's ecosystem.

Uniformitarianism

Uniformitarianism is a basic tenet of the science disciplines. It states that the processes which made the world the way it is today are still in effect. This means that careful observation and analysis of the natural processes occurring right now can provide information about the processes which formed the world as it is now known. Simply put, it says that "the present is the key to the past."

An associated (but perhaps less generally accepted) idea is that of **gradualism**, which says that the processes which created the world as it is known operated at the same rate that they do now.

The doctrine of **uniformitarianism** is applicable in all scientific disciplines, from geology to the life sciences to astronomy to physics. In geology, uniformitarianism supplanted the theory of catastrophism, which suggested that earth was formed by isolated, catastrophic events, such as Noah's flood.

Stratigraphic Correlation

The law of **superposition** states that in bodies of undisturbed sedimentary rocks, the strata at the bottom are older than the strata at the top. **Stratigraphic correlation** is a method used to determine the "correct" or natural stratigraphic position of rock beds which have been separated by disturbances such as metamorphic processes, orogenies, or plutonic formations. This is achieved through the identification of correspondence between two points in a characteristic such as fossil content, lithology (the physical characteristics of a rock), or geologic age. This practice of (theoretically) realigning beds which have been deformed is helpful in identification of the relative ages of rocks in a sedimentary rock sequence.

Important Terms

Geological stratum - a layer of rock which possesses certain attributes which distinguishes it from adjacent layers of rock. Such attributes include, but are not limited to, lithology, chemical composition, and mineralogy.

Stratigraphy - the study of the arrangement, form, distribution, composition, and succession of rock strata. Information gained from such study is then used to form hypotheses about the strata's origins, environments, relations to organic environments, relations to other geologic concepts, and ages.

Chronostratigraphy - an aspect of stratigraphy which focuses on the relative ages of geologic strata. Scientists examine the physical interrelations of strata, the relations of strata to the sequence of organic evolution, and radioactive ages of strata to determine their chronological sequence. When the relative ages of strata have been identified, scientists can examine the constituents and properties of those strata for clues about the sequence of events which made the world what it is today.

Record of the Earth's History

Rocks

One important way in which rocks provide a record of **earth's history** is through the study of **fossils**, which allows scientists to make inferences about the evolution of life on earth. However, the presentation of fossils is certainly not the only record of earth's history contained in rocks. For instance, the **chemical composition** of rock strata may give indications about the atmospheric and/or hydrospheric compositions at certain points in earth's history. Paleomagnetism constitutes another aspect of earth's historical record contained in rocks. Through the study of magnetic orientations of rocks formed at certain times in history, scientists learn more about the form and function of earth's magnetic field then and now.

Sediments

The study of the **sediments** which make up sedimentary rocks can reveal much about the environment in which they are formed. For example, a study of the **different types** of sediments in a bed, and the **ratios** in which they occur, can indicate the types of rocks exposed at the origination site and the relative abundances of each. Examination of the sorting of a sediment can reveal information about how far the particles traveled from their provenance, as well as the medium which carried the particles. For example, sediments transported by wind tend to be well-sorted, while water moves large particles which are often worn into spheres. The type of weathering experienced by particles in a sedimentary bed can reveal the climate from which they came—mechanical weathering tends to occur in cold and arid climates, while chemical weathering is more common in hot and humid climates. Interpreting the information supplied by sediment can, in turn, reveal information about past conditions on earth.

Soil

The study of **soil development** can give indications of the **age of certain sedimentary deposits**. For example, the study of soil led to the idea that multiple glaciations have occurred on the North American continent. Examination of the development level of certain areas of soil can also inform earth scientists about natural catastrophic events which have occurred in the past. Study of soil deposits also aided in the determination of how often "ice ages" can be expected to occur. Also, the presence of certain types of soil buried deep beneath the surface can provide indications of past climates.

Prehistoric Oceans

The elements present in the earliest oceans were quite different from those present in the Earth's hydrosphere today. This is largely due to the chemical composition of the atmosphere at that time. The oceans were formed when cooling caused atmospheric clouds to condense and produce rain. **Volcanic gasses** contributed elements such as sulfur and carbon dioxide to the air. Therefore, scientists suspect that the earliest oceans contained high levels of acids (for example, sulfuric acid, hydrochloric acid, and hydrofluoric acid), and low levels of the salts that inhabit the oceans today. The temperature in this early ocean was probably close to 100 degrees Celsius. As **carbon dioxide** began to dissolve in the water, it combined with carbonate ions to form limestone which was deposited on the ocean floor. Consequently, more carbon dioxide was trapped in these rocks. Eventually, **calcium carbonate** began to reduce the acidity of these early oceans. **Weathering** brought different minerals into the ocean, which began to increase its saltiness toward its current levels.

Radiometric Dating

Radiometric dating is one of the only methods currently available to determine the absolute age of an object such as a fossil or rock body. This process is possible when such an object contains isotopes, the products of radioactive decay. In radioactive decay, the atoms of certain unstable isotopes are transformed through the emissions of either electrons or alpha particles. This process occurs exponentially until it produces a stable final product. The rate of radioactive decay is measured in half-lives: after one half-life has passed, one-half of the atoms of the original element will have decayed. When scientists examine an object which contains isotopes with known half-life periods, they can determine the amount of the isotope that was present at the time of the object's origin. That figure can then be compared with the present level to determine the age of the object.

Gaia Hypothesis

Named for the Greek goddess who organized a living earth from chaos, the **Gaia hypothesis** states that the planet is a **living system**. While this idea is not scientific in the literal sense, it provides a metaphor which is useful in achieving an understanding of the interconnectedness of all of earth's systems. For example, increased levels of carbon dioxide in the atmosphere breed higher levels of plant growth, and these plants help to regulate the amount of carbon dioxide present in the atmosphere. Feedback mechanisms such as this were known before the formulation of the Gaia hypothesis. However, adherence to this idea requires one to study the planet as a whole, rather than focusing on only one of its many aspects in isolation. The fact that earth's atmosphere is quite different from those of the other planets led to the formulation of this idea.

Geologic Time

Geologic time may be measured absolutely using chronometric time, or relatively using chronostratic time. Measurements of chronometric time are achieved through **radiometric dating** and are expressed numerically in number of years. **Chronostratic time**, which places events in sequences, can be estimated through the study of rock bodies. According to the law of original horizontality, the original orientation of sedimentary beds is nearly always horizontal. Therefore, if one observes deformed or slanted strata, the event which disoriented the strata must have occurred after the strata were deposited. Also, a rock body that cuts across another must be newer than the rock body it intersects. Similarly, for a layer of rock to experience erosion and weathering, it must already exist on the surface. These destructive processes can lead to interruptions in the geologic record. Sometimes, sediments are deposited atop a weathered and eroded surface. Such an occurrence is called an unconformity. The most common method used to establish chronostratic time is through stratigraphy, as the name suggests.

Relative geologic time is divided into different units, including two recognized eons: the **Precambrian**, of which little is known due to limited fossil evidence that only reveals ultra-primitive life forms; and the **Phanerozoic**, for which fossil evidence is more abundant and reveals more evolved life forms. **Eons** are the largest units of geologic time.

Scientists also recognize three eras: the Paleozoic, the Mesozoic, and the Cenozoic. Eras contain periods, and periods contain epochs. These units are delineated largely by the conceptions used to divide historical time. They are arranged in a sequence through chronostratigraphy and classified largely on the basis of the fossils found in their associated strata.

Paleontology

Paleontology is the study of ancient plant and animal life. The bulk of information on this subject is provided by the fossil record, which consists of fossilized plants, animals, tracks, and chemical residues preserved in rock strata. There are three general subdivisions within the field of paleontology. The first, **paleozoology**, is the study of ancient animal life, including vertebrate and invertebrate specializations, as well as paleoanthropology, the study of fossil hominids. The second is **paleobotany**, the study of ancient plant life. The third, **micropaleontology**, is the study of microfossils. This field of scientific inquiry is useful in identifying the evolutionary processes that gave rise to present-day life forms. Paleontology also contributes to an understanding of the ways that environmental and geological factors affected evolution.

Evolution

Evolution is the process whereby organisms pass certain acquired traits to successive generations, affecting the attributes of later organisms and even leading to the creation of new species. Charles Darwin is the name often associated with the formulation of natural selection, a vital component of evolution as it is known today. **Natural selection** states that members of a species are not identical—due to their respective genetic make-ups, each individual will possess traits which make it stronger or weaker and more or less able to adapt. The other tenet of natural selection is that members of a species will always have to compete for scarce resources to survive. Therefore, organisms with traits which will help them survive are more likely to do so and produce offspring, passing along the "desirable" traits. Darwin suggested that this process, by creating groups of a species with increasingly different characteristics, would eventually lead to the formation of **a new species**.

Significant Events Leading to Evolution of Man

The **origination of life** is the most fundamental development in the history of life on Earth. Prokaryotic microfossils, the earliest fossils identified by paleontologists, are dated to near 3.5 billion years ago. However, the presence of large amounts of certain carbon and oxygen isotopes in sedimentary rocks dated at about 3.8 billion years ago may indicate the presence of organic material. The next significant event suggested by a drastic change in the fossil record is the huge diversification of species which occurred approximately 543 million years ago, near the end of the Precambrian eon and the beginning of the Phanerozoic. This theoretical evolutionary stage included higher-level tissue organization in multicellular organisms, the development of predator-prey relationships, and, most importantly, the development of skeletons. The final critical step toward the evolution of man is the emergence of life on land about 418 million years ago. This necessitated the evolution of structures which could breathe air, obtain and retain water on land, and support its own weight out of water.

Hydrologic Cycle

The **hydrologic (water) cycle** refers to the circulation of water in the Earth's hydrosphere (below the surface, on the surface, and above the surface of the Earth). This continuous process involves five physical actions. Evaporation entails the change of water molecules from a liquid to gaseous state. Liquid water on the Earth's surface (often contained in a large body of water) becomes water vapor and enters the atmosphere when its component molecules gain enough kinetic (heat) energy to escape the liquid form. As the vapor rises, it cools and therefore loses its ability to maintain the gaseous form. It begins to the process of condensation (the return to a liquid or solid state) and forms clouds. When the clouds become sufficiently dense, the water falls back to Earth as precipitation. Water is then either trapped in vegetation (interception) or absorbed into the surface (infiltration). Runoff, caused by gravity, physically moves water downward into oceans or other water bodies.

Evaporation

Evaporation is the change of state in a substance from a liquid to a gaseous form at a temperature below its boiling point (the temperature at which all of the molecules in a liquid are changed to gas through vaporization). Some of the molecules at the surface of a liquid always maintain enough heat energy to escape the cohesive forces exerted on them by neighboring molecules. At higher temperatures, the molecules in a substance move more rapidly, increasing their number with enough energy to break out of the liquid form. The rate of evaporation is higher when more of the surface area of a liquid is exposed (as in a large water body, such as an ocean). The amount of moisture already in the air also affects the rate of evaporation—if there is a significant amount of water vapor in the air around a liquid, some evaporated molecules will return to the liquid. The speed of the evaporation process is also decreased by increased atmospheric pressure.

Condensation

Condensation is the phase change in a substance from a gaseous to liquid form; it is the opposite of evaporation or vaporization. When temperatures decrease in a gas, such as water vapor, the material's component molecules move more slowly. The decreased motion of the molecules enables intermolecular cohesive forces to pull the molecules closer together and, in water, establish hydrogen bonds. Condensation can also be caused by an increase in the pressure exerted on a gas, which results in a decrease in the substance's volume (it reduces the distance between particles). In the hydrologic cycle, this process is initiated when warm air containing water vapor rises and then cools. This occurs due to convection in the air, meteorological fronts, or lifting over high land formations.

Precipitation

Precipitation is water that falls back to Earth's surface from the atmosphere. This water may be in the form of rain, which is water in the liquid form. Raindrops are formed in clouds due to the process of condensation. When the drops become too heavy to remain in the cloud (due to a decrease in their kinetic energy), gravity causes them to fall down toward Earth's surface. Extremely small raindrops are called drizzle. If the temperature of a layer of air through which rain passes on its way down is below the freezing point, the rain may take the form of sleet (partially frozen water). Precipitation may also fall in the form of snow, or water molecules sublimated into ice crystals. When clumps of snowflakes melt and refreeze, hail is formed. Hail may also be formed when liquid water accumulates on the surface of a snowflake and subsequently freezes.

Transportation of Water in the Water Cycle

In the **hydrologic cycle**, the principal movement of water in the atmosphere is its transport from the area above an ocean to an area over land. If this transport did not occur, the hydrologic cycle would be less a cycle than the vertical motion of water from the oceans to the atmosphere and back again. Some evaporated water is transported in the form of clouds consisting of condensed water droplets and small ice crystals. The clouds are moved by the jet stream (strong winds in the upper levels of the atmosphere that are related to surface temperatures) or by surface winds (land or sea breezes). Most of the water that moves through the atmosphere is water vapor (water in the gaseous form).

Review Video: Hydrologic Cycle
Visit mometrix.com/academy and enter code: 426578

Layers of the Atmosphere

The **atmosphere** consists of 78% nitrogen, 21% oxygen, and 1% argon. It also includes traces of water vapor, carbon dioxide and other gases, dust particles, and chemicals from Earth. The atmosphere becomes thinner the farther it is from the Earth's surface. It becomes difficult to breathe at about 3 km above sea level. The atmosphere gradually fades into space.

The main layers of the Earth's atmosphere (from lowest to highest) are:

- **Troposphere** (lowest layer): where life exists and most weather occurs; elevation 0–15 km
- **Stratosphere**: has the ozone layer, which absorbs UV radiation from the sun; hottest layer; where most satellites orbit; elevation 15–50 km
- **Mesosphere**: coldest layer; where meteors will burn up; elevation 50–80 km
- **Thermosphere**: where the international space station orbits; elevation 80–700 km
- **Exosphere** (outermost layer): consists mainly of hydrogen and helium; extends to ~10,000 km

Review Video: Earth's Atmosphere
Visit mometrix.com/academy and enter code: 417614

Tropospheric Circulation

Most weather takes place in the **troposphere**. Air circulates in the atmosphere by convection and in various types of "cells." Air near the equator is warmed by the Sun and rises. Cool air rushes under it, and the higher, warmer air flows toward Earth's poles. At the poles, it cools and descends to the surface. It is now under the hot air, and flows back to the equator. Air currents coupled with ocean currents move heat around the planet, creating winds, weather, and climate. Winds can change direction with the seasons. For example, in Southeast Asia and India, summer monsoons are caused by air being heated by the Sun. This air rises, draws moisture from the ocean, and causes daily rains. In winter, the air cools, sinks, pushes the moist air away, and creates dry weather.

Weather

Weather is the result of transfers of kinetic (heat) energy due to differences in temperature between objects as well as transfers of moisture in Earth's atmosphere. **Meteorology**, the study of weather, covers the same natural events as climatology, but observes them on a shorter time scale (usually no more than a few days). Rain, fog, snow, and wind are all examples of weather phenomena. The processes that occur at different stages in the hydrologic cycle form the basis of meteorological events. Most of the activity that produces the weather we experience on Earth takes place in the **troposphere**, the lowest level of the atmosphere. Atmospheric pressure, temperature, humidity, elevation, wind speed, and cloud cover are all factors in the study of weather.

Ozone Layer

The **Earth's ozone layer** is the region of the stratosphere with a high concentration of ozone (a form of oxygen) particles. These molecules are formed through the process of **photolysis**, which occurs when ultraviolet light from the sun collides with oxygen molecules (O_2) in the atmosphere. The ultraviolet radiation splits the oxygen atoms apart; when a free oxygen atom strikes an oxygen molecule, it combines with the molecule to create an **ozone particle** (O_3). Ozone molecules may be broken down by interaction with nitrogen-, chlorine-, and hydrogen-containing compounds, or by thermal energy from the sun. Under normal conditions, these creative and destructive processes balance the levels of ozone in the stratosphere. The concentration of ozone molecules in the atmosphere absorbs ultraviolet radiation, thus preventing this harmful energy from reaching the Earth's surface. Ozone particles form in the region of the atmosphere over the equator, which receives the most direct sunlight. Atmospheric winds then disperse the particles throughout the rest of the stratosphere.

Air Mass

An **air mass** is a body of air that exhibits consistent temperatures and levels of moisture throughout. These (usually large) pockets of air tend to come together under relatively still conditions, where air can remain in one place long enough to adopt the temperature and moisture characteristics of the land below it; this often occurs above wide areas of flat land. The region in which an air mass originates and the course of its motion are used to name it. For example, a maritime tropical air mass (denoted mT) is formed over the Gulf of Mexico (a tropical climate) and moves across the Atlantic Ocean (a maritime area). The conditions of an air mass will remain constant as long as the body is still, but when it moves across surfaces with different conditions, it may adopt those qualities. For example, polar air that moves over tropical land areas will be heated by the conditions below. Generally, maritime air masses contain high levels of moisture, and continental air masses are drier.

Meteorological Depression

A **meteorological depression** refers to a **low-pressure zone** (created by rising air) situated between 30- and 60-degrees latitude. These zones vary from approximately 321–3,218 kilometers in diameter. The rising air associated with a depression usually condenses at higher levels in the atmosphere and causes precipitation. Depressions are formed when warm air masses and cold air masses converge. At first, a single front (boundary between converging masses of air with different temperatures) separates the air masses.

A distortion similar to the crest of a water wave develops, creating a small center of low pressure. Then, differentiated warm and cold fronts develop from that center. A mass of warm air forms and rises over the body of cold air. The cold front and the cold air eventually catch up with the warm air, creating an occluded front and causing pressure to rise, effectually slowing the depression's movement. Depressions usually have life spans of four to seven days.

Prevailing Winds and Wind Belts

Wind (the horizontal movement of air with respect to Earth's surface) forms due to pressure gradients (differences) in the atmosphere. Air tends to move from areas of **high pressure** (such as the poles) to areas of **low pressure** (such as the tropics). Prevailing winds, or trade winds, are the winds (named in meteorology for the direction they come from) that blow most frequently in a particular region. For instance, the prevailing winds most common in the region from 90 to 60 degrees north latitude blow from the northeast, and are generally called the Polar Easterlies. Wind belts are created in areas where prevailing winds converge with other prevailing winds or air masses. The Inter-Tropical Convergence Zone (ITCZ), where air coming from tropical areas north and south of the equator come together, is an example of a wind belt.

Coriolis Force

The **Coriolis force**, which gives rise to the **Coriolis effect**, is not really a force at all. Rather, it appears to be there to us because the Earth is a rotating frame of reference and we are inside it. In the atmosphere, air tends to move from areas of high pressure to areas of lower pressure. This air would move in a straight line but for the Coriolis force, which appears to deflect the air and cause it to **swirl**. Really, however, the Earth moves underneath the wind, which creates the impression of swirling air to someone standing on the Earth's surface. The Coriolis force causes winds to swing to the right as they approach the Northern Hemisphere and to the left as they approach the Southern Hemisphere.

Air Stability in the Atmosphere

Air stability is the tendency for air to rise or fall through the atmosphere under its own power. Heated air rises because it is less dense than the surrounding air. As a pocket of air rises, however, it will expand and become cooler with changes in atmospheric pressure. If the ambient air into which rising air ascends does not cool as quickly with altitude as the rising air does, that air will rapidly become cooler (and heavier) than the surrounding air and descend back to its original position. The air in this situation is said to be stable. However, if the air into which the warm pocket rises becomes colder with increased altitude, the warm air will continue its ascent. In this case, the air is unstable. Unstable air conditions (such as those that exist in depressions) lead to the formation of large clouds of precipitation.

Clouds

The four main **types of clouds** are cirrus, cumulous, nimbus, and stratus. A **cirrus** cloud forms high in a stable atmosphere, generally at altitudes of 6,000 meters or higher. Temperatures at these altitudes (in the troposphere) decrease with increased altitude; therefore, the precipitation in a cirrus cloud adopts the form of ice crystals. These usually thin traces of clouds may indicate an approaching weather depression. A cumulous cloud is a stereotypical white, fluffy ball. **Cumulous** clouds are indicators of a stable atmosphere, and also of the vertical extent of convection in the atmosphere—condensation and cloud formation begin at the flat base of a cumulous cloud. The more humid the air, the lower a cumulous cloud will form. A **nimbus** cloud is, generally speaking, a rain cloud. Nimbus clouds are usually low, dark, and formless, sometimes spanning the entire visible sky. A **stratus** cloud is basically a cloud of fog which forms at a distance above the Earth's surface. This type of cloud forms when weak convective currents bring moisture just high enough to initiate condensation (if the temperature is below the dew point).

The four cloud subtypes are cumulonimbus, cirrostratus, altocumulus, and stratocumulus. A **cumulonimbus** cloud is produced by rapid convection in unstable air. This type of cloud (which is often dark) is formed as a large, tall "tower." Collections of these towers (squall lines) often signal a coming cold front. Thunderstorms often involve cumulonimbus clouds. A **cirrostratus** cloud is an ultra-thin formation with a white tint and a transparent quality. An **altocumulus** cloud forms at an altitude from 1,980 to 6,100 meters. Clouds of this type, which appear to be flattened spheres, often form in clumps, waves, or lines. A **stratocumulus** cloud forms as a globular mass or flake. Stratocumulus clouds usually come together in layers or clumps.

Review Video: Clouds
Visit mometrix.com/academy and enter code: 803166

Lightning

Lightning is a natural electrostatic discharge that produces light and releases electromagnetic radiation. It is believed that the separation of positive and negative charge carriers within a cloud is achieved by the polarization mechanism. The first step of this mechanism occurs when falling precipitation particles become **electrically polarized** after they move through the Earth's magnetic field. The second step of the polarization mechanism involves **electrostatic induction**, the process whereby electrically charged particles create charges in other particles without direct contact. Ice particles are charged though this method, and then energy-storing electric fields are formed between the charged particles. The positively-charged ice crystals tend to rise to the top of the cloud, effectively polarizing the cloud with positive charges on top and negative charges at the middle and bottom. When charged clouds conglomerate, an electric discharge (a lightning bolt) is produced, either between clouds or between a cloud and the Earth's surface.

Thunderstorms

A **thunderstorm** is a weather phenomenon that includes lightning, thunder, and usually large amounts of precipitation and strong winds. Thunder is the noise made by the rapid expansion and contraction of air due to the heat energy produced by lightning bolts. A thunderstorm develops when heating on the Earth's surface causes large amounts of air to rise into an unstable atmosphere. This results in large clouds of rain and ice crystals. The associated condensation releases high levels of heat, which in turn power the growth cycle of the cloud. The clouds created during thunderstorms are immense, sometimes reaching widths of several miles and extending to heights of 10,000 meters or more. The precipitation in such clouds eventually becomes heavy enough to fall against the updraft of unstable air; the consequent downpour is often short but intense. The differential speeds at which light and sound travel through the atmosphere enable one to estimate the distance between oneself and the storm by observing the interval between a lightning bolt and a thunderclap.

Hurricanes

Hurricanes form when several conditions are met: Oceanic water must be at least 26 degrees Celsius, the general circulation pattern of wind must be disrupted (this disruption usually takes the form of an atmospheric wave in the easterly trade winds), and the Coriolis force must be in effect. During hurricane season (June to November), easterly waves appear in the trade winds every few days. When such a wave occurs over a body of particularly warm, deep water, it is strengthened by the evaporation of warm air from below. Surrounding winds converge at the low-pressure zone created by the wave; air brought by these winds rises because it has nowhere else to go. The large body of warm, moist air rises high into the atmosphere and consequently condenses into huge clouds. As more and more humid air is drawn upward, this air begins to rotate around the area of low pressure. The storm continues to gain strength and may move toward land.

Review Video: Tornadoes
Visit mometrix.com/academy and enter code: 540439

El Nino

El Niño refers to the **unusual warming of surface waters** near the equatorial coast of South America. This phenomenon occurs during the winter approximately every two to seven years, lasting from a few weeks to a few months. El Nino can cause torrential rains, violent winds, drought, and dangerously high temperatures in surrounding areas. El Nino is caused by a reversal of the atmospheric pressures on the eastern and western sides of the Pacific (normally, pressure is high on the eastern side near South America and lower on the western side near the Indonesian coast). This reversal causes a wave of warm water to flow eastward and sea levels to fall on the western side. The changes in air pressure and ocean temperature cause moisture levels in the western Pacific to rise drastically while the region east of the Pacific experiences drought. The air pressure changes also weaken the region's trade winds, which normally serve to distribute heat and moisture.

Monsoons and Savannahs

The term **monsoon** refers to a unique pattern of moving air and currents that occurs when winds reverse direction with a change in season. India and Southeast Asia experience the most intense monsoons. This area lies between tropical and subtropical climate zones. During the winter season, northeasterly winds (which are generally dry) move from high-pressure subtropical areas to lower-pressure tropical areas. During the summer season, the continents of India and Asia heat up, creating a low-pressure zone. This causes winds to reverse and blow southwesterly across the

Indian Ocean, accumulating high levels of moisture, thereby creating large amounts of precipitation during this season.

Savannahs also exist between wet equatorial and dry subtropical climate zones. These regions are characterized by vegetation consisting mainly of shrubs and grass. Savannahs experience dry weather throughout most of the year. A single, brief rainy season that occurs when the Sun is directly above the region interrupts prolonged dry spells.

INFLUENCE OF MOUNTAINS ON CLIMATE

At the level of local climate, the presence of mountains forces air to rise to travel above them; this contributes to increased formation of clouds and consequently, increases in levels of precipitation. Mountain chains can affect regional and even global climates by deflecting airflow. The Coriolis force causes most of Earth's atmospheric airflow to move east and west. Therefore, the presence of north-south–oriented mountain chains can alter general circulation patterns. For example, the Rocky Mountains force air to move northward; the air cools near the North Pole before blowing back down. This causes winter temperatures in Canada and parts of the United States to be very cold.

HUMIDITY AND CLOUD COVER

Humidity is a measure of the amount of water vapor in the air. **Specific humidity** is the expression of humidity as a ratio of aqueous vapor to dry air; it is expressed as a ratio of mass of water vapor per unit mass of natural (dry) air. **Absolute humidity** measures the mass of water vapor in a given volume of moist air or gas; it is expressed in grams per cubic foot or per cubic meter. The equilibrium (or saturated) vapor pressure of a gas is the vapor pressure (created by the movement of molecules) of water vapor when air is saturated with water vapor. **Relative humidity**, usually expressed as a percentage, is the ratio of the vapor pressure of water in air (or another gas) to the equilibrium vapor pressure. In other words, it is a ratio of the mass of water per volume of gas and the mass per volume of a saturated gas. Cloud cover refers to the amount of sky blocked by clouds at a given location.

MEASURING WEATHER

Weather can be measured by a variety of methods. The simplest include measurement of rainfall, sunshine, pressure, humidity, temperature, and cloudiness with basic instruments such as thermometers, barometers, and rain gauges. However, the use of radar (which involves analysis of microwaves reflecting off of raindrops) and satellite imagery grants meteorologists a look at the big picture of weather across, for example, an entire continent. This helps them understand and make predictions about current and developing weather systems. Infrared (heat-sensing) imaging allows meteorologists to measure the temperature of clouds above ground. Using weather reports gathered from different weather stations spread over an area, meteorologists create synoptic charts. The locations and weather reports of several stations are plotted on a chart; analysis of the pressures reported from each location, as well as rainfall, cloud cover, and so on, can reveal basic weather patterns.

GLOBAL WARMING

The **natural greenhouse effect** of the atmosphere is beneficial to life on Earth; it keeps temperatures on the planet 33 degrees higher than they would be without this phenomenon. Originally, this helped sustain life. However, it has been discovered in the last 20 years that this effect is being intensified by the actions of humans. In the twentieth century, certain activities of mankind, including the burning of fossils fuels like coal and oil, have resulted in an **increase in the levels of greenhouse gases** (such as methane and carbon dioxide) being released into the atmosphere. Also, increasing deforestation has affected the number of photosynthesis-practicing plants. The combined effect of these trends is a higher-than-normal concentration of greenhouse gases in the atmosphere. This, in turn, produces the effect of global warming. The average temperature at the Earth's surface has gone up 0.6 degrees Celsius in the last 100 years. Continuation of this trend is likely to have a detrimental effect on many of the planet's ecosystems, including that of human beings.

Earth's Rotation

The **Earth rotates** west to east about its axis, an imaginary straight line that runs nearly vertically through the center of the planet. This rotation (which takes 23 hours, 56 minutes, and 5 seconds) places each section of the Earth's surface in a position facing the Sun for a period of time, thus creating the alternating periods of light and darkness we experience as **day and night**. This rotation constitutes a sidereal day; it is measured as the amount of time required for a reference star to cross the meridian (an imaginary north-south line above an observer). Each star crosses the meridian once every (sidereal) day. Since the speed at which Earth rotates is not exactly constant, we use the mean solar day (a 24-hour period) in timekeeping rather than the slightly variable sidereal day.

Sun

The **Sun** is the vital force of life on Earth; it is also the central component of our solar system. It is basically a sphere of extremely hot gases (close to 15 million degrees at the core) held together by gravity. Some of these gaseous molecules are ionized due to the high temperatures. The balance between its gravitational force and the pressure produced by the hot gases is called **hydrostatic equilibrium**. The source of the solar energy that keeps the Sun alive and plays a key role in the perpetuation of life on Earth is located in the Sun's core, where nucleosynthesis produces heat energy and photons. The Sun's atmosphere consists of the photosphere, the surface visible from Earth, the chromosphere, a layer outside of and hotter than the photosphere, the transition zone (the region where temperatures rise between the chromosphere and the corona), and the corona, which is best viewed at x-ray wavelengths. A solar flare is an explosive emission of ionized particles from the Sun's surface.

Review Video: The Sun
Visit mometrix.com/academy and enter code: 699233

Earth's Revolution Around the Sun

Like all celestial objects in our solar system, planet Earth revolves around the Sun. This process takes approximately 365 1/4 days, the period of time that constitutes a calendar year. The path of the orbit of Earth around the Sun is not circular but **elliptical**. Therefore, the distances between the Earth and the Sun at points on either extreme of this counterclockwise orbit are not equal. In other words, the distance between the two objects varies over the course of a year. At **perihelion**, the minimum heliocentric distance, Earth is 147 million kilometers from the Sun. At **aphelion**, the maximum heliocentric distance, Earth is 152 million kilometers from the Sun. This movement of the Earth is responsible for the apparent annual motions of the Sun (in a path referred to as the ecliptic) and other celestial objects visible from Earth's surface.

Review Video: Astronomy
Visit mometrix.com/academy and enter code: 640556

Review Video: Solar System
Visit mometrix.com/academy and enter code: 273231

SEASONS

The combined effects of Earth's revolution around the Sun and the tilt of the planet's rotational axis create the **seasons**. Earth's axis is not perfectly perpendicular to its orbital plane; rather, it is **tilted** about 23.5 degrees. Thus, at different times of the year, certain areas of the surface receive different amounts of sunlight. For example, during the period of time in Earth's orbit when the Northern Hemisphere is tipped toward the Sun, it is exposed to higher amounts of nearly direct sunlight than at any other time of year (days are longer, and the direction of Sun's rays striking the surface is nearly perpendicular). This period of time is summer in the Northern Hemisphere and winter in the Southern Hemisphere; on the opposite side of the orbit, the seasons are reversed in each hemisphere.

Review Video: Earth's Tilt and Seasons
Visit mometrix.com/academy and enter code: 602892

SUMMER AND WINTER SOLSTICES

The **summer solstice** occurs when Earth's orbital position and axial tilt point the North Pole most directly toward the Sun. This happens on or near June 21 each year. On this day in the Northern Hemisphere, the Sun appears to be directly overhead (at its zenith) at 12:00 noon. The entire Arctic Circle (the north polar region above approximately 66.5 degrees north latitude) is bathed in sunlight for a complete solar day. The North Pole itself experiences constant daylight for six full months. Conversely, the **winter solstice** occurs when the South Pole is oriented most directly toward the Sun. This phenomenon, which falls on or near December 22 each year, orients the Sun as viewed from the Northern Hemisphere at its lowest point above the horizon.

EQUINOXES

The **ecliptic** (the Sun's apparent path through the sky) crosses Earth's equatorial plane twice during the year; these intersections occur when the North Pole is at a right angle from the line connecting the Earth and the Sun. At these times, the two hemispheres experience equal periods of light and dark. These two points in time are respectively referred to as the vernal (spring) equinox (on or about March 21) and the autumnal (fall) equinox (on or about September 23). A calendar year is measured as the length of time between vernal equinoxes.

MOON

Earth's Moon is historically one of the most studied celestial bodies. Its mass is approximately 1.2% of the Earth's mass, and its radius is just over one-fourth of the size of the Earth's radius. Measurements of the Moon's density suggest that its characteristics are similar to those of the rocks that make up Earth's crust. The **landscape** of the Moon consists mostly of mountains and craters formed by collisions of this surface with meteors and other interplanetary materials. The Moon's crust (estimated to be 50 to 100 kilometers in thickness) is made up of a layer of regolith (lunar soil) supported by a layer of loose rocks and gravel. Beneath the crust is a mantle made up of a solid lithosphere and a semiliquid asthenosphere. The Moon's **core** (the innermost 500 kilometers of the body) is not as dense as that of the Earth. The Moon is made up mostly of refractory elements with high melting and boiling points with low levels of heavy elements such as iron.

FORMATION THEORIES

The **fission model** of Moon origin suggests that the Moon is actually a piece of the Earth that split off early during the planet's formation. In this model, a portion of the Earth's mantle fissioned off during a liquid stage in its formation, creating the Moon. According to the **capture model**, the Moon formed elsewhere in the solar system and was subsequently captured by the Earth's gravitational field. The **double-impact model** states that the Earth and the Moon formed during the same period of time from the same accretion material. Each of these theories has its strengths, but none of them can explain all of the properties of the Moon and its relationship to the Earth. Recently, a fourth (widely accepted) hypothesis has been suggested, which involves the **collision** between the Earth and a large asteroid. This hypothetical collision is said to have released a large amount of Earth's crustal material into its orbit; the Moon accreted from that material and the material displaced from the asteroid due to the collision.

EARTH-MOON SYSTEM

While the Moon is commonly referred to as a satellite of the Earth, this is not entirely accurate. The ratio of the masses of the two bodies is much larger than that of any other planet-satellite system. Also, the Moon does not truly **revolve** around the Earth. Rather, the two bodies revolve around a common center of mass beneath the surface of the Earth (approximately 4,800 kilometers from Earth's core). The **orbital planes** of the Moon and the Earth are nearly aligned; therefore, the Moon moves close to the ecliptic, as seen from Earth. Due to the Moon's synchronous rotation (its rotation period and orbital period are equal); the same side of the Moon is always facing Earth. This occurs because of the **mutual gravitational** pull between the two bodies.

PHASES

The **sidereal period** of the Moon (the time it takes the Moon to orbit the Earth with the fixed stars as reference points) is about 27 days. The **lunar month** (or synodic period) is the period of time required for the Moon to return to a given alignment as observed from the Earth with the Sun as a reference point; this takes 29 days, 12 hours, 44 minutes, and 28 seconds. A discrepancy exists between the two periods of time because the Earth and the Moon move at the same time. Sunlight reflected off of the Moon's surface at different times during the lunar month causes its apparent shape to change. The sequence of the Moon's shapes is referred to as the **phases of the Moon**. The full Moon can be viewed when the body is directly opposite from the Sun. The opposite end of the cycle, the new Moon, occurs when the Moon is not visible from Earth because it is situated between the Earth and the Sun.

CONFIGURATIONS

The **configurations of the Moon** describe its position with respect to the Earth and the Sun. We can thus observe a correlation between the phases of the Moon and its configuration. The Moon is at **conjunction** at the time of the new Moon—it is situated in the same direction as the Sun. **Quadrature** (which signals the first quarter phase) is the position of the Moon at a right angle between the Earth-Sun line; we see exactly half of the Moon's sunlit hemisphere. This is the **waxing crescent phase**, in which we see more of the Moon each night. Then comes opposition (which occurs when the Moon lies in the direction opposite the Sun)—we see the full Moon. After this point, the Moon enters its **waning gibbons phase** as it travels back toward quadrature. When it reaches that point again, it has entered the third-quarter phase. Finally, as the Moon circles back toward conjunction, it is in its waning crescent phase.

TERRESTRIAL PLANETS

The term **terrestrial planets** refers to the four planets closest to the Sun (Mercury, Venus, Earth, and Mars). They are classified together because they share many similarities that distinguish them from the giant planets. The terrestrial planets have **high densities and atmospheres** that constitute a small percentage of their total masses. These atmospheres consist mostly of heavy elements, such as carbon dioxide, nitrogen, and water, and are maintained by the gravitational field of the planets (which could not prevent hydrogen from escaping). These planets exhibit magnetic fields of varying intensity. An important characteristic that distinguishes the terrestrial planets from the giant planets is the evidence of various levels of internally generated activity, which caused these planets to evolve from their original states. These processes are thought to have been caused by constant meteoritic impacts during the first few hundred million years of the planets' existence. Radioactive decay of certain isotopes increased the internal temperatures of these planets, leading to volcanic activity on all of the terrestrial planets except Venus.

Mercury

Mercury, the smallest interior planet, is the least well known of the four. This is due to its close proximity to the Sun and high temperatures. Mercury's atmosphere is not very dense; this means that the planet's surface experiences wide temperature differentials from day to night. Mercury's density is close to that of Earth. As the smallest planet known to have experienced planetary evolution, Mercury's internal activity ceased (it became extinct) thousands of millions of years ago. The size of the planet is relevant because less massive bodies cool more quickly than larger ones after cessation of radioactivity. Mercury's surface is characterized by craters produced by meteoritic impact.

Venus

Venus is comparable to Earth in both mass and density. Venus is the brightest planet in the sky (partially due to the fact that it is proximate to the Sun), which makes exploration of its surface difficult. This planet's atmosphere consists mainly of carbon dioxide, with trace amounts of water and carbon oxide molecules, as well as high levels of sulfuric, nitric, and hydrofluoric acids in the clouds that characterize this atmosphere. The concentration of clouds, coupled with the chemical makeup of Venus's atmosphere, result in a strong greenhouse effect at the planet's surface. This surface consists of large plains (thought to be created by either volcanic activity, which remains unproven, or by meteoritic impacts) and large impact craters. The materials that compose Venus's surface are highly radioactive. Some astronomers have suggested past single-plate tectonic activity; again, however, the planet's dense atmosphere makes valid surface observation quite difficult.

Mars

Mars and Earth exhibit many similarities. For example, Mars has an internal structure that includes a central metallic core, a mantle rich in olivine and iron oxide, and a crust of hydrated silicates. Martian soil consists largely of basalts and clay silicate, with elements of sulfur, silicon oxide, and iron oxide. The planet's surface belies high levels of past volcanic activity (though, due to its relatively small mass, it is probably extinct). In fact, Mars is home to the largest known volcano in the solar system. The Martian landscape also includes two major basins, ridges and plateaus, and, most notably, apparent evidence of fluvial (water-based) erosion landforms, such as canyons and canals. It is possible that the past pressures and temperatures on Mars allowed water to exist on the red planet. Some have gone so far as to suggest that this planet was a site of biochemical evolution. So far, however, no evidence of life has been found.

Mars's Satellites

Two Martian satellites have been observed: **Phobos** and **Deimos**. Each of these bodies is ellipsoidal; the circular orbits of the two satellites lie in Mars's equatorial plane. The gravitational forces between this planet and Phobos and Deimos have caused both satellites to settle into synchronous rotation (the same parts of their surfaces are always facing Mars). This feature exerts a braking force on Phobos's orbit. In other words, its orbit is decreasing in size. The relationship between Deimos and Mars is similar to the Earth-Moon system, in which the radius of the satellite's orbit is gradually growing. The differential compositions and densities of Mars and its satellites indicate that Phobos and Deimos probably did not break off from Mars.

Giant Planets

The **large diameters** of Jupiter, Saturn, Uranus, and Neptune gave rise to the name of the category into which they fall. The **hypothetical icy cores** of these planets cause them to exhibit primary atmospheres, because the large levels of mass they accreted prevented even the lightest elements from escaping their gravitational pulls. The atmospheres of the giant planets thus consist mostly of hydrogen and helium. The giant planets do not have solid surfaces like those of the terrestrial planets. Jupiter probably consists of a core (made of ice and rock) surrounded by a layer of metallic hydrogen, which is covered by a convective atmosphere of hydrogen and helium. Saturn is believed to have the same type of core and hydrogen mantle, enriched by the helium missing from the atmosphere, surrounded by a differentiation zone and a hydrogenic atmosphere. Uranus and Neptune probably have the same type of core, surrounded by ionic materials, bounded by methane-rich molecular envelopes. Uranus is the only giant planet that exhibits no evidence of internal activity.

Rings

Each of the four giant planets exhibits **rings**. These are flat disks of fragmented material that orbit just next to their respective planets. Many of the giant planets' smaller satellites are embedded in these rings. There are two main hypotheses regarding the formation of such rings. One theory suggests that the tidal force exerted on a satellite by its planet may surpass the **Roche limit** (the point at which particle cohesion is no longer possible) and break the satellite into fragments, which then collide and become smaller. This material then spreads out and forms a ring. An alternate theory of the formation of the rings of the giant planets suggests that there was unaccreted material left over after the formation of these planets. Below the Roche limit (within a certain vicinity to the planet), these particles could not join together to form satellites and would consequently settle into orbital rings.

Satellites

Each of the giant planets possesses a number of **satellites**. **Jupiter** has over 50 known satellites—they are grouped according to size. Each of the four largest satellites of Jupiter exhibits evidence of internal activity at some point in their evolutions. In fact, Io, the densest satellite and the one closest to Jupiter, is the only celestial body besides Earth known to be currently volcanically active. **Saturn** has 21 satellites. Titan, the second-largest known satellite, has its own atmosphere. The other six largest of Saturn's satellites all have icy surfaces; some of these show evidence of past internal activity. The smaller 14 are relatively unknown. **Uranus** has five satellites. Each of them displays evidence of geological activity, in the form of valleys, smoothed surfaces, cliffs, mountains, and depressions. **Neptune** has eight known satellites. The larger, Triton, is similar to Titan in that it has an atmosphere. The other seven satellites of Neptune are relatively unknown.

Pluto and Charon

Though **Charon** was originally considered a satellite of Pluto, the ninth planet in the solar system, it now appears that the two are more accurately described as a **double-planet system** (largely because of the similarity in the sizes of the two). It is believed that these bodies formed from the solar nebula like most other objects in the solar system. Pluto has a highly irregular orbit, which places it closer to the Sun than Neptune for periods of time. In sharp contrast to its giant neighbors, this planet's density is higher than that of water ice. The surface of Pluto consists of high levels of methane absorbed into ice, with trace amounts of carbon oxide and nitrogen. Charon resembles the major Uranian satellites more so than it does Pluto. It consists of water ice with a siliceous or hydrocarbonate contaminant.

KEPLER'S LAWS

Kepler's laws are a collection of observations about the motion of planets in the solar system. Formulated by Johannes Kepler in the 1600s, these laws are still vital to our understanding of the way the universe works. **Kepler's first law** states that each planet moves in its own elliptical path and that all of these orbits have the Sun as their singular focal point. Before Kepler's discovery, astronomers had assumed that planetary orbits were circular (because the heavens were assumed to be geometrically perfect). **Kepler's second law** says that a straight line between a planet and the Sun sweeps out equal areas in equal time. In other words, planets move quickest in the part of their orbit that is closest to the Sun, and vice versa. **Kepler's third law** states that the further a planet is from the Sun, the longer its orbital period will be. In mathematical terms, the square of a planet's period is inversely proportional to the cube of the radius of its orbit.

STELLAR OBSERVATION

The observation of stars relates to one of three stellar properties: position, brightness, and spectra. **Positional stellar observation** is principally performed through study of the positions of stars on multiple photographic plates. Historically, this type of analysis was done through measurement of the angular positions of the stars in the sky. **Parallax** of a star is its apparent shift in position due to the revolution of the Earth about the Sun; this property can be used to establish the distance to a star. Observation of the **brightness** of a star involves the categorization of stars according to their magnitudes. There is a fixed intensity ratio between each of the six magnitudes. Since stars emit light over a range of wavelengths, viewing a star at different wavelengths can give an indication of its temperature. The analysis of stars' **spectra** provides information about the temperatures of stars—the higher a star's temperature, the more ionized the gas in its outer layer. A star's spectrum also relates to its chemical composition.

BINARY STAR

Binary star systems, of which about fifty percent of the stars in the sky are members, consist of two stars that orbit each other. The orbits of and distances between members of a binary system vary. A **visual binary** is a pair of stars that can be visually observed. Positional measurements of a visual binary reveal the orbital paths of the two stars. Astronomers can identify astrometric binaries through long-term observation of a visible star—if the star appears to wobble, it may be inferred that it is orbiting a companion star that is not visible. An **eclipsing binary** can be identified through observation of the brightness of a star. Variations in the visual brightness of a star can occur when one star in a binary system passes in front of the other. Sometimes, variations in the spectral lines of a star occur because it is in a binary system. This type of binary is a spectroscopic binary.

Review Video: Types of Stars
Visit mometrix.com/academy and enter code: 831934

HERTZSPRUNG-RUSSELL DIAGRAM

The **Hertzsprung-Russell (H-R) diagram** was developed to explore the relationships between the luminosities and spectral qualities of stars. This diagram involves plotting these qualities on a graph, with absolute magnitude (luminosity) on the vertical and spectral class on the horizontal. Plotting a number of stars on the H-R diagram demonstrates that stars fall into narrowly defined regions, which correspond to stages in stellar evolution. Most stars are situated in a diagonal strip that runs from the top-left (high temperature, high luminosity) to the lower-right (low temperature, low luminosity). This diagonal line shows stars in the main sequence of evolution (often called dwarfs). Stars that fall above this line on the diagram (low temperature, high luminosity) are believed to be much larger than the stars on the main sequence (because their high luminosities are not due to higher temperatures than main sequence stars); they are termed giants and supergiants. Stars below the main sequence (high temperature, low luminosity) are called white dwarfs. The H-R diagram is useful in calculating distances to stars.

Stellar Evolution

The life cycle of a star is closely related to its **mass**—low-mass stars become white dwarfs, while high-mass stars become **supernovae**. A star is born when a **protostar** is formed from a **collapsing interstellar cloud**. The temperature at the center of the protostar rises, allowing nucleosynthesis to begin. **Nucleosynthesis**, or hydrogen-burning through fusion, entails a release of energy. Eventually, the star runs out of fuel (hydrogen). If the star is relatively low mass, the disruption of hydrostatic equilibrium allows the star to contract due to gravity. This raises the temperature just outside the core to a point at which nucleosynthesis and a different kind of fusion (with helium as fuel) that produces a carbon nucleus can occur. The star swells with greater energy, becoming a red giant. Once this phase is over, gravity becomes active again, shrinking the star until the degeneracy pressure of electrons begins to operate, creating a white dwarf that will eventually burn out. If the star has a high mass, the depletion of hydrogen creates a supernova.

Supernova

When a star on the main sequence runs out of hydrogen fuel, it begins to burn helium (the by-product of nucleosynthesis). Once helium-burning is complete in a massive star, the mass causes the core temperature to rise, enabling the fusion of carbon, then silicon, and a succession of other atomic nuclei, each of which takes place in a new shell further out of the core. When the fusion cycle reaches iron (which cannot serve as fuel for a nuclear reaction), an iron core begins to form, which accumulates over time. Eventually, the temperature and pressure in the core become high enough for electrons to interact with protons in the iron nuclei to produce neutrons. In a matter of moments, this reaction is complete. The core falls and collides with the star's outer envelope, causing a massive explosion (a supernova). This continues until the neutrons exert degeneracy pressure; this creates a pulsar. In more massive stars, nothing can stop the collapse, which ends in the creation of a black hole.

Meteoroid

A **meteoroid** is a small, solid fragment of material in the solar system. An enormous number of these objects are present in the system. The term meteor is used to refer to such a body when it enters the Earth's atmosphere. Interaction (friction) between meteors and the upper levels of the atmosphere cause them to break up; most disintegrate before they reach the surface. The heat associated with frictional forces causes meteors to glow, creating the phenomena of shooting stars. The meteors that are large enough to avoid complete disintegration, and can therefore travel all the way down through the atmosphere to Earth's surface, are termed meteorites. Analysis of these fragments indicates that these bodies originate from the Moon, Mars, comets, and small asteroids that cross Earth's orbital path. The forceful impacts of meteorites on Earth's surface compress, heat, and vaporize some of the materials of the meteorite as well as crustal materials, producing gases and water vapor.

Asteroid

An **asteroid** is a small, solid planet (planetoid) that orbits the Sun. The orbital paths of most asteroids are between the orbits of Jupiter and Mars. Many of these bodies have been studied extensively and given names; those in the main belt (which tend to be carbonaceous) are classified into subgroups based on their distance from a large, named asteroid (for example, Floras, Hildas, Cybeles). **Atens** are asteroids whose orbits lie between the Earth and the Sun, and Apollos are asteroids with orbits that mimic Earth's. Asteroids may also be classified based on their composition. **C-type** asteroids exhibit compositions similar to that of the Sun and are fairly dark. S-type asteroids are made up of nickel-iron and iron- and magnesium-silicates; these are relatively bright. **Bright asteroids** made up exclusively of nickel-iron are classified as M-type. Observation of the relative brightness of an asteroid allows astronomers to estimate its size.

Interstellar Medium

The **interstellar**, or interplanetary, **medium** (the space between planets and stars) is populated by comets, asteroids, and meteoroids. However, particles exist in this medium on an even smaller scale. Tiny solid bodies (close to a millionth of a meter in diameter) are called **interplanetary dust**. The accumulation of this material in arctic lakes, for example, allows scientists to study it. Such analysis has revealed that these grains are most likely miniscule fragments of the **nuclei of dead comets**. They possess low density, for they are really many microscopic particles stuck together. The interplanetary dust refracts sunlight, which produces a visible (but faint) glow in parts of the sky populated by clouds of this dust. The interstellar medium also contains particle remnants of **dead stars** and **gases** (such as hydrogen molecules ionized by ultraviolet photons). **Black holes** (objects that collapse under their own gravitational forces), which trap photons, are also believed to populate the interstellar medium. Black holes are a form of dark matter.

Dark Matter

Observations of the **gravitational force** in the solar system (based on Kepler's laws) have indicated for years that there are bodies in the system that we cannot see. **Dark matter** (sometimes called missing matter) is thought to account for the unseen masses, though its exact nature is unknown. Some dark matter may simply be **ordinary celestial bodies** too small to be observed from Earth, even with technology such as high-powered telescopes. The presence of MACHOs (massive compact halo objects) has been noted through observation of distant galaxies—at certain times astronomers can discern dips in the brightness of these galaxies, thought to be caused by a large object (a MACHO) passing between Earth and the galaxy under observation. Some have postulated that dark matter is made up of **WIMPs** (weakly interacting massive particles), which do not interact with photons or other forms of electromagnetic radiation; these particles are hypothetical, because astronomers cannot detect or study them.

Eclipses

Eclipses occur when one celestial body obscures the view of another, either partially or completely. A **solar eclipse**, or eclipse of the Sun by the Moon, happens when the Moon passes directly in front of the Sun (as observed from Earth). Alternately, a **lunar eclipse** occurs when the Moon is situated in the Earth's shadow and is therefore completely invisible. These events do not happen every month because of the differential between the orbital planes of the Moon and the Earth—the Moon's orbit is about five degrees off from the ecliptic. The Moon's orbital path is subject to the same precession that occurs in the Earth's rotational axis; this causes the occasional intersection of the orbital planes of the two bodies. Therefore, eclipses are produced by a combination of the effects of the precession of the Moon's orbit, the orbit itself, and the Earth's orbit.

Newton's Law of Gravitation

Newton's law of gravitation (sometimes referred to as the law of universal gravitation) states that the force of gravity operates as an attractive force between all bodies in the universe. Prior to Newton's formulation of this law, scientists believed that two gravitational forces were at work in the universe—that gravity operated differently on Earth than it did in space. Newton's discovery served to unify these two conceptions of gravity. This law is expressed as a mathematical formula:

$F = \frac{GMm}{D^2}$, in which F is the gravitational force, M and m are the masses of two bodies, D is the distance between them, and G is the gravitational constant ($6.67 \times 10^{-11} \frac{\text{m}^3}{\text{kg s}}$). The gravitational attraction between two objects, therefore, depends on the distance between them and their relative masses. Newton's law of gravitation served to clarify the mechanisms by which Kepler's laws operated. In effect, Newton proved Kepler's laws to be true through the development of this law.

Milky Way

The **Milky Way**, which houses the Earth's solar system, is a spiral galaxy. It consists of a central bulging disk, the center of which is referred to as a **nucleus**. Most of a galaxy's visible light comes from stars in this region. The disk is surrounded by a halo of stars and star clusters that spread above, next to, and beneath the nucleus. **Globular clusters** (dense, spherical clusters of ancient stars) are often found in the halo. Spiral arms of high-luminosity stars (from which this type of galaxy gets its name) fan out from the nucleus as well, with stars that are less bright in between. Interstellar dust populates the entire galaxy between celestial bodies. The entire galaxy rotates about the center. While Earth, the Sun, and its solar system are located on the disk, we are far from the center of the Milky Way. The galaxy's mass, determined through the application of Kepler's third law to the Sun's orbit, is about 1,011 solar masses.

Structures of Galaxies

Elliptical galaxies are roughly spherical. Within this category, subgroups based on the degree of flattening exhibited in the galaxy's shape range from E0 (spherical) to E7 (flat). A dwarf elliptical galaxy has a spheroidal shape, with low mass and low luminosity. An S0 galaxy is similar in shape to a spiral galaxy, but lacks spiral arms. Spiral galaxies such as the Milky Way are characterized by disk-like nuclei with spiral arms. Subtypes of this category are determined by the tightness of the spiral arms and the size of the nucleus; a spiral galaxy of Sa type has a large nucleus and tightly wound arms, and an Sc-type galaxy consists of a small nucleus with open spiral arms. A barred spiral galaxy exhibits an elongated nucleus. The subtypes of barred spiral galaxies are determined like those of spiral galaxies. Some irregular galaxies (type I) display a loose spiral structure with high levels of disorganization. Other irregular galaxies (type II) can be of any shape.

Model of the Inflationary Universe

Hubble's law states that the speed at which a galaxy appears to be moving away from the Earth is proportional to its distance from Earth. This relatively simple formula ($v = Hr$, where v is the **velocity of a receding galaxy**, r is its distance from Earth, and H is the Hubble constant) had an important implication at the time that it was developed—the universe is expanding. This fact, in turn, implies that the universe began at a **specific point** in the past. This model suggests that a random conglomeration of quarks and leptons, along with the strong force (all the forces in the universe unified as one), existed in the very dense, very hot, early universe. When the universe was a certain age (about 10–35 seconds old), the strong force separated out from the mass. This enabled the rapid expansion of the particles that formed the universe.

Big Bang Theory

The **theory of the big bang** expands upon the model of the **inflationary universe**. This theory hypothesizes that the early universe consisted of elementary particles, high energy density and high levels of pressure and heat. This single mass experienced a **phase change** (similar to that of freezing water) when it cooled and expanded. This transition caused the early universe to expand exponentially; this period of growth is called **cosmic inflation**. As it continued to grow, the temperature continued to fall. At some point, **baryogenesis** (an unknown process in which quarks and gluons become baryons, such as protons and neutrons) occurred, somehow creating the distinction between matter and antimatter. As the universe continued to cool, the **elementary forces** reached their present form, and **elementary particles** engaged in big bang **nucleosynthesis** (a process that produced helium and deuterium nuclei). **Gravity** became the predominant force governing interactions between particles; this enabled increasing accretion of particles of matter, which eventually formed the universal constituents as we recognize them today.

Life Science

Biochemical Pathways

Autotrophs that use light to produce energy use **photosynthesis** as a biochemical pathway. In eukaryotic autotrophs photosynthesis takes place in chloroplasts. Prokaryotic autotrophs that use inorganic chemical reactions to produce energy use **chemosynthesis** as a biochemical pathway. Heterotrophs require food and use **cellular respiration** to release energy from chemical bonds in the food. All organisms use cellular respiration to release energy from stored food. Cellular respiration can be aerobic or anaerobic. Most eukaryotes use cellular respiration that takes place in the mitochondria.

Photosynthesis

Photosynthesis is a food-making process that occurs in three processes: light-capturing events, light-dependent reactions, and light-independent reactions. In light-capturing events, the thylakoids of the chloroplasts, which contain chlorophyll and accessory pigments, absorb light energy and produce excited electrons. Thylakoids also contain enzymes and electron-transport molecules. Molecules involved in this process are arranged in groups called photosystems. In light-dependent reactions, the excited electrons from the light-capturing events are moved by electron transport in a series of steps in which they are used to split water into hydrogen and oxygen ions. The oxygen is released, and the $NADP^+$ bonds with the hydrogen atoms and forms NADPH. ATP is produced from the excited elections. The light-independent reactions use this ATP, NADPH, and carbon dioxide to produce sugars.

Review Video: Photosynthesis
Visit mometrix.com/academy and enter code: 227035

C_3 and C_4 Photosynthesis

Plants undergo an additional process during photosynthesis that is known as photorespiration. Photorespiration is a wasteful process that uses energy and decreases sugar synthesis. This process occurs when the enzyme rubisco binds to oxygen rather than atmospheric carbon dioxide. There are three different processes that plants use to fix carbon during photosynthesis and these include C_3, C_4, and crassulacean acid metabolism (CAM). Some plants, such as C_4 and CAM plants, can decrease photorespiration and therefore minimize energy lost while C_3 plants, which make up more than 85% of plants, have no special adaptations to stop photorespiration from occuring. C_3 and C_4 plants are named for the type of carbon molecule (three-carbon or four-carbon) that is made during the first step of the reaction. The first step of the C_3 process involves the formation of two three-carbon molecules (3-phosphoglycerate; 3-PGA) from carbon dioxide being fixed by the enzyme. The first step of C_4 photosynthesis is carbon dioxide beign fixed by the enzyme PEP carboxylase, which unlike rubisco does not have the ability to bind to oxygen. This fixation forms a four-carbon molecule (oxaloaceate) and these initial steps occur in the mesophyll cell. Next, oxaloacetate is converted into a malate, a molecule that can enter the bundle sheath cells, and then is broken down to release carbon dioxide. From there, the carbon dioxide is fixed by rubisco as it undergoes the Calvin cycle seen in C_3 photosynthesis. Because C_4 plants undergo an initial step that allows carbon dioxide to be more readily available, with the use of malate, photorespiration is minimized.

Crassulacean Acid Metabolism

Crassulacean acid metabolism (CAM) is a form of photosynthesis adapted to dry environments. While C_4 plants separate the Calvin cycle via space, or by having different cells for different functions and processes, CAM plants separate the processes by time of day. During the night, pores of the plant leaves, called stomata, open to receive carbon dioxide, which combines with PEP carboxylase to form oxaloacetate. Oxaloacetate is eventually converted into malate, which is stored in vacuoles until the next day. During the following day, the stomata are closed and the malate is transported to chloroplasts, where malate is broken down into pyruvate (three-carbon molecule) and carbon dioxide. The carbon dioxide released from malate is used in photosynthesis during the daytime. One advantage of the CAM cycle is that it minimizes loss of water through the stomata during the daytime. A second advantage is that concentrating carbon dioxide in the chloroplasts in this manner increases the efficiency of the enzyme rubisco to fix carbon dioxide and complete the Calvin cycle.

Review Video: Photosynthesis in Chemistry
Visit mometrix.com/academy and enter code: 227035

Aerobic Respiration

Aerobic cellular respiration is a series of enzyme-controlled chemical reactions in which oxygen reacts with glucose to produce carbon dioxide and water, releasing energy in the form of adenosine triphosphate (ATP). Cellular respiration occurs in a series of three processes: glycolysis, the Krebs cycle, and the electron-transport system.

Review Video: Aerobic Respiration
Visit mometrix.com/academy and enter code: 770290

Glycolysis

Glycolysis is a series of enzyme-controlled chemical reactions that occur in the cell's cytoplasm. Each glucose molecule is split in half to produce two pyruvic acid molecules, four ATP molecules, and two NADH molecules. Because two ATP molecules are used to split the glucose molecule, the net ATP yield for glycolysis is two ATP molecules.

Review Video: Glycolysis
Visit mometrix.com/academy and enter code: 466815

Krebs Cycle

The **Krebs cycle** is also called the citric acid cycle or the tricarboxylic acid cycle (TCA). It is a **catabolic pathway** in which the bonds of glucose and occasionally fats or lipids are broken down and reformed into ATP. It is a respiration process that uses oxygen and produces carbon dioxide, water, and ATP. Cells require energy from ATP to synthesize proteins from amino acids and replicate DNA. The cycle is acetyl CoA, citric acid, isocitric acid, ketoglutaric acid (products are amino acids and CO_2), succinyl CoA, succinic acid, fumaric acid, malic acid, and oxaloacetic acid. One of the products of the Krebs cycle is NADH, which is then used in the electron chain transport system to manufacture ATP. From glycolysis, pyruvate is oxidized in a step linking to the Krebs cycle. After the Krebs cycle, NADH and succinate are oxidized in the electron transport chain.

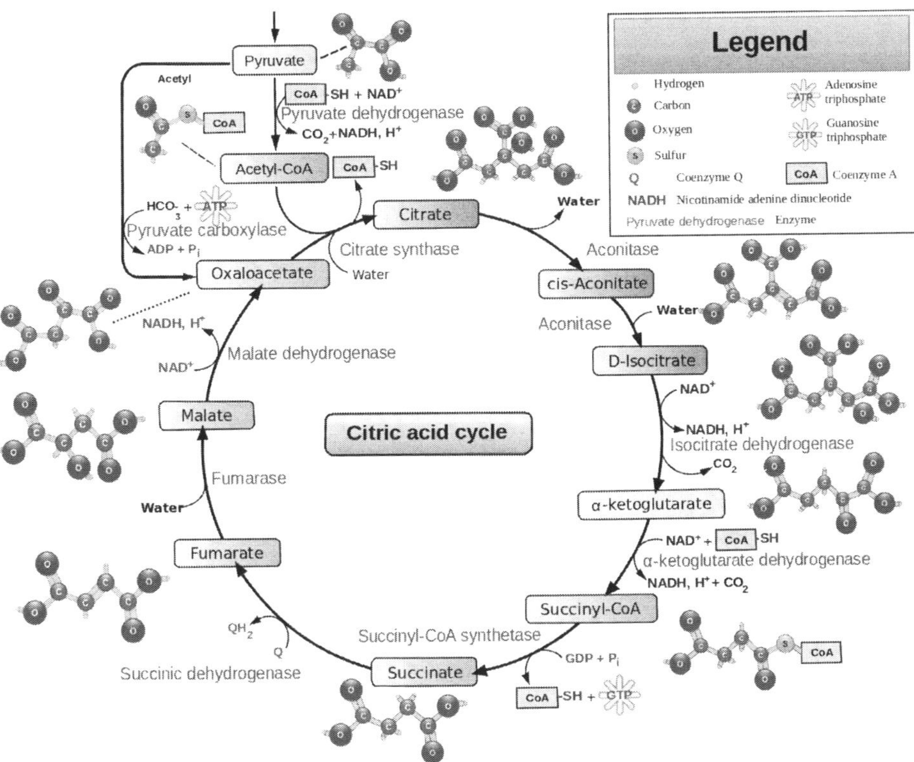

Electron Transport Chain

The **electron transport chain** is part of phosphorylation, whereby electrons are transported from enzyme to enzyme until they reach a final acceptor. The electron transport chain includes a series of oxidizing and reducing molecules involved in the release of energy. In **redox reactions**, electrons are removed from a substrate (oxidative) and H^+ (protons) can also be simultaneously removed. A substrate gains electrons during reduction. For example, when glucose is oxidized, electrons are lost and energy is released. There are enzymes in the membranes of mitochondria. The electrons are carried from one enzyme to another by a co-enzyme. Protons are also released to the other side of the membrane. For example, FAD and $FADH_2$ are used in oxidative phosphorylation. FAD is reduced to $FADH_2$. Electrons are stored there and then sent onward, and the $FADH_2$ becomes FAD again. In aerobic respiration, the final electron acceptor is O_2. In anaerobic respiration, it is something other than O_2.

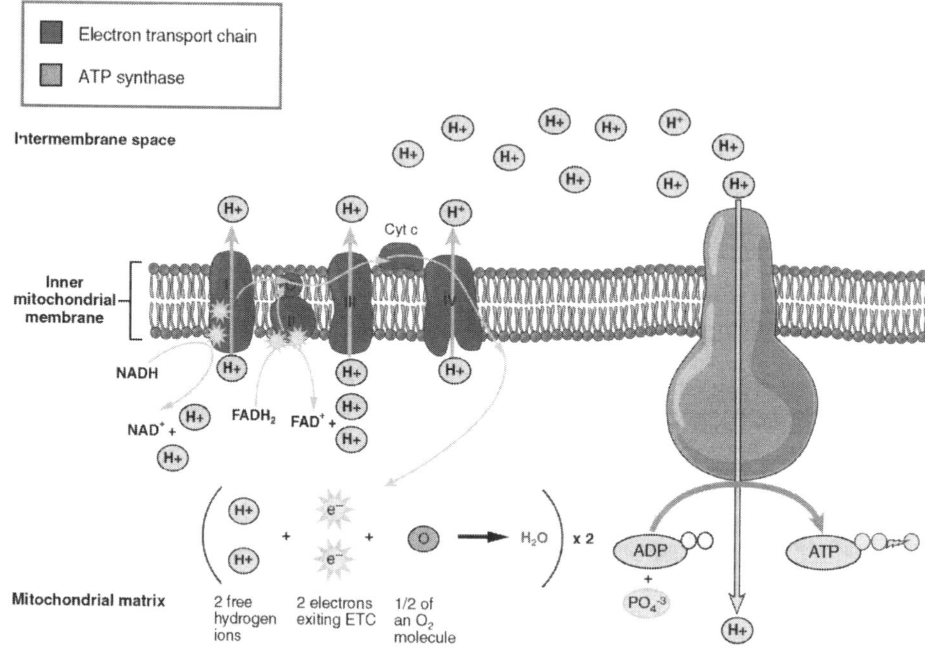

Fermentation

Fermentation is an anaerobic reaction in which glucose is only partially broken down. It releases energy through the oxidation of sugars or other types of organic molecules. Oxygen is sometimes involved, but not always. It is different from respiration in that it uses neither the Krebs cycle nor the electron transport chain and the final electron acceptor is an organic molecule. It uses **substrate-level phosphorylation** to form ATP. NAD^+ is reduced to NADH and NADH further reduces pyruvic acid to various end products. Fermentation can lead to excess waste products and is less efficient than aerobic respiration. **Homolactic fermentation** refers to lactic acid fermentation in which the sugars are converted to lactic acid only (there is one end product). In **heterolactic fermentation**, the sugars are converted to a range of products.

Examples of Fermentation

Lactic acid fermentation is the breakdown of glucose and six-carbon sugars into lactic acid to release energy. It is an anaerobic process, meaning that it does not require oxygen. It can occur in muscle cells and is also performed by streptococcus and lactobacillus bacteria. It can also be used to making yogurt and other food products.

Alcohol fermentation is the breakdown of glucose and six-carbon sugars into ethanol and carbon dioxide to release energy. It is an anaerobic process. It is performed by yeast and used in the production of alcoholic beverages.

Chemosynthesis

Chemosynthesis is the food-making process of chemoautotrophs in extreme environments such as deep-sea-vents, or hydrothermal vents. Unlike photosynthesis, chemosynthesis does not require light. In general, chemosynthesis involves the oxidation of inorganic substances to make a sugar, but there are several species that use different pathways or processses. For example, sulfur bacteria live near or in deep-sea vents and oxidize hydrogen sulfide released from those vents to make a sugar. Instead of sunlight, chemosynthesis uses the energy stored in the chemical bonds of chemicals such as hydrogen sulfide to produce food. During chemosynthesis, the electrons that are removed from the inorganic molecules are combined with carbon dioxide and oxygen to produce sugar, sulfur, and water. Some bacteria use metal ions such as iron and magnesium to obtain the needed electrons. For example, methanobacteria such as those found in human intestines combine carbon dioxide and hydrogen gas and release methane as a waste product. Nitrogen bacteria such as nitrogen-fixing bacteria in the nodules of legumes convert atmospheric nitrogen into nitrates.

Prokaryotes and Eukaryotes

Sizes and Metabolism

Cells of the domains of Bacteria and Archaea are **prokaryotes**. Bacteria cells and Archaea cells are much smaller than cells of eukaryotes. Prokaryote cells are usually only 1 to 2 micrometers in diameter, but eukaryotic cells are usually at least 10 times and possibly 100 times larger than prokaryotic cells. Eukaryotic cells are usually 10 to 100 micrometers in diameter. Most prokaryotes are unicellular organisms, although some prokaryotes live in colonies. Because of their large surface-area-to-volume ratios, prokaryotes have a very high metabolic rate. **Eukaryotic cells** are much larger than prokaryotic cells. Due to their larger sizes, they have a much smaller surface-area-to-volume ratio and consequently have much lower metabolic rates.

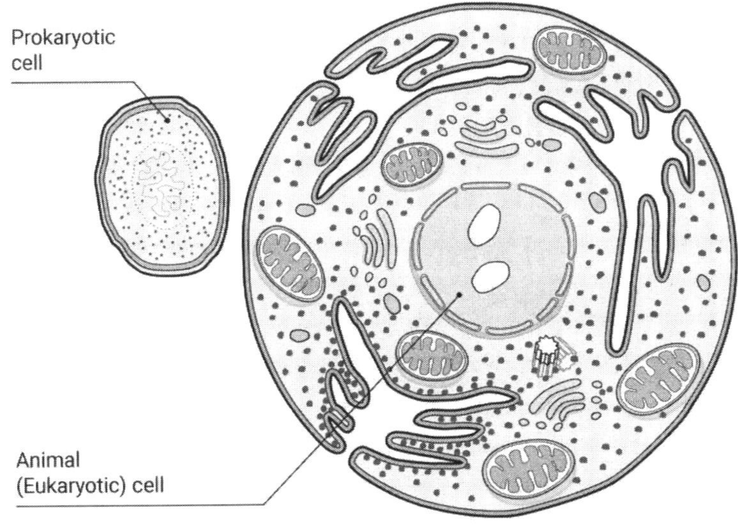

Review Video: Eukaryotic and Prokaryotic
Visit mometrix.com/academy and enter code: 231438

Review Video: Cell Structure
Visit mometrix.com/academy and enter code: 591293

Membrane-Bound Organelles

Prokaryotic cells are much simpler than eukaryotic cells. Prokaryote cells do not have a nucleus due to their small size and their DNA is located in the center of the cell in a region referred to as a **nucleoid**. Eukaryote cells have a **nucleus** bound by a double membrane. Eukaryotic cells typically have hundreds or thousands of additional **membrane-bound organelles** that are independent of the cell membrane. Prokaryotic cells do not have any membrane-bound organelles that are independent of the cell membrane. Once again, this is probably due to the much larger size of the eukaryotic cells. The organelles of eukaryotes give them much higher levels of intracellular division than is possible in prokaryotic cells.

Cell Walls

Not all cells have cell walls, but most prokaryotes have cell walls. The cell walls of organisms from the domain Bacteria differ from the cell walls of the organisms from the domain Archaea. Some eukaryotes, such as some fungi, some algae, and plants, have cell walls that differ from the cell walls of the Bacteria and Archaea domains. The main difference between the cell walls of different domains or kingdoms is the composition of the cell walls. For example, most bacteria have cell walls outside of the plasma membrane that contains the molecule peptidoglycan. **Peptidoglycan** is a large polymer of amino acids and sugars. The peptidoglycan helps maintain the strength of the cell wall. Some of the Archaea cells have cell walls containing the molecule pseudopeptidoglycan, which differs in chemical structure from the peptidoglycan but basically provides the same strength to the cell wall. Some fungi cell walls contain **chitin**. The cell walls of diatoms, a type of yellow algae, contain silica. Plant cell walls contain cellulose, and woody plants are further strengthened by lignin. Some algae also contain lignin. Animal cells do not have cell walls.

Chromosome Structure

Prokaryote cells have DNA arranged in a **circular structure** that should not be referred to as a chromosome. Due to the small size of a prokaryote cell, the DNA material is simply located near the center of the cell in a region called the nucleoid. A prokaryotic cell may also contain tiny rings of DNA called plasmids. Prokaryote cells lack histone proteins, and therefore the DNA is not actually packaged into chromosomes. Prokaryotes reproduce by binary fission, while eukaryotes reproduce by mitosis with the help of **linear chromosomes** and histone proteins. During mitosis, the chromatin is tightly wound on the histone proteins and packaged as a chromosome. The DNA in a eukaryotic cell is located in the membrane-bound nucleus.

Review Video: Chromosomes
Visit mometrix.com/academy and enter code: 132083

Cell Cycle Stages

The cell cycle consists of three stages: interphase, mitosis, and cytokinesis. **Interphase** is the longest stage of the cell cycle and involves the cell growing and making a copy of its DNA. Cells typically spend more than 90% of the cell cycle in interphase. Interphase includes two growth phases called G_1 and G_2. The order of interphase is the first growth cycle, **GAP 1** (G_1 phase), followed by the **synthesis phase** (S), and ending with the second growth phase, **GAP 2** (G_2 phase). During the G_1 phase of interphase, the cell increases the number of organelles by forming diploid cells. During the S phase of interphase, the DNA is replicated, and the chromosomes are doubled. During the G_2 phase of interphase, the cell synthesizes needed proteins and organelles, continues to increase in size, and prepares for mitosis. Once the G_2 phase ends, mitosis can begin.

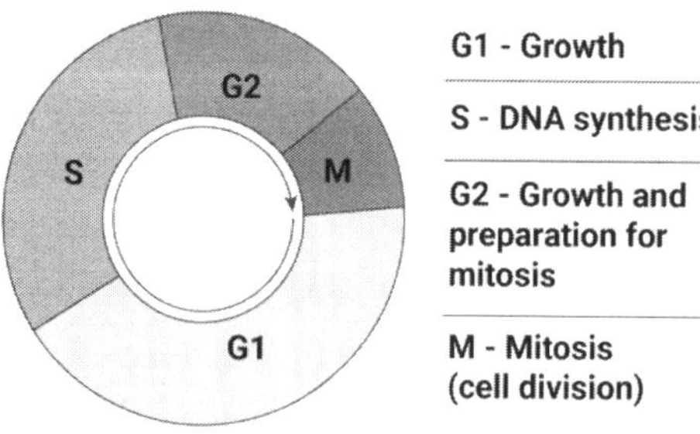

Mitosis

Mitosis is the asexual process of cell division. During mitosis, one parent cell divides into two identical daughter cells. Mitosis is used for growth, repair, and replacement of cells. Some unicellular organisms reproduce asexually by mitosis. Some multicellular organisms can reproduce by fragmentation or budding, which involves mitosis. Mitosis consists of four phases: prophase, metaphase, anaphase, and telophase. During **prophase**, the spindle fibers appear, and the DNA is condensed and packaged as chromosomes that become visible. The nuclear membrane also breaks down, and the nucleolus disappears. During **metaphase**, the spindle apparatus is formed and the centromeres of the chromosomes line up on the equatorial plane. During **anaphase**, the centromeres divide and the two chromatids separate and are pulled toward the opposite poles of the cell. During **telophase**, the spindle fibers disappear, the nuclear membrane reforms, and the DNA in the chromatids is decondensed.

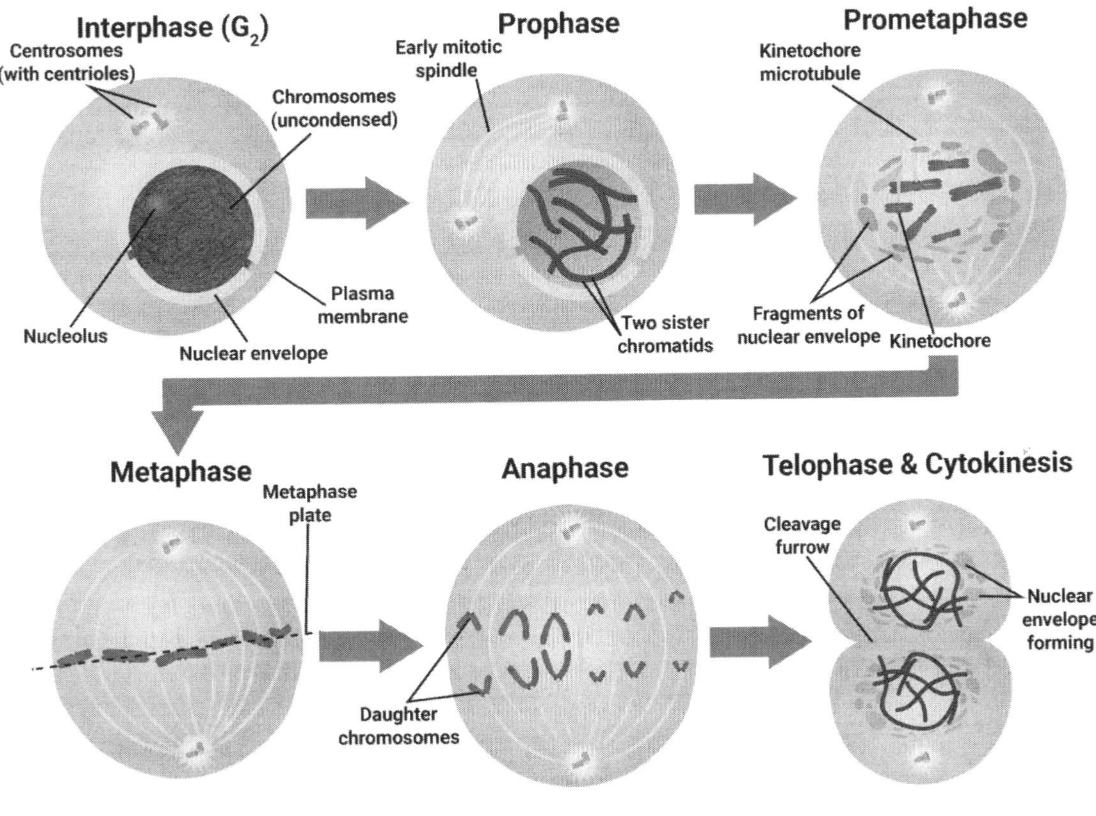

> **Review Video: Mitosis**
> Visit mometrix.com/academy and enter code: 849894

Cytokinesis

Cytokinesis is the dividing of the cytoplasm and cell membrane by the pinching of a cell into two new daughter cells at the end of mitosis. This occurs at the end of telophase when the actin filaments in the cytoskeleton form a contractile ring that narrows and divides the cell. In plant cells, a cell plate forms across the phragmoplast, which is the center of the spindle apparatus. In animal cells, as the contractile ring narrows, the cleavage furrow forms. Eventually, the contractile ring narrows down to the spindle apparatus joining the two cells and the cells eventually divide. Diagrams of the cleavage furrow of an animal cell and cell plate of a plant are shown below.

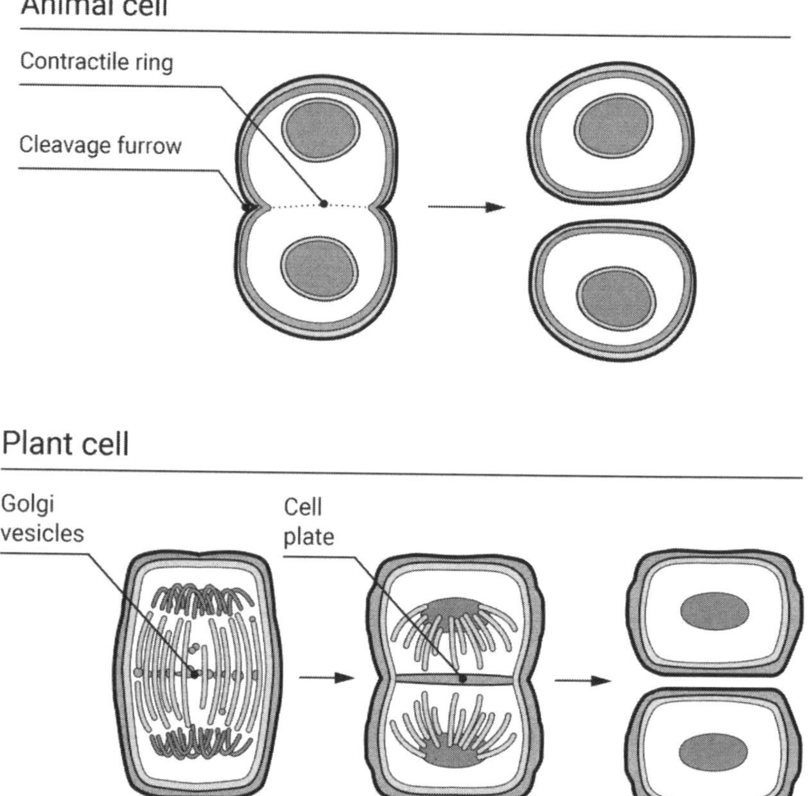

Meiosis

Meiosis is a type of cell division in which the number of chromosomes is reduced by half. Meiosis produces gametes, or egg and sperm cells. Meiosis occurs in two successive stages, which consist of a first mitotic division followed by a second mitotic division. During **meiosis I**, or the first meiotic division, the cell replicates its DNA in interphase and then continues through prophase I, metaphase I, anaphase I, and telophase I. At the end of meiosis I, there are two daughter cells that have the same number of chromosomes as the parent cell. During **meiosis II**, the cell enters a brief interphase but does not replicate its DNA. Then, the cell continues through prophase II, metaphase II, anaphase II, and telophase II. During prophase II, the unduplicated chromosomes split. At the end of telophase II, there are four daughter cells that have half the number of chromosomes as the parent cell.

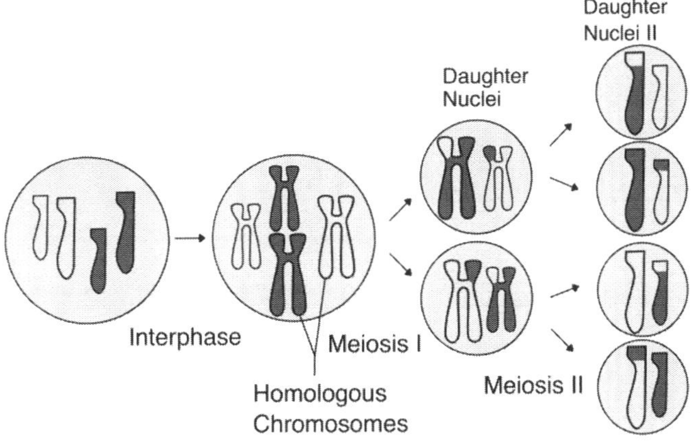

Review Video: Meiosis
Visit mometrix.com/academy and enter code: 247334

Cell Cycle Checkpoints

During the cell cycle, the cell goes through three checkpoints to ensure that the cell is dividing properly at each phase, that it is the appropriate time for division, and that the cell has not been damaged. The **first checkpoint** is at the end of the G_1 phase just before the cell undergoes the S phase, or synthesis. At this checkpoint, a cell may continue with cell division, delay the division, or rest. This **resting phase** is called G_0. In animal cells, the G_1 checkpoint is called **restriction**. Proteins called cyclin D and cyclin E, which are dependent on enzymes cyclin-dependent kinase 4 and cyclin-dependent kinase 2 (CDK4 and CDK2), respectively, largely control this first checkpoint. The **second checkpoint** is at the end of the G_2 phase just before the cell begins prophase during mitosis. The protein cyclin A, which is dependent on the enzyme CDK2, largely controls this checkpoint. During mitosis, the **third checkpoint** occurs at metaphase to check that the chromosomes are lined up along the equatorial plane. This checkpoint is largely controlled by cyclin B, which is dependent upon the enzyme CDK1.

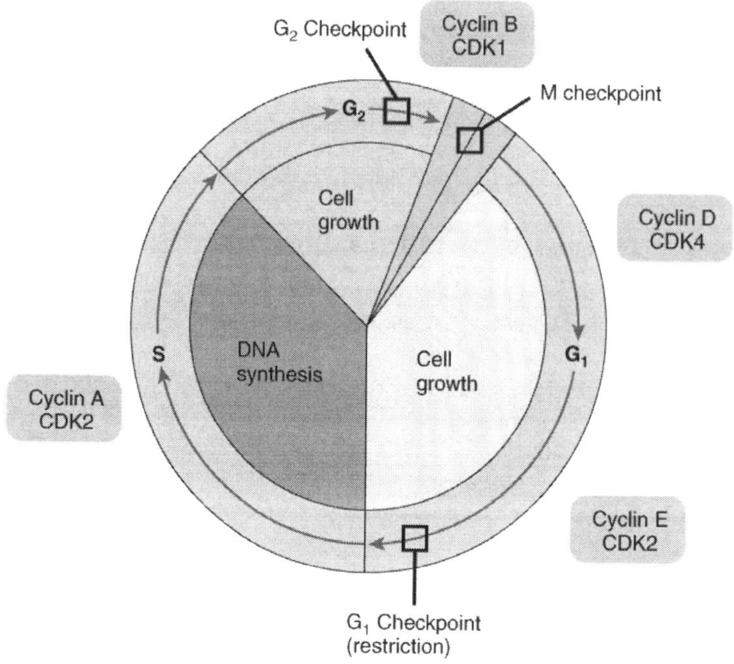

Mutations

Missense Mutations, Silent Mutations, and Nonsense Mutations

Mutations are changes in DNA sequences. **Point mutations** are changes in a single nucleotide in a DNA sequence. Three types of point mutations are missense, silent, and nonsense.

- **Missense mutations** result in a codon for a different amino acid. An example is mutating TGT (Cysteine codon) to TGG (Tryptophan codon).
- **Silent mutations** result in a codon for the same amino acid as the original sequence. An example is mutating TGT (Cysteine codon) to TGC (a different Cysteine codon).
- **Nonsense mutations** insert a premature stop codon, typically resulting in a non-functional protein. An example is mutating TGT (Cysteine codon) to TGA (STOP codon).

Review Video: Codons
Visit mometrix.com/academy and enter code: 978172

Frameshift Mutations and Inversion Mutations

Deletions and insertions can result in the addition of amino acids, the removal of amino acids, or cause a frameshift mutation. A **frameshift mutation** changes the reading frame of the mRNA (a new group of codons will be read), resulting in the formation of a new protein product. Mutations can also occur on the chromosomal level. For example, an **inversion** is when a piece of the chromosome inverts or flips its orientation.

Germline Mutations and Somatic Mutations

Mutations can occur in somatic (body) cells and germ cells (egg and sperm). **Somatic mutations** develop after conception and occur in an organism's body cells such as bone cells, liver cells, or brain cells. Somatic mutations cannot be passed on from parent to offspring. The mutation is limited to the specific descendent of the cell in which the mutation occurred. The mutation is not in the other body cells unless they are descendants of the originally mutated cell. Somatic mutations may cause cancer or diseases. Some somatic mutations are silent. **Germline mutations** are present at conception and occur in an organism's germ cells, which are only egg and sperms cells. Germline mutations may be passed on from parent to offspring. Germline mutations will be present in every cell of an offspring that inherits a germline mutation. Germline mutations may cause diseases. Some germline mutations are silent.

MUTAGENS

Mutagens are physical and chemical agents that cause changes or errors in DNA replication. Mutagens are external factors to an organism. Examples include ionizing radiation such as ultraviolet radiation, x-rays, and gamma radiation. Viruses and microorganisms that integrate their DNA into host chromosomes are also mutagens. Mutagens include environmental poisons such as asbestos, coal tars, tobacco, and benzene. Alcohol and diets high in fat have been shown to be mutagenic. Not all mutations are caused by mutagens. **Spontaneous mutations** can occur in DNA due to molecular decay.

LAW OF SEGREGATION

The **law of segregation** states that the alleles for a trait separate when gametes are formed, which means that only one of the pair of alleles for a given trait is passed to the gamete. This can be shown in monohybrid crosses, which can be used to show which allele is **dominant** for a single trait. A **monohybrid cross** is a genetic cross between two organisms with a different variation for a single trait. The first monohybrid cross typically occurs between two **homozygous** parents. Each parent is homozygous for a separate allele (gg or GG) for a particular trait. For example, in pea plants, green seeds (G) are dominant over yellow seeds(g). Therefore, in a genetic cross of two pea plants that are homozygous for seed color, the F_1 generation will be 100% **heterozygous** green seeds.

	g	g
G	Gg	Gg
G	Gg	Gg

Review Video: Gene & Alleles
Visit mometrix.com/academy and enter code: 363997

Review Video: Punnett Square
Visit mometrix.com/academy and enter code: 853855

MONOHYBRID CROSS FOR A CROSS BETWEEN TWO GG PARENTS

If the plants with the heterozygous green seeds are crossed, the F_2 generation should be 50% heterozygous green (Gg), 25% homozygous green (GG), and 25% homozygous yellow (gg).

	G	g
G	GG	Gg
g	Gg	gg

LAW OF INDEPENDENT ASSORTMENT

Mendel's law of independent assortment states that alleles of one characteristic or trait separate independently of the alleles of another characteristic. Therefore, the allele a gamete receives for one gene does not influence the allele received for another gene due to the allele pairs separating independently during gamete formation. This means that traits are transmitted independently of each other. This can be shown in dihybrid crosses.

GENE, GENOTYPE, PHENOTYPE, AND ALLELE

A **gene** is a portion of DNA that identifies how traits are expressed and passed on in an organism. A gene is part of the genetic code. Collectively, all genes form the **genotype** of an individual. The genotype includes genes that may not be expressed, such as recessive genes. The **phenotype** is the physical, visual manifestation of genes. It is determined by the basic genetic information and how genes have been affected by their environment.

An **allele** is a variation of a gene. Also known as a trait, it determines the manifestation of a gene. This manifestation results in a specific physical appearance of some facet of an organism, such as eye color or height. The genetic information for eye color is a gene. The gene variations responsible for blue, green, brown, or black eyes are called alleles. **Locus** (pl. loci) refers to the location of a gene or alleles.

Review Video: Genotype vs Phenotype
Visit mometrix.com/academy and enter code: 922853

DOMINANT AND RECESSIVE GENES

Gene traits are represented in pairs with an uppercase letter for the **dominant trait** (A) and a lowercase letter for the **recessive trait** (a). Genes occur in pairs (AA, Aa, or aa). There is one gene on each chromosome half supplied by each parent organism. Since half the genetic material is from each parent, the offspring's traits are represented as a combination of these. A dominant trait only requires one gene of a gene pair for it to be expressed in a phenotype, whereas a recessive requires both genes in order to be manifested. For example, if the mother's genotype is Dd and the father's is dd, the possible combinations are Dd and dd. The dominant trait will be manifested if the genotype is DD or Dd. The recessive trait will be manifested if the genotype is dd. Both DD and dd are **homozygous** pairs. Dd is **heterozygous**.

DIHYBRID CROSS FOR THE F_2 GENERATION OF A CROSS BETWEEN GGRR AND GGRR PARENTS

A **dihybrid cross** is a genetic cross for two traits that each have two alleles. For example, in pea plants, green seeds (G) are dominant over yellow seeds (g), and round seeds (R) are dominant over wrinkled seeds (r). In a genetic cross of two pea plants that are homozygous for seed color and seed shape (GGRR or ggRR), the F_1 generation will be 100% heterozygous green and round seeds (GgRr). If these F_1 plants (GgRr) are crossed, the resulting F_2 generation is shown below. Out of the 16 total genotypes for the cross of green, round seeds, there are only four possible phenotypes, or physical traits of the seed: green and round seed (GGRR, GGRr, GgRR, or GgRr), green and wrinkled seed (GGrr or Ggrr), yellow and round seed (ggRR or ggRr) , or yellow and wrinkled seed (ggrr). There are nine green and round seed plants, three green and wrinkled seed plants, three yellow and round seed plants, and only one yellow and wrinkled seed plant. This cross has a **9:3:3:1 ratio**.

	GR	**gR**	**Gr**	**gr**
GR	GGRR	GgRR	GGRr	GgRr
gR	GgRR	ggRR	GgRr	ggRr
Gr	GGRr	GgRr	GGrr	Ggrr
gr	GgRr	ggRr	Ggrr	ggrr

Pedigree

Pedigree analysis is a type of genetic analysis in which an inherited trait is studied and traced through several generations of a family to determine how that trait is inherited. A pedigree is a chart arranged as a type of family tree using symbols for people and lines to represent the relationships between those people. Squares usually represent males, and circles represent females. **Horizontal lines** represent a male and female mating, and the **vertical lines** beneath them represent their children. Usually, family members who possess the trait are fully shaded and those that are carriers only of the trait are half-shaded. Genotypes and phenotypes are determined for each individual if possible. The pedigree below shows the family tree of a family in which the first male who was red-green color blind mated with the first female who was unaffected. They had five children. The three sons were unaffected, and the two daughters were carriers.

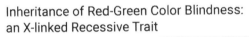

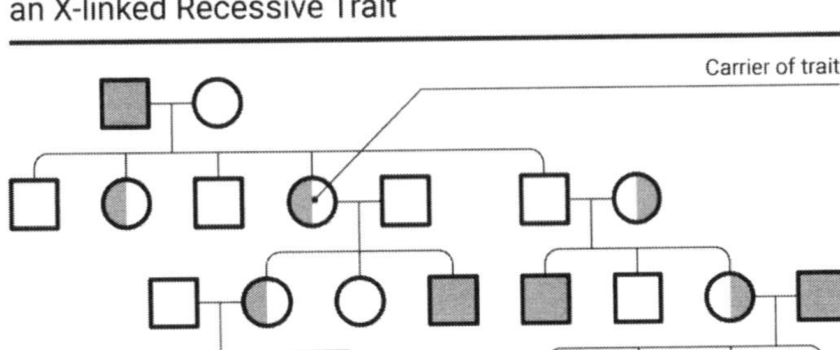

Genetic Drift

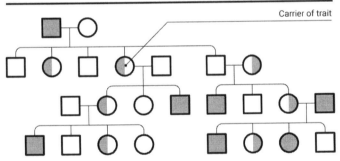

Genetic drift is a microevolutionary process that causes random changes in allele frequencies that are not the result of natural selection. Genetic drift can result in a loss of genetic diversity. Genetic drift greatly impacts small populations. Two special forms of genetic drift are the genetic bottleneck and the founder effect. A **genetic bottleneck** occurs when there is a drastic reduction in population due to some change such as overhunting, disease, or habitat loss. When a population is greatly reduced in size, many alleles can be lost. Even if the population size greatly increases again, the lost alleles represent lost genetic diversity. The **founder effect** occurs when one individual or a few individuals populate a new area such as an island. This new population is limited to the alleles of the founder(s) unless mutations occur or new individuals immigrate to the region.

Gene Flow

Gene flow is a microevolutionary process in which alleles enter a population by immigration and leave a population by emigration. Gene flow helps counter genetic drift. When individuals from one genetically distinct population immigrate to a different genetically distinct population, alleles and their genetic information are added to the new population. The added alleles will change the gene frequencies within the population. This increases genetic diversity. If individuals with rare alleles emigrate from a population, the genetic diversity is decreased. Gene flow reduces the genetic differences between populations.

Mechanisms of Evolution

Natural and Artificial Selection

Natural selection and artificial selection are both mechanisms of evolution. **Natural selection** is a process of nature in which a population can change over generations. Every population has variations in individual heritable traits and organisms best suited for survival typically reproduce and pass on those genetic traits to offspring to increase the likelihood of them surviving. Typically, the more advantageous a trait is, the more common that trait becomes in a population. Natural selection brings about evolutionary **adaptations** and is responsible for biological diversity. Artificial selection is another mechanism of evolution. **Artificial selection** is a process brought about by humans. Artificial selection is the selective breeding of domesticated animals and plants such as when farmers choose animals or plants with desirable traits to reproduce. Artificial selection has led to the evolution of farm stock and crops. For example, cauliflower, broccoli, and cabbage all evolved due to artificial selection of the wild mustard plant.

Sexual Selection

Sexual selection is a special case of natural selection in animal populations. **Sexual selection** occurs because some animals are more likely to find mates than other animals. The two main contributors to sexual selection are **competition** of males and **mate selection** by females. An example of male competition is in the mating practices of the redwing blackbird. Some males have huge territories and numerous mates that they defend. Other males have small territories, and some even have no mates. An example of mate selection by females is the mating practices of peacocks. Male peacocks display large, colorful tail feathers to attract females. Females are more likely to choose males with the larger, more colorful displays.

Coevolution

Coevolution describes a rare phenomenon in which two populations with a close ecological relationship undergo reciprocal adaptations simultaneously and evolve together, affecting each other's evolution. General examples of coevolution include predator and prey, or plant and pollinator, and parasites and their hosts. A specific example of coevolution is the yucca moths and the yucca plants. Yucca plants can only be pollinated by the yucca moths. The yucca moths lay their eggs in the yucca flowers, and their larvae grow inside the ovary.

Adaptive Radiation

Adaptive radiation is an evolutionary process in which a species branches out and adapts and fills numerous unoccupied ecological niches. The adaptations occur relatively quickly, driven by natural selection and resulting in new phenotypes and possibly new species eventually. An example of adaptive radiation is the finches that Darwin studied on the Galápagos Islands. Darwin recorded 13 different varieties of finches, which differed in the size and shape of their beaks. Through the process of natural selection, each type of finch adapted to the specific environment and specifically the food sources of the island to which it belonged. On newly formed islands with many unoccupied ecological niches, the adaptive radiation process occurred quickly due to the lack of competing species and predators.

> **Review Video: Organic Evolution**
> Visit mometrix.com/academy and enter code: 108959

Evidence Supporting Evolution

Molecular Evidence

Because all organisms are made up of cells, all organisms are alike on a fundamental level. Cells share similar components, which are made up of molecules. Specifically, all cells contain DNA and RNA. This should indicate that all species descended from a **common ancestor**. Humans and chimpanzees share approximately 98% of their genes in common, while humans and bacteria share approximately 7% of their genes in common suggesting that bacteria and humans are not closely related. Biologists have been able to use DNA sequence comparisons of modern organisms to reconstruct the "root" of the tree of life. The fact that RNA can store information, replicate itself, and code for proteins suggests that RNA could have could have evolved first, followed by DNA.

Homology

Homology is the similarity of structures of different species based on a similar anatomy in a common evolutionary ancestor. For instance, the forelimbs of humans, dogs, birds, and whales all have the same basic pattern of the bones. Specifically, all of these organisms have a humerus, radius, and ulna. They are all modifications of the same basic evolutionary structure from a common ancestor. Tetrapods resemble the fossils of extinct transitional animal called the *Eusthenopteron*. This would seem to indicate that evolution primarily modifies preexisting structures.

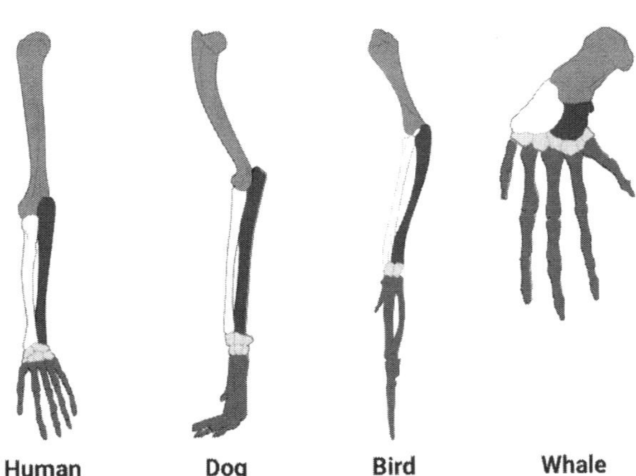

> **Review Video: Homologous vs Analogous Structures**
> Visit mometrix.com/academy and enter code: 355157

Embryology

The stages of **embryonic development** reveal homologies between species. These homologies are evidence of a **common ancestor**. For example, in chicken embryos and mammalian embryos, both include a stage in which slits and arches appear in the embryo's neck region that are strikingly similar to gill slits and gill arches in fish embryos. Adult chickens and adult mammals do not have gills, but this embryonic homology indicates that birds and mammals share a common ancestor with fish. As another example, some species of toothless whales have embryos that initially develop teeth that are later absorbed, which indicates that these whales have an ancestor with teeth in the adult form. Finally, most tetrapods have five-digit limbs, but birds have three-digit limbs in their wings. However, embryonic birds initially have five-digit limbs in their wings, which develop into a three-digit wing. Tetrapods such as reptiles, mammals, and birds all share a common ancestor with five-digit limbs.

ENDOSYMBIOSIS THEORY

The endosymbiosis theory is foundational to evolution. Endosymbiosis provides the path for prokaryotes to give rise to eukaryotes. Specifically, **endosymbiosis** explains the development of the organelles of mitochondria in animals and chloroplasts in plants. This theory states that some eukaryotic organelles such as mitochondria and chloroplasts originated as free living cells. According to this theory, primitive, heterotrophic eukaryotes engulfed smaller, autotrophic bacteria prokaryotes, but the bacteria were not digested. Instead, the eukaryotes and the bacteria formed a symbiotic relationship. Eventually, the bacteria transformed into mitochondrion or chloroplasts.

SUPPORTING EVIDENCE

Several facts support the endosymbiosis theory. Mitochondria and chloroplasts contain their own DNA and can both only arise from other preexisting mitochondria and chloroplasts. The genomes of mitochondria and chloroplasts consist of single, circular DNA molecules with no histones. This is similar to bacteria genomes, not eukaryote genomes. Also, the RNA, ribosomes, and protein synthesis of mitochondria and chloroplasts are remarkably similar to those of bacteria, and both use oxygen to produce ATP. These organelles have a double phospholipid layer that is typical of engulfed bacteria. This theory also involves a secondary endosymbiosis in which the original eukaryotic cells that have engulfed the bacteria are then engulfed themselves by another free-living eukaryote.

CONVERGENT EVOLUTION

Convergent evolution is the evolutionary process in which two or more unrelated species become increasingly similar in appearance. In convergent evolution, similar adaptations in these unrelated species occur due to these species inhabiting the same kind of environment. For example, the mammals shown below, although found in different parts of the world, developed similar appearances due to their similar environments.

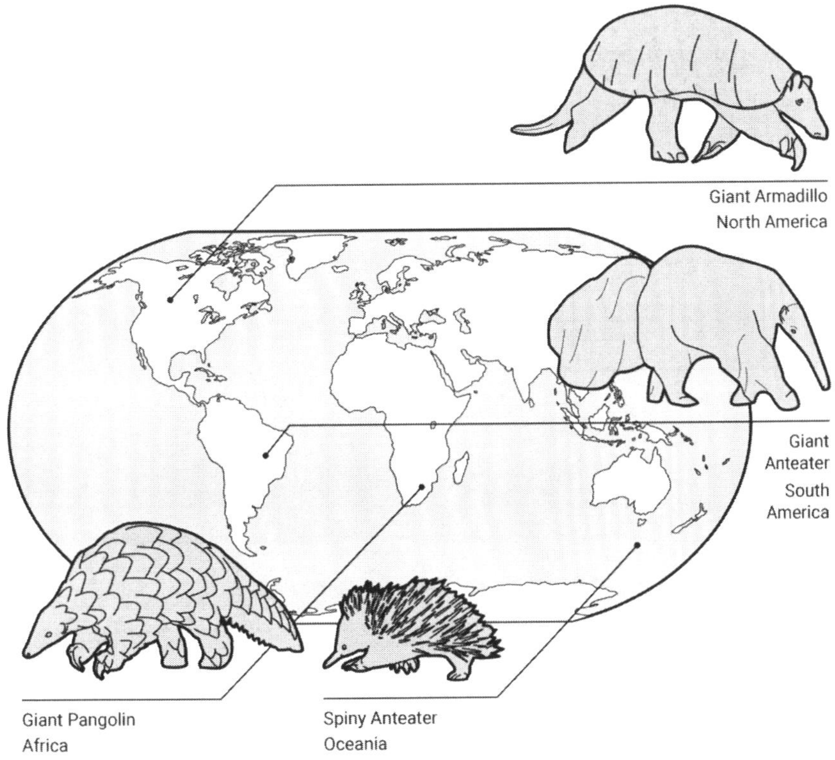

Divergent Evolution

Divergent evolution is the evolutionary process in which organisms of one species become increasingly dissimilar in appearance. As several small adaptations occur due to natural selection, the organisms will finally reach a point at which two new species are formed, also known as **speciation**. Then, these two species will further diverge from each other as they continue to evolve.

Adaptive radiation is an example of divergent evolution. Another example is the divergent evolution of the wooly mammoth and the modern elephant from a common ancestor.

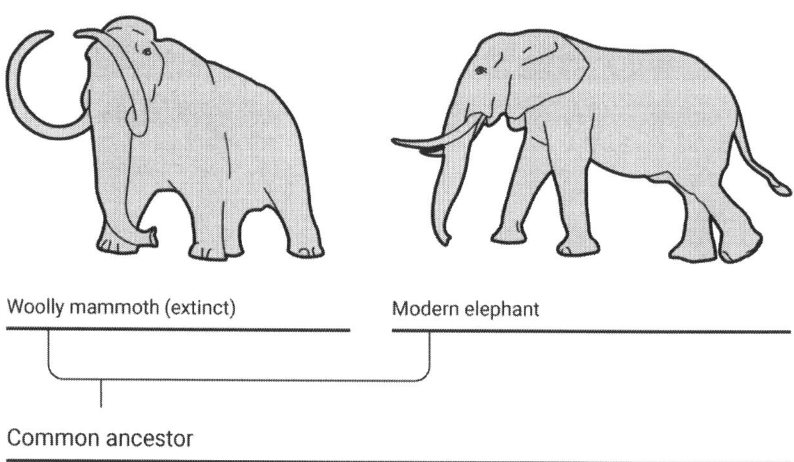

Fossil Record

The **fossil record** provides many types of support for evolution including comparisons from rock layers, transition fossils, and homologies with modern organisms. First, fossils from rock layers from all over the world have been compared, enabling scientists to develop a sequence of life from simple to complex. Based on the fossil record, the **geologic timeline** chronicles the history of all living things. For example, the fossil record clearly indicates that invertebrates developed before vertebrates and that fish developed before amphibians. Second, numerous transitional fossils have been found. **Transitional fossils** show an intermediate state between an ancestral form of an organism and the form of its descendants. These fossils show the path of evolutionary change. For example, many transition fossils documenting the evolutionary change from fish to amphibians have been discovered. In 2004, scientists discovered *Tiktaalik roseae*, or the "fishapod," which is a 375-million-year-old fossil that exhibits both fish and amphibian characteristics. Another example would be *Pakicetus,* an extinct land mammal, that scientists determined is an early ancestor of modern whales and dolphins based on the specialized structures of the inner ear. Most fossils exhibit homologies with modern organisms. For example, extinct horses are similar to modern horses, indicating a common ancestor.

Cephalization and Multicellularity

Cephalization is the evolutionary trend that can be summarized as "the evolution of the head." In most animals, nerve tissue has been concentrated into a brain at one end of an organism over many generations. Eventually, a head enclosing a brain and housing sensory organs was produced at one end of the organism. Many invertebrates, such as arthropods and annelids and all vertebrates, have undergone cephalization. However, some invertebrates, such as echinoderms and sponges, have not undergone cephalization, and these organisms literally do not have a head.

Another evolutionary trend is **multicellularity**. Life has evolved from simple, single-celled organisms to complex, multicellular organisms. Over millions of years, single-celled organisms gave rise to biofilms, which gave rise to multicellular organisms, which gave rise to all of the major phyla of multicellular organisms present today.

Explanations for the Origin of Life on Earth

Panspermia

The word *panspermia* is a Greek work that means "seeds everywhere." **Panspermia** is one possible explanation for the origin of life on Earth that states that "seeds" of life exist throughout the universe and can be transferred from one location to another. Three types of panspermia based on the seed-dispersal method have been proposed. **Lithopanspermia** is described as rocks or dust transferring microorganisms between solar systems. **Ballistic panspermia** is described as rocks or dust transferring microorganisms between planets within the same solar system. **Directed panspermia** is described as intelligent extraterrestrials purposely spreading the seeds to other planets and solar systems. The panspermia hypothesis only proposes the origin of life on Earth. It does not offer an explanation for the origin of life in the universe or explain the origin of the seeds themselves.

Abiotic Synthesis of Organic Compounds

Scientists have performed sophisticated experiments to determine how the first organic compounds appeared on Earth. First, scientists performed controlled experiments that closely resembled the conditions similar to an early Earth. In the classic **Miller–Urey experiment** (1953), the Earth's early atmosphere was simulated with water, methane, ammonia, and hydrogen that were stimulated by an electric discharge. The Miller–Urey experiment produced complex organic compounds including several amino acids, sugars, and hydrocarbons. Later experiments by other scientists produced nucleic acids. Recently, Jeffrey Bada, a former student of Miller, was able to produce amino acids in a simulation using the Earth's current atmospheric conditions with the addition of iron and carbonate to the simulation. This is significant because in previous studies using Earth's current atmosphere, the amino acids were destroyed by the nitrites produced by the nitrogen.

Atmospheric Composition

The early atmosphere of Earth had little or possibly no oxygen. Early rocks had high levels of iron at their surfaces. Without oxygen, the iron just entered into the early oceans as ions. In the same time frame, early photosynthetic algae were beginning to grow abundantly in the early ocean. During photosynthesis, the algae would produce oxygen gas, which oxidized the iron at the rocks' surfaces, forming an iron oxide. This process basically kept the algae in an oxygen-free environment. As the algae population grew much larger, it eventually produced such a large amount of oxygen that it could not be removed by the iron in the rocks. Because the algae at this time were intolerant to oxygen, the algae became extinct. Over time, a new iron-rich layer of sediments formed, and algae populations reformed, and the cycle began again. This cycle repeated itself for millions of years. Iron-rich layers of sediment alternated with iron-poor layers. Gradually, algae and other life forms evolved that were tolerant to oxygen, stabilizing the oxygen concentration in the atmosphere at levels similar to those of today.

Development of Self-Replication

Several hypotheses for the origin of life involve the self-replication of molecules. In order for life to have originated on Earth, proteins and RNA must have been replicated. Hypotheses that combine the replication of proteins and RNA seem promising. One such hypothesis is called **RNA world**. RNA world explains how the pathway of DNA to RNA to protein may have originated by proposing the reverse process. RNA world proposes that self-replicating RNA was the precursor to DNA. Scientists have shown that RNA can actually function both as a gene and as an enzyme and could therefore have carried genetic information in earlier life stages. Also, RNA can be transcribed into DNA using reverse transcription. In RNA world, RNA molecules self-replicated and evolved through recombination and mutations. RNA molecules developed the ability to act as enzymes. Eventually, RNA began to synthesize proteins. Finally, DNA molecules were copied from the RNA in a process of reverse transcription.

Historical and Current Kingdom Systems

In 1735 Carolus Linnaeus devised a two-kingdom classification system. He placed all living things into either the *Animalia* kingdom or the *Plantae* kingdom. Fungi and algae were classified as plants. Also, Linnaeus developed the binomial nomenclature system that is still used today. In 1866, Ernst Haeckel introduced a three-kingdom classification system, adding the *Protista* kingdom to Linnaeus's animal and plant kingdoms. Bacteria were classified as protists and cyanobacteria were still classified as plants. In 1938, Herbert Copeland introduced a four-kingdom classification system in which bacteria and cyanobacteria were moved to the *Monera* kingdom. In 1969, Robert Whittaker introduced a five-kingdom system that moved fungi from the plant kingdom to the *Fungi* kingdom. Some algae were still classified as plants. In 1977, Carl Woese introduced a six-kingdom system in which in the *Monera* kingdom was replaced with the *Eubacteria* kingdom and the *Archaebacteria* kingdom.

Domain Classification System

In 1990, Carl Woese introduced his domain classification system. **Domains** are broader groupings above the kingdom level. This system consists of three domains- *Archaea*, *Bacteria*, and *Eukarya*. All eukaryotes such as plants, animals, fungi, and protists are classified in the *Eukarya* domain. The *Bacteria* and *Archaea* domains consist of prokaryotes. Organisms previously classified in the *Monera* kingdom are now classified into either the *Bacteria* or *Archaea* domain based on their ribosomal RNA structure. Members of the *Archaea* domain often live in extremely harsh environments.

Review Video: Biological Classification Systems
Visit mometrix.com/academy and enter code: 736052

Viruses

Viruses are nonliving, infectious particles that act as parasites in living organisms. Viruses are acellular, which means that they lack cell structure. Viruses cannot reproduce outside of living cells. The structure of a virus is a nucleic acid genome, which may be either DNA or RNA, surrounded by a protective protein coat or **capsid**. In some viruses, the capsid may be surrounded by a lipid membrane or envelope. Viruses can contain up to 500 genes and have various shapes. They usually are too small to be seen without the aid of an electron microscope. Viruses can infect plants, animals, fungi, protists, and bacteria. Viruses can attack only specific types of cells that have specific receptors on their surfaces. Viruses do not divide or reproduce like living cells. Instead, they use the host cell they infect by "reprogramming" it, using the nucleic acid genome, to make more copies of the virus. The host cell usually bursts to release these copies.

Review Video: Viruses
Visit mometrix.com/academy and enter code: 984455

Bacteria

Bacteria are small, prokaryotic, single-celled organisms. Bacteria have a circular loop of DNA (plasmid) that is not contained within a nuclear membrane. Bacterial ribosomes are not bound to the endoplasmic reticulum, as in eukaryotes. A cell wall containing peptidoglycan surrounds the bacterial plasma membrane. Some bacteria such as pathogens are further encased in a gel-like, sticky layer called the **capsule**, which enhances their ability to cause disease. Bacteria can be autotrophs or heterotrophs. Some bacterial heterotrophs are saprophytes that function as decomposers in ecosystems. Many types of bacteria share commensal or mutualistic relationships with other organisms. Most bacteria reproduce asexually by binary fission. Two identical daughter cells are produced from one parent cell. Some bacteria can transfer genetic material to other bacteria through a process called conjugation, while some bacteria can incorporate DNA from the environment in a process called transformation.

PROTISTS

Protists are small, eukaryotic, single-celled organisms. Although protists are small, they are much larger than prokaryotic bacteria. Protists have three general forms, which include plantlike protists, animal-like protists, and fungus-like protists. **Plantlike protists** are algae that contain chlorophyll and perform photosynthesis. Animal-like protists are **protozoa** with no cell walls that typically lack chlorophyll and are grouped by their method of locomotion, which may use flagella, cilia, or a different structure. **Fungus-like protists**, which do not have chitin in their cell walls, are generally grouped as either slime molds or water molds. Protists may be autotrophic or heterotrophic. Autotrophic protists include many species of algae, while heterotrophic protists include parasitic, commensal, and mutualistic protozoa. Slime molds are heterotrophic fungus-like protists, which consume microorganisms. Some protists reproduce sexually, but most reproduce asexually by binary fission. Some reproduce asexually by spores while others reproduce by alternation of generations and require two hosts in their life cycle.

FUNGI

Fungi are nonmotile organisms with eukaryotic cells and contain chitin in their cell walls. Most fungi are multicellular, but a few including yeast are unicellular. Fungi have multicellular filaments called **hyphae** that are grouped together into the mycelium. Fungi do not perform photosynthesis and are considered heterotrophs. Fungi can be parasitic, mutualistic or free living. Free-living fungi include mushrooms and toadstools. Parasitic fungi include fungi responsible for ringworm and athlete's foot. Mycorrhizae are mutualistic fungi that live in or near plant roots increasing the roots' surface area of absorption. Almost all fungi reproduce asexually by spores, but most fungi also have a sexual phase in the production of spores. Some fungi reproduce by budding or fragmentation.

> **Review Video: Feeding Among Heterotrophs**
> Visit mometrix.com/academy and enter code: 836017
>
> **Review Video: Kingdom Fungi**
> Visit mometrix.com/academy and enter code: 315081

PLANTS

Plants are multicellular organisms with eukaryotic cells containing cellulose in their cell walls. Plant cells have chlorophyll and perform photosynthesis. Plants can be vascular or nonvascular. **Vascular plants** have true leaves, stems, and roots that contain xylem and phloem. **Nonvascular plants** lack true leaves, stems and roots and do not have any true vascular tissue but instead rely on diffusion and osmosis to transport most of materials or resources needed to survive. Almost all plants are autotrophic, relying on photosynthesis for food. A small number do not have chlorophyll and are parasitic, but these are extremely rare. Plants can reproduce sexually or asexually. Many plants reproduce by seeds produced in the fruits of the plants, while some plants reproduce by seeds on cones. One type of plant, ferns, reproduce by a different system that utilizes spores. Some plants can even reproduce asexually by vegetative reproduction.

Review Video: Kingdom Plantae
Visit mometrix.com/academy and enter code: 710084

Structure, Organization, Modes of Nutrition, and Reproduction of Animals

Animals are multicellular organism with eukaryotic cells that do not have cell walls surrounding their plasma membranes. Animals have several possible structural body forms. Animals can be relatively simple in structure such as sponges, which do not have a nervous system. Other animals are more complex with cells organized into tissues, and tissues organized into organs, and organs even further organized into systems. Invertebrates such as arthropods, nematodes, and annelids have complex body systems. Vertebrates including fish, amphibians, reptiles, birds, and mammals are the most complex with detailed systems such as those with gills, air sacs, or lungs designed to exchange respiratory gases. All animals are heterotrophs and obtain their nutrition by consuming autotrophs or other heterotrophs. Most animals are motile, but some animals move their environment to bring food to them. All animals reproduce sexually at some point in their life cycle. Typically, this involves the union of a sperm and egg to produce a zygote.

Review Video: Kingdom Animalia
Visit mometrix.com/academy and enter code: 558413

Characteristics of the Major Animal Phyla

Body Planes

Animals can exhibit bilateral symmetry, radial symmetry, or asymmetry. With **bilateral symmetry**, the organism can be cut in half along only one plane to produce two identical halves. Most animals, including all vertebrates such as mammals, birds, reptiles, amphibians, and fish, exhibit bilateral symmetry. Many invertebrates including arthropods and crustaceans also exhibit bilateral symmetry. With **radial symmetry**, the organism can be cut in half along several planes to produce two identical halves. Starfish, sea urchins, and jellyfish exhibit radial symmetry. With **asymmetry**, the organism exhibits no symmetry. Very few organisms in the animal phyla exhibit asymmetry, but a few species of sponges are asymmetrical.

Body Cavities

Animals can be grouped based on their types of body cavities. A **coelom** is a fluid-filled body cavity between the alimentary canal and the body wall. The three body plans based on the formation of the coelom are coelomates, pseudocoelomates, and acoelomates. **Coelomates** have a true coelom located within the mesoderm. Most animals including arthropods, mollusks, annelids, echinoderms, and chordates are coelomates. **Pseudocoelomates** have a body cavity called a pseudocoelom. **Pseudocoeloms** are not considered true coeloms. Pseudocoeloms are located between mesoderm and endoderm instead of actually in the mesoderm as in a true coelom. Pseudocoelomates include roundworms and rotifers. **Acoelomates** do not have body cavities. Simple or primitive animals such as sponges, jellyfish, sea anemones, hydras, flatworms, and ribbon worms are acoelomates.

Modes of Reproduction

Animals can reproduce sexually or asexually. Most animals reproduce sexually. In **sexual reproduction**, males and females have different reproductive organs that produce **gametes**. Males have testes that produce sperm, and females have ovaries that produce eggs. During fertilization, a sperm cell unites with an egg cell, forming a **zygote**. Fertilization can occur internally such as in most mammals and birds or externally such as aquatic animals such as fish and frogs. The zygote undergoes cell division, which develops into an embryo and eventually develops into an adult organism. Some embryos develop in eggs such as in fish, amphibians, reptiles, and birds. Some mammals are **oviparous** meaning that they lay eggs, but most are **viviparous** meaning they have a uterus in which the embryo develops. One particular type of mammal called **marsupials** give birth to an immature fetus that finishes development in a pouch. However, there are some animals reproduce **asexually**. For example, hydras reproduce by budding, and starfish and planarians can reproduce by fragmentation and regeneration. Some fish, frogs, and insects can even reproduce by parthenogenesis, which is a type of self-reproduction without fertilization.

Modes of Temperature Regulation

Animals can be classified as either homeotherms or poikilotherms. **Homeotherms**, also called warm-blooded animals or **endotherms**, maintain a constant body temperature regardless of the temperature of the environment. Homeotherms such as mammals and birds have a high metabolic rate because a lot of energy is needed to maintain the constant temperature. **Poikilotherms**, also called cold-blooded animals or **ectotherms**, do not maintain a constant body temperature. Their body temperature fluctuates with the temperature of the environment. Poikilotherms such as arthropods, fish, amphibians, and reptiles have metabolic rates that fluctuate with their body temperature.

Review Video: Basic Characteristics of Organisms
Visit mometrix.com/academy and enter code: 314694

Organizational Hierarchy within Multicellular Organisms

Cells are the smallest living units of organisms. Tissues are groups of cells that work together to perform a specific function. Organs are groups of tissues that work together to perform a specific function. Organ systems are groups of organs that work together to perform a specific function. An organism is an individual that contains several body systems.

Cells

Cells are the basic structural units of all living things. Cells are composed of various molecules including proteins, carbohydrates, lipids, and nucleic acids. All animal cells are eukaryotic and have a nucleus, cytoplasm, and a cell membrane. Organelles include mitochondria, ribosomes, endoplasmic reticulum, Golgi apparatuses, and vacuoles. Specialized cells are numerous, including but not limited to, various muscle cells, nerve cells, epithelial cells, bone cells, blood cells, and cartilage cells. Cells are grouped to together in tissues to perform specific functions.

Tissues

Tissues are groups of cells that work together to perform a specific function. Tissues can be grouped into four broad categories: muscle tissue, connective tissue, nerve tissue, and epithelial tissue. Muscle tissue is involved in body movement. **Muscle tissues** can be composed of skeletal muscle cells, cardiac muscle cells, or smooth muscle cells. Skeletal muscles include the muscles commonly called biceps, triceps, hamstrings, and quadriceps. Cardiac muscle tissue is found only in the heart. Smooth muscle tissue provides tension in the blood vessels, controls pupil dilation, and aids in peristalsis. **Connective tissues** include bone tissue, cartilage, tendons, ligaments, fat, blood, and lymph. **Nerve tissue** is located in the brain, spinal cord, and nerves. **Epithelial tissue** makes up the layers of the skin and various membranes. Tissues are grouped together as organs to perform specific functions.

Organs and Organ Systems

Organs are groups of tissues that work together to perform specific functions. **Organ systems** are groups of organs that work together to perform specific functions. Complex animals have several organs that are grouped together in multiple systems. In mammals, there are 11 major organ systems: integumentary system, respiratory system, cardiovascular system, endocrine system, nervous system, immune system, digestive system, excretory system, muscular system, skeletal system, and reproductive system.

Maintenance of Homeostasis in Organisms

Role of Feedback Mechanisms

Homeostasis is the regulation of internal chemistry to maintain a constant internal environment. This state is controlled through various feedback mechanisms that consist of receptors, an integrator, and effectors. **Receptors** such as mechanoreceptors or thermoreceptors in the skin detect the stimuli. The **integrator** such as the brain or spinal cord receives the information concerning the stimuli and sends out signals to other parts of the body. The **effectors** such as muscles or glands respond to the stimulus. Basically, the receptors receive the stimuli and notify the integrator, which signals the effectors to respond.

Feedback mechanisms can be negative or positive. **Negative-feedback** mechanisms are mechanisms that provide a decrease in response with an increase in stimulus that inhibits the stimulus, which in turn decreases the response. **Positive-feedback** mechanisms are mechanisms that provide an increase in response with an increase in stimulus, which actually increases the stimulus, which in turn increases the response.

Role of Hypothalamus

The hypothalamus plays a major role in the homoeostasis of vertebrates. The **hypothalamus** is the central portion of the brain just above the brainstem and is linked to the endocrine system through the pituitary gland. The hypothalamus releases special hormones that influence the secretion of pituitary hormones. The hypothalamus regulates the fundamental physiological state by controlling body temperature, hunger, thirst, sleep, behaviors related to attachment, sexual development, fight-or-flight stress response, and circadian rhythms.

Role of Endocrine System and Hormones

All vertebrates have an **endocrine system** that consists of numerous ductless glands that produce hormones to help coordinate many functions of the body. **Hormones** are signaling molecules that are received by receptors. Many hormones are secreted in response to signals from the pituitary gland and hypothalamus gland. Other hormones are secreted in response to signals from inside the body. Hormones can consist of amino acids, proteins, or lipid molecules such as steroid hormones. Hormones can affect target cells, which have the correct receptor that is able to bind to that particular hormone. Most cells have receptors for more than one type of hormone. Hormones are distributed to the target cells in the blood by the cardiovascular system. Hormones incorporate feedback mechanisms to help the body maintain homeostasis.

Role of Antidiuretic Hormone

Antidiuretic hormone (ADH) helps maintain homeostasis in vertebrates. ADH is produced by the posterior pituitary gland, and it regulates the reabsorption of water in the kidneys and concentrates the urine. The stimulus in this feedback mechanism is a drop in blood volume due to water loss. This signal is picked up by the hypothalamus, which signals the pituitary gland to secrete ADH. ADH is carried by the cardiovascular system to the nephrons in the kidneys signaling them to reabsorb more water and send less out as waste. As more water is reabsorbed, the blood volume increases, which is monitored by the hypothalamus. As the blood volume reaches the set point, the hypothalamus signals for a decrease in the secretion of ADH, and the cycle continues.

Role of Insulin and Glucagon

Insulin and glucagon are hormones that help maintain the glucose concentration in the blood. Insulin and glucagon are secreted by the clumps of endocrine cells called the **pancreatic islets** that are located in the pancreas. Insulin and glucagon work together to maintain the blood glucose level. **Insulin** stimulates cells to remove glucose from the blood. **Glucagon** stimulates the liver to convert glycogen to glucose. After eating, glucose levels increase in the blood. This stimulus signals the pancreas to stop the secretion of glucagon and to start secreting insulin. Cells respond to the insulin and remove glucose from the blood, lowering the level of glucose in the blood. Later, after eating, the level of glucose in the blood decreases further. This stimulus signals the pancreas to secrete glucagon and decrease the secretion of insulin. In response to the stimulus, the liver converts glycogen to glucose, and the level of glucose in the blood rises. When the individual eats, the cycle begins again.

Thermoregulation

Animals exhibit many adaptations that help them achieve homeostasis, or a stable internal environment. Some of these adaptions are behavioral. Most organisms exhibit some type of behavioral **thermoregulation**. Thermoregulation is the ability to keep the body temperature within certain boundaries. The type of behavioral thermoregulation depends on whether the animal is an endotherm or an ectotherm. **Ectotherms** are "cold-blooded," and their body temperature changes with their external environment. To regulate their temperature, ectotherms often move to an appropriate location. For example, fish move to warmer waters while animals will climb to higher grounds. **Diurnal ectotherms** such as reptiles often bask in the sun to increase their body temperatures. Butterflies are **heliotherms** in that they derive nearly all of their heat from basking in the sun. **Endotherms** are "warm-blooded" and maintain a stable body temperature by internal means. However, many animals that live in hot environments have adapted to the nocturnal lifestyle. Desert animals are often nocturnal to escape high daytime temperatures. Other nocturnal animals sleep during the day in underground burrows or dens.

Gamete Formation

Gametogenesis is the formation of gametes, or reproductive cells. Gametes are produced by meiosis. **Meiosis** is a special type of cell division that consists of two consecutive mitotic divisions referred to as meiosis I and meiosis II. **Meiosis I** is a reduction division in which a diploid cell is reduced to two haploid daughter cells that contain only one of each pair of homologous chromosomes. During **meiosis II**, those haploid cells are further divided to form four haploid cells. **Spermatogenesis** in males produces four viable sperm cells from each complete cycle of meiosis. **Oogenesis** produces four daughter cells, but only one is a viable egg and the other three are polar bodies.

Fertilization

Fertilization is the union of a sperm cell and an egg cell to produce a zygote. Many sperm may bind to an egg, but only one joins with the egg and injects its nuclei into the egg. Fertilization can be external or internal. **External fertilization** takes place outside of the female's body. For example, many fish, amphibians, crustaceans, mollusks, and corals reproduce externally by **spawning** or releasing gametes into the water simultaneously or right after each other. Reptiles and birds reproduce by **internal fertilization**. All mammals except monotremes (e.g. platypus) reproduce by internal fertilization.

Embryonic Development

Embryonic development in animals is typically divided into four stages: cleavage, patterning, differentiation, and growth. **Cleavage** occurs immediately after fertilization when the large single-celled zygote immediately begins to divide into smaller and smaller cells without an increase in mass. A hollow ball of cells forms a blastula. Next, during patterning, gastrulation occurs. During gastrulation, the cells are organized into three primary germ layers: ectoderm, mesoderm, and endoderm. Then, the cells in these layers differentiate into special tissues and organs. For example, the nervous system develops from the ectoderm. The muscular system develops from the mesoderm. Much of the digestive system develops from the endoderm. The final stage of embryonic development is growth and further tissue specialization. The embryo continues to grow until ready for hatching or birth.

Postnatal Growth

Postnatal growth occurs from hatching or birth until death. The length of the postnatal growth depends on the species. Elephants can live 70 years, but mice only about 4 years. Right after animals are hatched or born, they go through a period of rapid growth and development. In vertebrates, bones lengthen, muscles grow in bulk, and fat is deposited. At maturity, bones stop growing in length, but bones can grow in width and repair themselves throughout the animal's lifetime, and muscle deposition slows down. Fat cells continue to increase and decrease in size throughout the animal's life. Growth is controlled by genetics but is also influenced by nutrition and disease. Most animals are sexually mature in less than two years and can produce offspring.

Vascular and Nonvascular Plants

Vascular plants, also referred to as **tracheophytes**, have dermal tissue, meristematic tissue, ground tissues, and vascular tissues. Nonvascular plants, also referred to as **bryophytes**, do not have the vascular tissue xylem and phloem. Vascular plants can grow very tall, whereas nonvascular plants are short and close to the ground. Vascular plants can be found in dry regions, but nonvascular plants typically grow near or in moist areas. Vascular plants have leaves, roots, and stems, but nonvascular plants have leaf-like, root-like, and stem-like structures that do not have true vascular tissue. Nonvascular plants have hair-like **rhizoids**, that act like roots by anchoring them to the ground and absorbing water. Vascular plants include angiosperms, gymnosperms, and ferns. Nonvascular plants include mosses and liverworts.

Flowering Versus Nonflowering Plants

Angiosperms and gymnosperms are both vascular plants. **Angiosperms** are flowering plants, and **gymnosperms** are non-flowering plants. Angiosperms reproduce by seeds that are enclosed in an ovary, usually in a fruit, while gymnosperms reproduce by unenclosed or "naked" seeds on scales, leaves, or cones. Angiosperms can be further classified as either monocots or dicots, depending on if they have one or two cotyledons, respectively. Angiosperms include grasses, garden flowers, vegetables, and broadleaf trees such as maples, birches, elms, and oaks. Gymnosperms include conifers such as pines, spruces, cedars, and redwoods.

Review Video: Fruits in Flowering Plants
Visit mometrix.com/academy and enter code: 867090

Monocots and Dicots

Angiosperms can be classified as either monocots or dicots. The seeds of **monocots** have one cotyledon, and the seeds of **dicots** have two cotyledons. The flowers of monocots have petals in multiples of three, and the flowers of dicots have petals in multiples of four or five. The leaves of monocots are slender with parallel veins, while the leaves of dicots are broad and flat with branching veins. The vascular bundles in monocots are distributed throughout the stem, whereas the vascular bundles in dicots are arranged in rings. Monocots have a **fibrous root system**, and dicots have a **taproot system**.

Plant Dermal Tissue

Plant dermal tissue is called the epidermis, and is usually a single layer of closely-packed cells that covers leaves and young stems. The epidermis protects the plant by secreting the cuticle, which is a waxy substance that helps prevent water loss and infections. The epidermis in leaves has tiny pores called **stomata**. Guard cells in the epidermis control the opening and closing of the stomata. The epidermis usually does not have chloroplasts. The epidermis may be replaced by periderm in older plants. The **periderm** is also referred to as bark. The layers of the periderm are cork cells or phellem, phelloderm, and cork cambium or phellogen. Cork is the outer layer of the periderm and consists of nonliving cells. The periderm protects the plant and provides insulation.

Plant Vascular Tissue

The two major types of plant vascular tissue are xylem and phloem. Xylem and phloem are bound together in vascular bundles. A meristem called vascular cambium is located between the xylem and phloem and produces new xylem and phloem. **Xylem** is made up of tracheids and vessel elements. All vascular plants contain tracheids, but only angiosperms contain vessel elements. Xylem provides support and transports water and dissolved minerals unidirectionally from the roots upward using processes like transpiration pull and root pressure. Phloem is made up of companion cells and sieve-tube cells. **Phloem** transports dissolved sugars produced during photosynthesis and other nutrients bidirectionally to non-photosynthetic areas of the plant. By active transport, the companion vessels move glucose in and out of the sieve-tube cells.

Plant Ground Tissue

The three major types of ground tissue are parenchyma tissue, collenchyma tissue, and sclerenchyma tissue. Most ground tissue is made up of parenchyma. **Parenchyma** is formed by parenchyma cells, and it function in photosynthesis, food storage, and tissue repair. The inner tissue of a leaf, mesophyll, is an example of parenchyma tissue. **Collenchyma** is made of collenchyma cells and provides support in roots, stems, and petioles. **Sclerenchyma** tissue is made of sclereid cells, which are more rigid than the collenchyma cells, and provides rigid support and protection. Plant sclerenchyma tissue may contain cellulose or lignin. Fabrics such as jute, hemp, and flax are made of sclerenchyma tissue.

Plant Meristematic Tissue

Meristems or meristematic tissues are regions of plant growth. The cells in meristems are undifferentiated and always remain **totipotent**, which means they can always develop into any type of special tissue. Meristem cells can divide and produce new cells, which can aid in the process of regenerating damaged parts. Cells of meristems reproduce asexually through mitosis or cell division that is regulated by hormones. The two types of meristems are lateral meristems and apical meristems. **Primary growth** occurs at **apical meristems**, located at the tip of roots and shoots, and increases the length of the plant. Primary meristems include the protoderm, which produces epidermis; the procambium, which produces cambium, or lateral meristems; xylem and phloem; and the ground meristem, which produces ground tissue including parenchyma. **Secondary growth** occurs at the lateral or secondary meristems and causes an increase in diameter or thickness.

Flowers

The primary function of flowers is to produce seeds for reproduction of the plant. Flowers have a **pedicel**, a stalk with a receptacle or enlarged upper portion, which holds the developing seeds. Flowers also can have sepals and petals. **Sepals** are leaflike structures that protect the bud. **Petals**, which are collectively called the corolla, help to attract pollinators. Plants can have stamens, pistils, or both depending on the type of plant. The **stamen** consists of the anther and filament. The end of the stamen is called the **anther** and is where pollen is produced. Pollen also contains sperm, which is needed in order for a proper plant zygot to form. The **pistil** consists of the stigma, style, and ovary. The ovary contains the ovules, which house the egg cells.

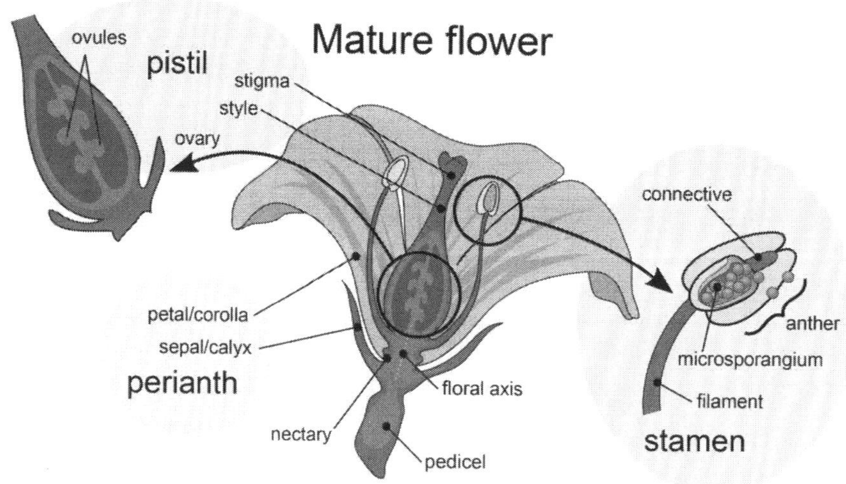

Stems

Plants can have either woody or nonwoody (herbaceous) stems. **Woody** stems consist of wood, or bark, as a structural tissue, while **herbaceous** stems are very flexible. The stem is divided into nodes and internodes. Buds are located at the nodes and may develop into leaves, roots, flowers, cones, or more stems. Stems consist of dermal tissue, ground tissue, and vascular tissue. **Dicot** stems have vascular bundles distributed through the stem. **Monocots** have rings of vascular bundles. Stems have four main functions: (1) they provide support to leaves, flowers, and fruits; (2)

they transport materials in the xylem and phloem; (3) they store food; and (4) they have meristems, which provide all of the new cells for the plant.

MONOCOT	DICOT
Single Cotyledon	 Two Cotyledon 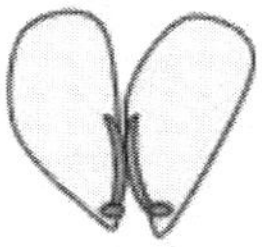
Long Narrow Leaf Parallel Veins	 Broad Leaf Network of Veins 
Vascular Bundles Scattered	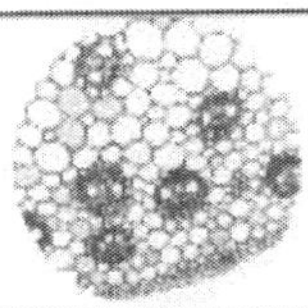 Vascular Bundles in a Ring 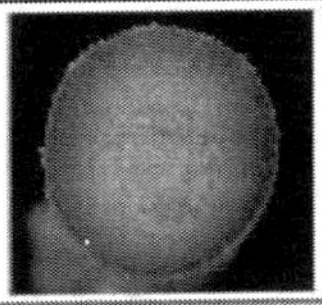
Floral Parts in Multiples of 3	 Floral Parts in Multiples of 4 or 5 

LEAVES

The primary function of a **leaf** is to manufacture food through photosynthesis. The leaf consists of a flat portion called the **blade** and a stalk called the **petiole**. The edge of the leaf is called the margin and can be entire, toothed, or lobed. Veins transport food and water and make up the skeleton of the leaf. The large central vein is called the **midrib**. The blade has an upper and lower epidermis. The epidermis is covered by a protective cuticle. The lower epidermis contains many stomata, which are pores that allow air to enter and leave the leaf. Stomata also regulate transpiration. The middle portion of the leaf is called the **mesophyll**. The mesophyll consists of the palisade mesophyll and the spongy mesophyll. Most photosynthesis occurs in chloroplasts located in the palisade mesophyll.

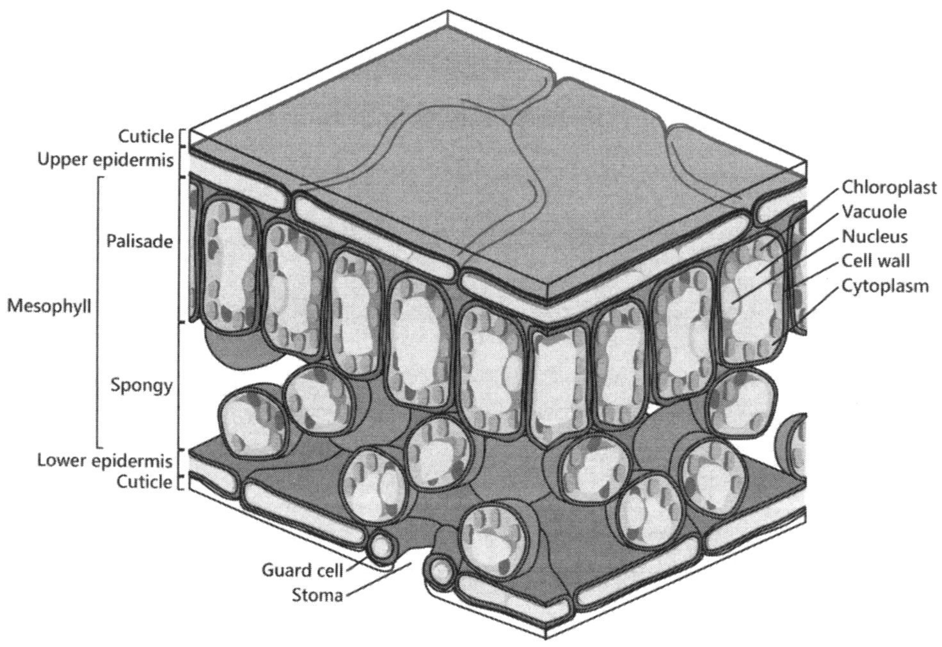

Roots

The primary functions of roots are to anchor the plant, absorb materials, and store food. The two basic types of root systems are taproot systems and fibrous root systems. **Taproot systems** have a primary root with many smaller secondary roots. **Fibrous root systems**, which lack a primary root, consist of a mass of many small secondary roots. The root has three main regions: the area of maturation, the area of elongation, and the area of cell division or the meristematic region. The root is covered by an epidermal cell, some of which develops into root hairs. **Root hairs** absorb water and minerals by osmosis, and capillary action helps move the water upward through the roots to the rest of the plant. The center of the root is the **vascular cylinder**, which contains the xylem and phloem. The vascular cylinder is surrounded by the cortex where the food is stored. Primary growth occurs at the root tip. Secondary growth occurs at the vascular cambium located between the xylem and phloem.

Pollination Strategies

Pollination is the transfer of pollen from the anther of the stamen to the stigma of the pistil on the same plant or on a different plant. Pollinators can be either **abiotic** (not derived from a living organism) or **biotic** (derived from a living organism). Abiotic pollinators include wind and water. Approximately 20% of pollination occurs by abiotic pollinators. For example, grasses are typically pollinated by wind, and aquatic plants are typically pollinated by water. Biotic pollinators include insects, birds, mammals, and occasionally reptiles. Most biotic pollinators are insects. Many plants have colored petals and strong scents, which attract insects. Pollen rubs off on the insects and is transferred as they move from plant to plant.

Seed Dispersal Methods

Methods of **seed dispersal** can be abiotic or biotic. Methods of seed dispersal include gravity, wind, water, and animals. Some plants produce seeds in fruits that get eaten by animals and then are distributed to new locations in the animals' waste. Some seeds (e.g. dandelions) have structures to aid in dispersal by wind. Some seeds have barbs that get caught in animal hair or bird feathers and are then carried to new locations by the animals. Interestingly, some animals bury seeds for food storage but do not return for the seeds. The seeds of aquatic plants can be dispersed by water, while the seeds of plants near rivers, streams, lakes, and beaches (e.g. coconuts) are also often dispersed by water. Some plants, in a method called **mechanical dispersal**, can propel or shoot their seeds away from them even up to several feet. For example, touch-me-nots and violets utilize mechanical dispersal.

ALTERNATION OF GENERATIONS

Alternation of generations, also referred to as **metagenesis**, contains both a sexual phase and an asexual phase in the life cycle of the plant. Mosses and ferns reproduce by alternation of generations: the sexual phase is called the **gametophyte**, and the asexual phase is called the **sporophyte**. During the sexual phase, a sperm fertilizes an egg to form a zygote. By mitosis, the zygote develops into the sporophyte. The sporangia in the sori of the sporophyte produce the spores through meiosis. The spores germinate and by mitosis produce the gametophyte.

Review Video: Asexual Reproduction
Visit mometrix.com/academy and enter code: 565616

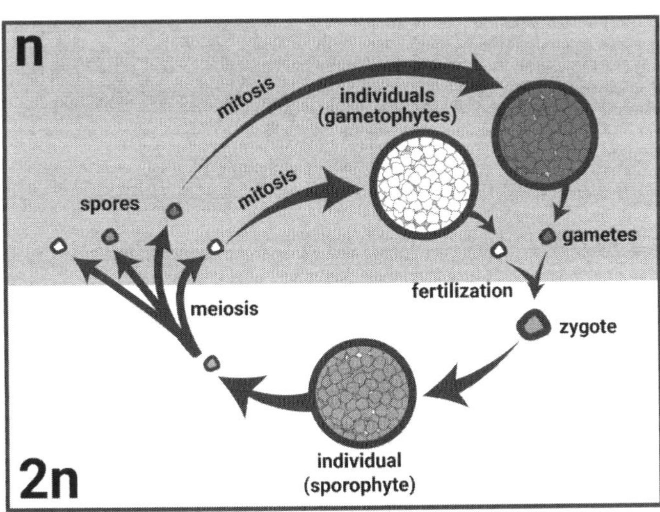

OBTAINING AND TRANSPORTING WATER AND INORGANIC NUTRIENTS

Inorganic nutrients and water enter plants through the root hair and travel to the xylem. Once the water, minerals, and salts have crossed the endodermis, they must be moved upward through the xylem by water uptake. Most of a plant's water is lost through the stomata by transpiration. This loss is necessary to provide the tension needed to pull the water and nutrients up through the xylem. In order to maintain the remaining water that is necessary for the functioning of the plant, guard cells control the stomata. Whether an individual stoma is closed or open is controlled by two guard cells. When the guard cells lose water and become flaccid, they collapse together, closing the stoma. When the guard cells swell with water and become turgid, they move apart, opening the stoma.

USE OF ROOTS

Plant roots have numerous root hairs that absorb water and inorganic nutrients such as minerals and salts. Root hairs are thin, hair-like outgrowths of the root's epidermal cells that exponentially increase the root's surface area. Water molecules cross the cell membranes of the root hairs by

osmosis and then travel on to the vascular cylinder. Inorganic nutrients are transported across the cell membranes of the root endodermis by **active transport**. The endodermis is a single layer of cells that the water and nutrients must pass through by osmosis or active transport. To control mineral uptake by the roots, Casparian strips act as an extracellular diffusion barrier, and forces nutrients to be pulled into the plant. While water passes through by osmosis, mineral uptake is controlled by transport proteins.

USE OF XYLEM

The xylem contains dead, water-conducting cells called tracheids and vessels. The movement of water upward through the tracheids and vessels is explained by the **cohesion-tension theory**. First, water is lost through evaporation of the plant's surface through transpiration. This can occur at any surface exposed to air but is mainly through the stomata in the epidermis. This transpiration puts the water inside the xylem in a state of tension. Because water is cohesive due to the strong hydrogen bonds between molecules, the water is pulled up the xylem as long as the water is transpiring.

GLUCOSE PRODUCED DURING PHOTOSYNTHESIS

Plants produce glucose, a simple carbohydrate or monosaccharide, during photosynthesis. Plants do not transport glucose molecules directly, but instead glucose undergoes reactions to form sucrose, starch, and cellulose which are then used in different ways. Glucose is joined to a fructose molecule to form **sucrose**, a disaccharide, which is transported in sap. Like glucose, sucrose is also considered a simple carbohydrate. Starches and cellulose are complex carbohydrates consisting of long chains of glucose molecules called polysaccharides. Plants use **starch** to store glucose, and **cellulose** for rigidity in cell walls.

USE OF PHLOEM TO TRANSPORT PRODUCTS OF PHOTOSYNTHESIS

The movement of sugars and other materials from the leaves to other tissues throughout the plants is called **translocation**. Nutrients are translocated from **sources**, or areas with excess sugars such as mature leaves, to **sinks**, areas where sugars are needed (i.e. roots or developing seeds). Phloem vessels are found in the vascular bundles along with the xylem. Phloem contains conducting cells called sieve elements, which are connected end to end in sieve tubes. **Sieve tubes** carry sap from sugar sources to sugar sinks. Phloem sap contains mostly sucrose dissolved in water. The sap can also contain proteins, amino acids, and hormones. Some plants transport sugar alcohols. Loading the sugar into the sieve tubes causes water to enter the tubes by osmosis, creating a higher hydrostatic pressure at the source end of the tube. This pressure is what causes nutrients to move upward towards the sink areas. Sugar is removed from the sieve tube at the sink end and the solute potential is increased, thus causing water to leave the phloem. This process is referred to as the **pressure-flow mechanism**.

BIOSPHERE

COMPONENTS

The **biosphere** is the region of the earth inhabited by living things. The components of the biosphere from smallest to largest are organisms, populations, communities, ecosystems, and biomes. Organisms of the same species make up a **population**. All of the populations in an area make up the **community**. The community combined with the physical environment for a region forms an **ecosystem**. Several ecosystems are grouped together to form large geographic regions called **biomes**.

POPULATION

A **population** is a group of all the individuals of one species in a specific area or region at a certain time. A **species** is a group of organisms that can breed and produce fertile offspring. There may be many populations of a specific species in a large geographic region. **Ecologists** study the size, density, and growth rate of populations to determine their stability. Population size continuously changes with births, deaths, and migrations. The population density is the number of individuals per unit of area. Growth rates for a population may be exponential or logistic. Ecologists also study how the individuals are dispersed within a population. Some species form clusters, while others are evenly or randomly spaced. However, every population has limiting factors. Changes in the environment or geography can reduce or limit population size. The individuals of a population interact with each other and with other organisms in the community in various ways, including competition and predation, which have direct impacts population size.

COMMUNITY INTERACTIONS

A **community** is all of the populations of different species that live in an area and interact with each other. Community interaction can be intraspecific or interspecific. **Intraspecific interactions** occur between members of the same species. **Interspecific interactions** occur between members of different species. Different types of interactions include competition, predation, and symbiosis. Communities with high diversity are more complex and more stable than communities with low diversity. The level of diversity can be seen in a food web of the community, which shows all the feeding relationships within the community.

ECOSYSTEMS

An **ecosystem** is the basic unit of ecology. An ecosystem is the sum of all the biotic and abiotic factors in an area. **Biotic factors** are all living things such as plants, animals, fungi, and microorganisms. **Abiotic factors** include the light, water, air, temperature, and soil in an area. Ecosystems obtain the energy they need from sunlight. Ecosystems also contain biogeochemical cycles such as the hydrologic cycle and the nitrogen cycle. Ecosystems are generally classified as either terrestrial or aquatic. All of the living things within an ecosystem are called its community. The number and variety of living things within a community describes the ecosystem's **biodiversity**. However, each ecosystem can only support a limited number of organisms known as the **carrying capacity**.

SYMBIOSIS

Many species share a special nutritional relationship with another species, called **symbiosis**. The term symbiosis means "living together." In symbiosis, two organisms share a close physical relationship that can be helpful, harmful, or neutral for each organism. Three forms of symbiotic relationships are parasitism, commensalism, and mutualism. **Parasitism** is a relationship between two organisms in which one organism is the parasite, and the other organism is the host. The parasite benefits from the relationship because the parasite obtains its nutrition from the host. The host is harmed from the relationship because the parasite is using the host's energy and giving nothing in return. For example, a tick and a dog share a parasitic relationship in which the tick is the parasite, and the dog is the host. **Commensalism** is a relationship between two organisms in which one benefits, and the other is not affected. For example, a small fish called a remora can attach to the belly of a shark and ride along. The remora is safe under the shark, and the shark is not affected. **Mutualism** is a relationship between two organisms in which both organisms benefit. For example, a rhinoceros usually can be seen with a few tick birds perched on its back. The tick birds are helped by the easy food source of ticks, and the rhino benefits from the tick removal.

PREDATION

Predation is a special nutritional relationship in which one organism is the predator, and the other organism is the prey. The predator benefits from the relationship, but the prey is harmed. The predator hunts and kills the prey for food. The predator is specially adapted to hunt its prey, and the prey is specially adapted to escape its predator. While predators harm (kill) their individual prey, predation usually helps the prey species. Predation keeps the population of the prey species under control and prevents them from overshooting the carrying capacity, which often leads to starvation. Also, predation usually helps to remove weak or slow members of the prey species leaving the healthier, stronger, and better adapted individuals to reproduce. Examples of predator-prey relationships include lions and zebras, snakes and rats, and hawks and rabbits.

COMPETITION AND TERRITORIALITY

Competition is a relationship between two organisms in which the organisms compete for the same vital resource that is in short supply. Typically, both organisms are harmed, but one is usually harmed more than the other, which provides an avenue for natural selection. Organisms compete for resources such as food, water, mates, and space. **Interspecific competition** is between members of different species, while **intraspecific competition** is between members of the same species. **Territoriality** can be considered to be a type of interspecific competition for space. Many animals including mammals, birds, reptiles, fish, spiders, and insects have exhibited territorial behavior. Once territories are established, there are fewer conflicts between organisms. For example, a male redwing blackbird can establish a large territory. By singing and flashing his red patches, he is able to warn other males to avoid his territory, and they can avoid fighting.

ALTRUISTIC BEHAVIORS BETWEEN ANIMALS

Altruism is a self-sacrificing behavior in which an individual animal may serve or protect another animal. For example, in a honey bee colony there is one queen with many workers (females). There are also drones (males), but only during the mating seasons. Adult workers do all the work of the hive and will die defending it. Another example of altruism is seen in a naked mole rat colony. Each colony has one queen that mates with a few males, and the rest of the colony is nonbreeding and lives to service the queen, her mates, and her offspring.

Review Video: Mutualism, Commensalism, and Parasitism
Visit mometrix.com/academy and enter code: 757249

ENERGY FLOW IN THE ENVIRONMENT

USING TROPHIC LEVELS WITH AN ENERGY PYRAMID

Energy flow through an ecosystem can be tracked through an energy pyramid. An **energy pyramid** shows how energy is transferred from one trophic level to another. **Producers** always form the base of an energy pyramid, and the consumers form successive levels above the producers. Producers only store about 1% of the solar energy they receive. Then, each successive level only uses about 10% of the energy of the previous level. That means that **primary consumers** use about 10% of the energy used by primary producers, such as grasses and trees. Next, **secondary**

consumers use 10% of primary consumers' 10%, or 1% overall. This continues up for as many trophic levels as exist in a particular ecosystem.

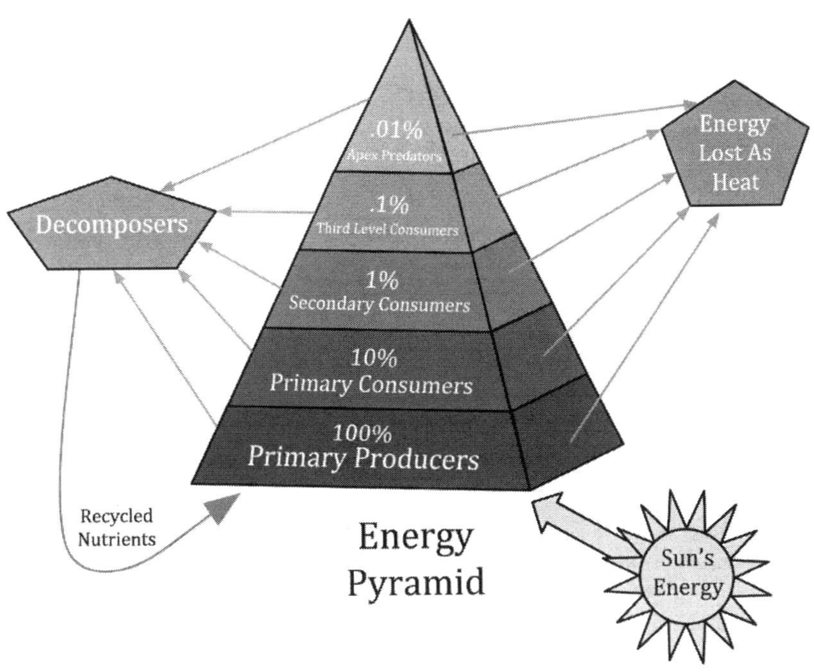

Food Web

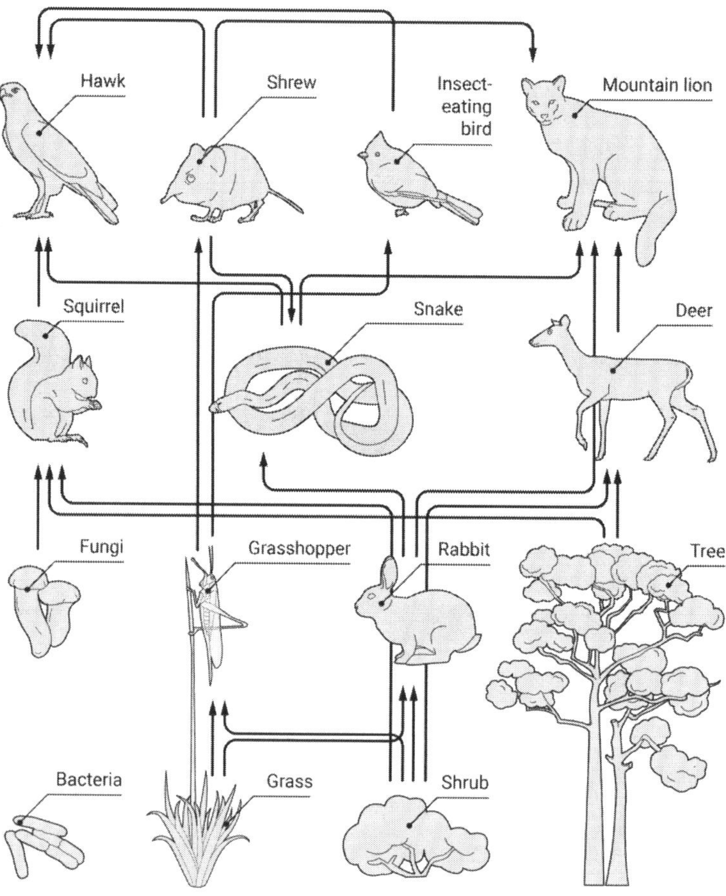

Energy flow through an ecosystem can be illustrated by a **food web**. Energy moves through the food web in the direction of the arrows. In the food web, producers such as grass, trees, and shrubs use energy from the sun to produce food through photosynthesis. Herbivores or primary consumers such as squirrels, grasshoppers, and rabbits obtain energy by eating the producers. Secondary consumers, which are carnivores such as snakes and shrews, obtain energy by eating the primary consumers. Tertiary consumers, which are carnivores such as hawks and mountain lions, obtain energy by eating the secondary consumers. Note that the hawk and the mountain lion can also be considered quaternary consumers in this food web if a different food chain within the web is followed.

Review Video: <u>Food Webs</u>
Visit mometrix.com/academy and enter code: 853254

Physical Science

Basic Equation for Work

The equation for **work** (W) is fairly simple: $W = F \times d$, where F is the force exerted and d is the displacement of the object on which the force is exerted. For the simplest case, when the vectors of force and displacement have the same direction, the work done is equal to the product of the magnitudes of the force and displacement. If this is not the case, then the work may be calculated as $W = Fd\cos\theta$, where θ is the angle between the force and displacement vectors. If force and displacement have the same direction, then work is positive; if they are in opposite directions, however, work is negative; and if they are perpendicular, the work done by the force is zero.

For example, if a man pushes a block horizontally across a surface with a constant force of 10 N for a distance of 20 m, the work done by the man is 200 N-m or 200 J. If instead the block is sliding and the man tries to **slow its progress** by pushing against it, his work done is –200 J, since he is pushing in the direction opposite the motion. Also, if the man pushes vertically downward on the block while it slides, his work done is zero, since his force vector is perpendicular to the displacement vector of the block.

It is important to note in each of these cases that neither the mass of the block nor the elapsed time is considered when calculating the amount of work done by the man.

Review Video: Work
Visit mometrix.com/academy and enter code: 681834

Power

Put simply, **power** is the **rate at which work is done**. Power, like work, is a scalar quantity. If we know the amount of work, W, that has been performed in a given amount of time, Δt, then we may find average power, $P_{avg} = W/\Delta t$. If we are instead looking for the instantaneous power, there are two possibilities. If the force on an object is constant, and the object is moving at a constant velocity, then the instantaneous power is the same as the average power. If either the force or the velocity is varying, the instantaneous power should be computed by the equation $P = Fv$, where F and v are the instantaneous force and velocity. This equation may also be used to compute average power if the force and velocity are constant. Power is typically expressed in joules per second, or watts.

Simple Machines

Simple machines include the inclined plane, lever, wheel and axle, and pulley. These simple machines have no internal source of energy. More complex or compound machines can be formed from them. Simple machines provide a force known as a mechanical advantage and make it easier to accomplish a task. The inclined plane enables a force less than the object's weight to be used to push an object to a greater height. A lever enables a multiplication of force. The wheel and axle allows for movement with less resistance. Single or double pulleys allow for easier direction of force. The wedge and screw are forms of the inclined plane. A wedge turns a smaller force working over a greater distance into a larger force. The screw is similar to an incline that is wrapped around a shaft.

Review Video: Simple Machines
Visit mometrix.com/academy and enter code: 950789

Mechanical Advantage

A certain amount of **work** is required to move an object. The amount cannot be reduced, but by changing the way the work is performed a **mechanical advantage** can be gained. A certain amount of work is required to raise an object to a given vertical height. By getting to a given height at an angle, the effort required is reduced, but the distance that must be traveled to reach a given height is increased. An example of this is walking up a hill. One may take a direct, shorter, but steeper route, or one may take a more meandering, longer route that requires less effort. Examples of wedges include doorstops, axes, plows, zippers, and can openers.

Levers

A **lever** consists of a bar or plank and a pivot point or fulcrum. Work is performed by the bar, which swings at the pivot point to redirect the force. There are three types of levers: first, second, and third class. Examples of a **first-class lever** include balances, see-saws, nail extractors, and scissors (which also use wedges). In a **second-class lever** the fulcrum is placed at one end of the bar and the work is performed at the other end. The weight or load to be moved is in between. The closer to the fulcrum the weight is, the easier it is to move. Force is increased, but the distance it is moved is decreased. Examples include pry bars, bottle openers, nutcrackers, and wheelbarrows. In a **third-class lever** the fulcrum is at one end and the positions of the weight and the location where the work is performed are reversed. Examples include fishing rods, hammers, and tweezers.

Review Video: Levers
Visit mometrix.com/academy and enter code: 103910

Wheel and Axle

The center of a **wheel and axle** can be likened to a fulcrum on a rotating lever. As it turns, the wheel moves a greater distance than the axle, but with less force. Obvious examples of the wheel and axle are the wheels of a car, but this type of simple machine can also be used to exert a greater force. For instance, a person can turn the handles of a winch to exert a greater force at the turning axle to move an object. Other examples include steering wheels, wrenches, faucets, waterwheels, windmills, gears, and belts. **Gears** work together to change a force. The four basic types of gears are spur, rack and pinion, bevel, and worm gears. The larger gear turns slower than the smaller, but exerts a greater force. Gears at angles can be used to change the direction of forces.

Review Video: Wheel and Axle
Visit mometrix.com/academy and enter code: 574045

Pulleys

A **single pulley** consists of a rope or line that is run around a wheel. This allows force to be directed in a downward motion to lift an object. This does not decrease the force required, just changes its direction. The load is moved the same distance as the rope pulling it. When a **combination pulley** is used, such as a double pulley, the weight is moved half the distance of the rope pulling it. In this way, the work effort is doubled. Pulleys are never 100% efficient because of friction. Examples of pulleys include cranes, chain hoists, block and tackles, and elevators.

Kinetic Energy

The **kinetic energy of an object** is that quality of its motion that can be related in a qualitative way to the amount of work performed on the object. Kinetic energy can be defined as $KE = \frac{mv^2}{2}$, in which m is the mass of an object and v is the magnitude of its velocity. Kinetic energy cannot be negative, since it depends on the square of velocity. Units for kinetic energy are the same as those for work: joules. Kinetic energy is a scalar quantity.

Changes in kinetic energy occur when a force does work on an object, such that the speed of the object is altered. This change in kinetic energy is equal to the amount of work that is done, and can be expressed as $W = KE_f - KE_i = \Delta KE$. This equation is commonly referred to as the work-kinetic energy theorem. If there are several different forces acting on the object, then W in this equation is simply the total work done by all the forces, or by the net force. This equation can be very helpful in solving some problems that would otherwise rely solely on Newton's laws of motion.

Potential Energy

Potential energy is the amount of energy that can be ascribed to a body or bodies based on configuration. There are a couple of different kinds of potential energy. **Gravitational potential energy** is the energy associated with the separation of bodies that are attracted to one another gravitationally. Any time you lift an object, you are increasing its gravitational potential energy. Gravitational potential energy can be found by the equation $PE = mgh$, where m is the mass of an object, g is the gravitational acceleration, and h is its height above a reference point, most often the ground.

Another kind of potential energy is **elastic potential energy**; elastic potential energy is associated with the compression or expansion of an elastic, or spring-like, object. Physicists will often refer to potential energy as being stored within a body, the implication being that it could emerge in the future.

Review Video: Potential and Kinetic Energy
Visit mometrix.com/academy and enter code: 491502

Conservative and Non-Conservative Forces

Forces that change the state of a system by changing kinetic energy into potential energy, or vice versa, are called **conservative forces**. This name arises because these forces conserve the **total amount of kinetic and potential energy**. Every other kind of force is considered non-conservative. One example of a conservative force is gravity. Consider the path of a ball thrown straight up into the air. Since the ball has the same amount of kinetic energy when it is thrown as it does when it returns to its original location (known as completing a closed path), gravity can be said to be a conservative force. More generally, a force can be said to be conservative if the work it does on an object through a closed path is zero. Frictional force would not meet this standard, of course, because it is only capable of performing negative work.

One-Dimensional Analysis of Work Done By a Variable Force

If the force on an object varies across the distance the object is moved, then a simple product will not yield the work. If we consider the work performed by a variable force in one dimension, then we are assuming that the directions of the force and the displacement are the same. The magnitude of the force will depend on the position of the particle. In order to calculate the amount of work performed by a variable force over a given distance, we should first divide the total displacement into a number of intervals, each with a width of Δx. We may then say that the amount of work performed during any one interval is $\Delta W = F_{avg}\Delta x$, where F_{avg} is the average force over the interval Δx. We can then say that the total amount of work performed is the sum of all work performed during the various intervals. By reducing the interval to an infinitesimal length, we obtain the integral:

$$W = \int_{x_1}^{x_2} F_x dx$$

This integral requires that the force be a known function of x.

Work Performed by a Spring

If we move a block attached to a spring from point x_i to point x_f, we are doing work on the block, and the spring is also doing work on the block. To determine the work done by the spring on the block, we can substitute F from Hooke's law into our equation for work performed by a variable force, and arrive at this measure: $W = \frac{k(x_i^2 - x_f^2)}{2}$. This work will be positive if $x_i^2 > x_f^2$, and negative if the opposite is true. If $x_i = 0$ and we decide to call the final position x, then we may change our equation: $W = \frac{-kx^2}{2}$. It is important to keep in mind that this is the work done by the spring. The work done by the force that moves the block to its final position will be a positive quantity.

Like all simple harmonic oscillators, springs operate by **storing and releasing potential energy**. The amount of energy being stored or released by a spring is equal to the magnitude of the work done by the spring during that same operation. The total potential energy stored in a spring can be calculated as $PE = \frac{kx^2}{2}$. Neglecting the effects of friction and drag, an object oscillating on a spring will continue to do so indefinitely, since total mechanical energy (kinetic and potential) is conserved. In such a situation, the period of oscillation can be calculated as $T = 2\pi \times \sqrt{\frac{m}{k}}$.

Displacement

When something changes its location from one place to another, it is said to have undergone **displacement**. If we can determine the original and final position of the object, then we can determine the total displacement with this simple equation:

$$\Delta \boldsymbol{x} = final\ position - original\ position$$

If the object has moved in the positive direction, then the final position will be greater than the original position, so we can say that the change was positive. If the final position is less than the original, however, displacement will be negative. Displacement along a straight line is a very simple example of a vector quantity; it has both a magnitude and a direction. If an object travels from position $x = -5$ cm to $x = 5$ cm, it has undergone a displacement of 10 cm. If it traverses the same path in the opposite direction, its displacement is −10 cm. A vector that spans the object's displacement in the direction of travel is known as a displacement vector, with units of length.

Review Video: Displacement
Visit mometrix.com/academy and enter code: 236197

Determining Position

In order to determine anything about the **motion of an object**, we must first **locate it**. In other words, we must be able to describe its position relative to some reference point, often called an **origin**. If we consider the origin as the zero point of an axis, then the positive direction of the axis will be the direction in which measuring numbers are getting larger, and the negative direction is that in which the numbers are getting smaller. If a particle is located 5 cm from the origin in the positive direction of the x-axis, its location is said to be $x = 5$ cm. If another particle is 5 cm from the origin in the negative direction of the x-axis, its position is $x = -5$ cm. These two particles are 10 cm apart. A vector whose starting point is the origin and whose endpoint is the location of an object is that object's position vector, with units of length.

VELOCITY

INSTANTANEOUS VELOCITY

There are two types of velocity that are commonly considered in physics: **average velocity** and **instantaneous velocity**. In order to obtain the *instantaneous velocity* of an object, we must find its average velocity and then try to decrease Δt as close as possible to zero. As Δt decreases, it approaches what is known as a *limiting value*, bringing the average velocity very close to the instantaneous velocity. Instantaneous velocity is most easily discussed in the context of calculus-based physics.

AVERAGE VELOCITY

If we want to calculate the *average velocity* of an object, we must know two things. First, we must know its **displacement**, or the **distance** it has covered. Second, we must know the **time it took to cover this distance**. Once we have this information, the formula for average velocity is quite simple: $\boldsymbol{v}_{avg} = \frac{(x_f - x_i)}{(t_f - t_i)}$, where the subscripts i and f denote the initial and final values of the position and time. In other words, the average velocity is equal to the change in position divided by the change in time. This calculation will indicate the average distance that was covered per unit of time. **Average velocity is a vector** and will always point in the same direction as the displacement vector (since time is a scalar and always positive).

ACCELERATION

Acceleration is the **change in the velocity** of an object. Like velocity, acceleration may be computed as an average or an instantaneous quantity. To calculate average acceleration, we may use this simple equation: $\boldsymbol{a}_{avg} = \frac{v_f - v_i}{t_f - t_i}$, where the subscripts i and f denote the initial and final values of the velocity and time. The so-called instantaneous acceleration of an object can be found by reducing the time component to the limiting value until instantaneous velocity is approached. Acceleration will be expressed in units of distance divided by time squared; for instance, meters per second squared. Like position and velocity, acceleration is a vector quantity and will therefore have both magnitude and direction.

Review Video: Velocity and Acceleration
Visit mometrix.com/academy and enter code: 671849

KINEMATICS

KINEMATIC EQUATIONS

The phenomenon of constant acceleration allows physicists to construct a number of helpful equations. Perhaps the most fundamental equation of an object's motion is the **position equation**:

$$x = x_i + \boldsymbol{v}_i t + \frac{1}{2}\boldsymbol{a}t^2$$

If the object is starting from rest at the origin, this equation reduces to $x = \frac{at^2}{2}$. The position equation can be rearranged to give the **displacement equation**:

$$\Delta \boldsymbol{x} = \boldsymbol{v}_i t + \frac{1}{2}\boldsymbol{a}t^2$$

If the object's acceleration is unknown, the position or displacement may be found by the equation:

$$\Delta \boldsymbol{x} = \frac{(\boldsymbol{v}_f + \boldsymbol{v}_i)t}{2}$$

If the position of an object is unknown, the velocity may be found by the equation:

$$\boldsymbol{v} = \boldsymbol{v}_i + \boldsymbol{a}t$$

Similarly, if the time is unknown, the velocity after a given displacement may be found by the equation:

$$\boldsymbol{v} = \sqrt{(\boldsymbol{v}_i{}^2 + 2\boldsymbol{a}\Delta \boldsymbol{x})}$$

Projectile Motion

When we discuss **projectile motion**, we are referring to the movement of an object through two dimensions during a free fall. Two-dimensional motion may be described using the same equations as one-dimensional motion, but two equations must be considered simultaneously. For basic equations for projectile motion, it is often assumed that the rate of gravitational acceleration on the earth is $\boldsymbol{g} = 9.8 \text{ m/s}^2$, and that the effect of air resistance can be ignored (Note: take care with the sign on gravitational acceleration make sure that it always points toward the earth). If a projectile is launched under such ideal conditions, we may say that its initial velocity is $\boldsymbol{v}_0 = v_0 \cos\theta\,\mathbf{i} + v_0 \sin\theta\,\mathbf{j}$. These two velocity components are sometimes written as $\boldsymbol{v}_{0x}$ and $\boldsymbol{v}_{0y}$, respectively.

Example: If a cannon located at a height of 5 m above ground level fires a cannonball 250 m/s at an angle of $\frac{\pi}{6}$ from the horizontal, how far will the cannonball travel before hitting the ground?

When the cannonball hits the ground, it has been displaced by -5 m in the y-direction. Solving for the components of initial velocity yields $\boldsymbol{v}_{0x} = 216.5 \text{ m/s}$ and $\boldsymbol{v}_{0y} = 125 \text{ m/s}$. Setting up the y-direction displacement equation results in the following: $-5 = 125t_f - 4.9t_f{}^2$. Solving for t_f yields an impact time of around 25.5 seconds. To find the horizontal distance covered, simply set up the displacement equation for the x-direction: $\Delta \boldsymbol{x} = \boldsymbol{v}_{0x}t_f + \frac{1}{2}\boldsymbol{a}_x\left(t_f\right)^2$. Since we ignore the effects of air resistance, acceleration in the x-direction is zero, yielding a flight distance of 5,530 m.

Review Video: Projectile Motion
Visit mometrix.com/academy and enter code: 719700

Uniform Circular Motion

We may say that a particle is in **uniform circular motion** when it is traveling in a circle, or circular arc, and at a constant speed. Crucially, we must note that such a particle is accelerating, even though the magnitude of its velocity does not change. This is because velocity is a vector, and consequently, any change in its direction is an acceleration. So, if we take two points on an arc of radius, r, separated by an angle, θ, and want to determine the time it will take a particle to move between these two points at a constant speed, $|\boldsymbol{v}|$, we can use the equation: $\Delta t = \frac{r\theta}{|v|}$. The quantity $\frac{|v|}{r}$ is often written as $\boldsymbol{\omega}$, or angular velocity, having units of radians per second, so the time may also be computed as $\Delta t = \frac{\theta}{\omega}$. The speed, or absolute value of the velocity, of an object in uniform circular motion is also called the tangential speed, because the object is always moving in a direction tangent to the circle. Similarly, an increase in the magnitude of this velocity is called **tangential acceleration**.

A very important component of uniform motion is the centripetal acceleration. This is the acceleration that changes the direction of the velocity vector to follow the circular arc. It is directed toward the center of the circle or arc and is described by $\boldsymbol{a}_c = \frac{|v|^2}{r} = r\boldsymbol{\omega}^2$.

Relative Motion and Inertial Reference Frames

When we describe motion as being **relative**, we mean that it can only be measured in relation to something else. If a moving object is considered as it relates to some stationary object or arbitrary location, it will have a different measured velocity than it would if it were compared to some other object that is itself in motion. In other words, the measure of an object's velocity depends entirely on the reference frame from which the measurement is taken. When performing measurements of this kind, we may use any reference point we like. However, once we have decided on a reference point, we must be consistent in using it as the basis for all of our measurements, or else we will go astray. Additionally, if we want to be able to apply Newton's laws of motion or Galilean principles of relativity, we must select an **inertial reference frame**: that is, a reference frame that is not accelerating or rotating. A car traveling at a constant speed in a straight line is an inertial reference frame. A car moving in uniform circular motion is not.

An object's velocity with respect to a frame fixed to the earth can be computed by measuring its velocity from any inertial reference frame and combining that velocity by vector addition with the velocity of the inertial frame with respect to the earth. For instance, if a man is traveling in the x-direction at 20 m/s, and he throws a rock out the window at a relative velocity of 15 m/s in the y-direction, the rock's velocity with respect to the earth is found by adding the two vectors:

$$\boldsymbol{v}_r = 20\mathbf{i} + 15\mathbf{j} \text{ m/s}$$

Newton's Laws

Newton's First Law

Before Newton formulated his laws of mechanics, it was generally assumed that some force had to act on an object continuously in order to make the object move at a **constant velocity**. Newton, however, determined that unless some other force acted on the object (most notably friction or air resistance), it would continue in the direction it was pushed at the same velocity forever. In this light, a body at rest and a body in motion are not all that different, and Newton's first law makes little distinction. It states that a body at rest will tend to remain at rest, while a body in motion will tend to remain in motion. This phenomenon is commonly referred to as **inertia**, the tendency of a body to remain in its present state of motion. In order for the body's state of motion to change, it must be acted on by a non-zero net force. **Net force** is the vector sum of all forces acting on a body.

If this vector sum is zero, then there is no unbalanced force, and the body will remain in its present state of motion. It is important to remember that this law only holds in inertial reference frames.

Review Video: Newton's First Law of Motion
Visit mometrix.com/academy and enter code: 590367

NEWTON'S SECOND LAW

Newton's second law states that an **object's acceleration** is directly proportional to the net force acting on the object, and inversely proportional to the object's mass. It is generally written in equation form $\boldsymbol{F} = m\boldsymbol{a}$, where $\boldsymbol{F}$ is the net force acting on a body, m is the mass of the body, and $\boldsymbol{a}$ is its acceleration. It is important to note from this equation that since the mass is always a positive quantity, the acceleration vector is always pointed in the same direction as the net force vector. Of course, in order to apply this equation correctly, one must clearly identify the body to which it is being applied. Once this is done, we may say that $\boldsymbol{F}$ is the vector sum of all forces acting on that body, or the net force. This measure includes only those forces that are external to the body; any internal forces, in which one part of the body exerts force on another, are discounted. Newton's second law somewhat encapsulates his first, because it includes the principle that if no net force is acting on a body, the body will not accelerate. As was the case with his first law, Newton's second law may only be applied in inertial reference frames.

Review Video: Newton's Second Law of Motion
Visit mometrix.com/academy and enter code: 737975

NEWTON'S THIRD LAW

Newton's third law of motion is quite simple: **for every force, there is an equal and opposite force**. When a hammer strikes a nail, the nail hits the hammer just as hard. If we consider two objects, A and B, then we may express any contact between these two bodies with the equation $\boldsymbol{F}_{AB} = -\boldsymbol{F}_{BA}$. It is important to note in this kind of equation that the order of the subscripts denotes which body is exerting the force. Although the two forces are often referred to as the **action** and **reaction** forces, in physics there is really no such thing. There is no implication of cause and effect in the equation for Newton's third law. At first glance, this law might seem to forbid any movement at all. We must remember, however, that these equal, opposite forces are exerted on different bodies with different masses, so they will not cancel each other out.

Review Video: Newton's Third Law of Motion
Visit mometrix.com/academy and enter code: 838401

STATIC AND KINETIC FRICTIONAL FORCES

In order to illustrate the concept of friction, let us imagine a book resting on a table. As it sits there, the force of its **weight** ($\boldsymbol{W}$) is equal and opposite to the **normal force** ($\boldsymbol{N}$). If, however, we were to exert a force ($\boldsymbol{F}$) on the book, attempting to push it to one side, a **frictional force** ($\boldsymbol{f}$) would arise, equal and opposite to our force. This kind of frictional force is known as *static frictional force*. As we increase our force on the book, however, we will eventually cause it to accelerate in the direction of our force. At this point, the frictional force opposing us will be known as *kinetic frictional force*. For the most part, kinetic frictional force is lower than static frictional force, and so the amount of force needed to maintain the movement of the book will be less than that needed to initiate movement. For wheels and spherical objects on a surface, static friction at the point of contact allows them to roll, but there is a frictional force that resists the rolling motion as well, due primarily to deformation effects in the rolling material. This is known as rolling friction, and tends to be much smaller than either static or kinetic friction.

Equilibrium

We may say that an object is in a **state of equilibrium** when it has a **constant linear momentum** P at its center of mass, and when **angular momentum L is also constant about the center of mass**. In other words, a wheel may be in equilibrium when it is spinning at a constant speed, and a hockey puck may be in equilibrium as it slides across ice. These are both examples of **dynamic equilibrium**. The phrase **static equilibrium**, however, is reserved for objects in which both linear and angular momentum are at zero. An object sitting on a table could be considered as being in static equilibrium.

Using Equilibrium Conditions

For a **body in equilibrium**, the net force vector and the net torque vector will both be equal to zero. For the most common cases, two-dimensional systems, these conditions can be fully expressed by one or two force summation equations and one torque summation equation. Torque summations may be taken about any point on the body, though strategic placement can make calculations simpler. To determine the **torque exerted by a force**, simply multiply the magnitude of the force by the perpendicular distance to the point of interest. It will be necessary to decide in advance which direction of torque (clockwise or counterclockwise) will be considered positive.

For example, if we have a bar of known mass, m, that is suspended by cables at each end and whose center of mass is two thirds of the way along its length, L, we can use the equilibrium conditions to determine the tension in each cable. Gravity exerts a force of $-m\boldsymbol{g}$ on the bar's center of mass. Translational equilibrium conditions tell us that $\boldsymbol{T}_1 + \boldsymbol{T}_2 - m\boldsymbol{g} = 0$. Setting the total torque about the center of mass equal to zero, considering counterclockwise torque to be positive, yields the equation $\boldsymbol{T}_2\left(\frac{L}{3}\right) - \boldsymbol{T}_1\left(\frac{2L}{3}\right) = 0$. Solving these equations results in $\boldsymbol{T}_1 = \frac{m\boldsymbol{g}}{3}$ and $\boldsymbol{T}_2 = \frac{2m\boldsymbol{g}}{3}$. This result makes sense since the center of mass is closer to the second cable.

Translational and Rotational Equilibrium

If a body is in **translational equilibrium**, then its linear momentum will be constant, and there will be a net force of zero. Likewise, a body in rotational equilibrium will have a constant angular momentum, and again there will be a net torque of zero. Both of these equations are vector equations, and as such are both equivalent to three scalar equations for the three dimensions of motion, though in most instances, only one or two dimensions will be considered at a time. We may say that the two requirements for a body to be in equilibrium are that the vector sum of all the external forces acting on the body must be zero, and the vector sum of all the external torques acting on the body must also be zero. Conversely, if we are told that a body is in equilibrium, we may assume that both of these conditions will hold, and that we can use them to find unknown forces or torques.

Friction

The **first property of friction** is that, if the body does not move when horizontal force $\boldsymbol{F}$ is applied, then the static frictional force is exactly equal and opposite to $\boldsymbol{F}$. Static frictional force has a maximum value, however, which is expressed as $\boldsymbol{f}_{s,max} = \mu_s \boldsymbol{N}$, in which μ_s is the coefficient of static friction, and $\boldsymbol{N}$ is the magnitude of the normal force. If the magnitude of $\boldsymbol{F}$ should exceed the maximum value of static friction, the body will begin to move. Once the body has begun to slide, the frictional force will generally decrease. The value to which the frictional force will diminish is expressed as $\boldsymbol{f}_k = \mu_k \boldsymbol{N}$, in which μ_k is the coefficient of kinetic friction. For objects inclined to roll, such as balls or wheels, there is a rolling frictional force that resists the continued rolling of such an object. This force is expressed by $\boldsymbol{f}_r = \mu_r \boldsymbol{N}$, in which μ_r is the coefficient of rolling friction. All of these frictional coefficients are dimensionless. Since the value of the frictional force depends on the interaction of the body and the surface, it is usually described as friction between the two.

Review Video: Friction
Visit mometrix.com/academy and enter code: 716782

APPLYING CONSERVATION OF ROTATIONAL ENERGY AND ANGULAR MOMENTUM

A metal hoop of mass m and radius r is released from rest at the top of a hill of height h. Assuming that it rolls without sliding and does not lose energy to friction or drag, what will be the hoop's angular and linear velocities upon reaching the bottom of the hill?

The hoop's initial energy is all potential energy, $PE = mgh$. As the hoop rolls down, all of its energy is converted to **translational** and **rotational kinetic energy**. Thus, $mgh = \frac{1}{2}m\boldsymbol{v}^2 + \frac{1}{2}I\boldsymbol{\omega}^2$. Since the moment for a hoop is $I = mr^2$, and $\boldsymbol{\omega} = \frac{\boldsymbol{v}}{r}$, the equation becomes $mgh = \frac{1}{2}m\boldsymbol{v}^2 + \frac{1}{2}mr^2\left(\frac{\boldsymbol{v}^2}{r^2}\right)$, which further simplifies to $gh = \boldsymbol{v}^2$. Thus, the resulting velocity of the hoop is $\boldsymbol{v}_f = \sqrt{gh}$, with an angular velocity of $\boldsymbol{\omega}_f = \frac{\boldsymbol{v}_f}{r}$. Note that if you were to forget about the energy converted to rotational motion, you would calculate a final velocity of $\boldsymbol{v}_f = \sqrt{2gh}$, which is the **impact velocity** of an object dropped from height h.

Angular momentum, $\boldsymbol{L}$, of an object is defined as its moment of inertia multiplied by its angular velocity, or $\boldsymbol{L} = I\boldsymbol{\omega}$. Consider a planet orbiting the sun with an elliptical orbit where the small radius is r_S and large radius is r_L. Find the angular velocity of the planet when it is at distance r_S from the sun if its velocity at r_L is $\boldsymbol{\omega}_L$.

Since the size of a planet is almost insignificant compared to the interplanetary distances, the planet may be treated as a single particle of mass m, giving it a moment about the sun of $I = mr^2$. Since the gravitational force is incapable of exerting a net torque on an object, we can assume that the planet's angular momentum about the sun is a constant, $\boldsymbol{L}_L = \boldsymbol{L}_S$. Thus, $m{r_L}^2\boldsymbol{\omega}_L = m{r_S}^2\boldsymbol{\omega}_S$. Solving this equation for $\boldsymbol{\omega}_S$ yields $\boldsymbol{\omega}_S = \boldsymbol{\omega}_L\left(\frac{r_L}{r_S}\right)^2$.

MASS-ENERGY RELATIONSHIP

Because mass consists of atoms, which are themselves formed of subatomic particles, there is an energy inherent in the composition of all mass. If all the atoms in a given mass were formed from their most basic particles, it would require a significant input of energy. This rest energy is the energy that Einstein refers to in his famous mass-energy relation $E = mc^2$, where c is the speed of light in a vacuum. In theory, if all the subatomic particles in a given mass were to spontaneously split apart, it would give off energy $E = mc^2$. For example, if this were to happen to a single gram of mass, the resulting outburst of energy would be $E = 9 \times 10^{13}$ J, enough energy to heat more than 200,000 cubic meters of water from the freezing point to the boiling point.

In some nuclear reactions, small amounts of mass are converted to energy. The amount of energy released can be calculated through the same relation, $E = mc^2$. Most such reactions involve mass losses on the order of 10^{-30} kg.

WEIGHT

Too often, **weight** is confused with **mass**. Strictly speaking, weight is the force pulling a body towards the center of a nearby astronomical body. Of course, in the case of most day-to-day operations for human beings, that astronomical body is the earth. The reason for weight is primarily a gravitational attraction between the masses of the two bodies. The SI unit for weight is the Newton. In general, we will be concerned with situations in which bodies with mass are located where the free-fall acceleration is g. In these situations, we may say that the magnitude of the weight vector is $\boldsymbol{W} = mg$. As a vector, weight can be expressed as either $-mg\mathbf{j}$ or $-W\mathbf{j}$, in which **j** is the direction on the axis pointing away from the earth.

Review Video: Mass, Weight, Volume, Density, and Specific Gravity
Visit mometrix.com/academy and enter code: 920570

Common Means of Transferring Electrical Charge

Charge is transferred in three common ways: conduction, induction, and friction. **Conduction**, as the name implies, takes place between conductive materials. There must be a point of contact between the two materials and a potential difference, such as when a battery is connected to a circuit. **Induction** also requires conductive materials. It occurs due to one material encountering a varying magnetic field. This can be the result of a changing magnetic field or the material moving within a constant magnetic field. Charge transfer due to **friction** does not require conductive materials. When two materials are rubbed together, electrons may be transferred from one to the other, leaving the two materials with equal and opposite charges. This is observed when shoes are dragged across a carpeted floor.

Review Video: Charging by Conduction
Visit mometrix.com/academy and enter code: 502661

Conductors, Insulators, and Semiconductors

In many materials, electrons are able to move freely; these are known as **conductors**. Due to their atomic structure and delocalized electrons, **metals** tend to be the best conductors, particularly copper and silver. Highly conductive wires are instrumental in creating low-resistance pathways for electrons to travel along within a circuit.

Other materials naturally inhibit the movement of charge and are known as **insulators**. Their electrons are tightly held by the individual constituent atoms. Glass, pure water, wood, and plastic are all insulators. Insulators are necessary in circuits to prevent charge from escaping to undesirable places, such as an operator's hand. For this reason, most highly conductive materials are covered by insulators.

Semiconductors, as the name suggests, are materials that only partially conduct electrical charge. The elements silicon and germanium are both common semiconductors, and are frequently used in microelectronic devices because they allow for tight control of the rate of conduction. In many cases, the conduction ability of semiconductors can be controlled by adjusting the temperature of the material.

Electric Current

An **electric current** is simply an **electric charge in motion**. Electric current cannot exist unless there is a difference in electric potential. If, for instance, we have an isolated conducting loop, it will be at the same potential throughout. If, however, we insert a battery into this loop, then the conducting loop will no longer be at a single electric potential. A flow of electrons will result and will very quickly reach a steady state. At that point, it will be completely analogous to steady-state fluid flow. A current is quantified by the amount of charge that is transferred in a given amount of time. The SI unit for current is the ampere (A), equal to a coulomb of charge per second.

Review Video: Electric Charge
Visit mometrix.com/academy and enter code: 323587

Electromotive Force and Common EMF Devices

A force that maintains a potential difference between two locations in a circuit is known as an **electromotive force.** A device that creates this force is referred to as an EMF device. The most common EMF device is the battery. **Batteries** operate by converting chemical energy stored in the electrolyte, the internal chemical material, into electrical energy. The reaction causes a lack of electrons on the cathode, and when the circuit is connected, they flow from the anode, creating a flow of current. The electrolyte's composition also determines whether the battery is classified as acidic or alkaline, and wet or dry. Another EMF device is the **photocell**, also commonly called the solar cell, since most photocells are powered by the sun. These operate by absorbing photons, which cause the electrons to be excited and flow in a current, a process of converting light energy into electrical energy. A third type of EMF device is the **generator**. This device converts mechanical energy to electrical energy. A generator may be powered by such diverse sources as gasoline engines, flowing water, or even manually powered cranks. These devices utilize a rotating shaft to spin a coil within a magnetic field, creating a potential difference by induction.

Ohm's Law

If we were to apply the exact same potential difference between the ends of two geometrically similar rods, one made of copper and one made of glass, we would create vastly different currents. This is because these two substances have different **resistances**. Ohm's Law describes the relation between applied voltage and induced current, $V = IR$. This is one of the most important tools of circuit analysis. Resistance, then, can be calculated as $R = \frac{V}{I}$. The SI unit for resistance is the **ohm** (Ω), equal to a volt per ampere. When a conductor is placed into a circuit to provide a specific resistance, it is known as a resistor. For a given potential difference, the greater the resistance is to the current, the smaller the current will be.

If we wish to look instead at the quality of the material of which the resistor is made, then we must consider resistivity. **Resistivity**, ρ, is a physical property of every material, which, if known, can be used to size a resistor for a specific resistance. Resistance is dictated by both the material and the dimensions of the resistor, given by the relation $R = \frac{\rho L}{\mathrm{A}}$, where L is the effective length of the resistor and A is the effective cross-section. Alternatively, an unknown resistivity may be calculated by rearranging the equation as $\rho = \frac{RA}{L}$.

The resistivity will often change with temperature. In these cases, the relevant resistivity may be calculated $\rho = p_{ref}\left(1 + \alpha\left(T - T_{ref}\right)\right)$, where α is the resistivity proportionality constant and T is the material temperature.

Review Video: Resistance of Electric Currents
Visit mometrix.com/academy and enter code: 668423

Energy and Power

Electric circuits operate by **transferring** electrical energy from one location in the circuit to another. Some devices in a circuit can store and release energy while other devices, like resistors, simply dissipate energy. **Power** is a measure of the rate at which energy is stored, released, transferred, or dissipated. It is measured in watts (W), or joules per second. Power is calculated by $P = VI$. The amount of power being released by a 9-V battery producing a current of 5 A is 45 W. When calculating the amount of power dissipated by a resistor, Ohm's Law allows two other equations for power, $P = I^2R = \frac{V^2}{R}$.

When power consumption over long periods of time needs to be measured, it will often be measured in units of kilowatt-hours, which is the amount of energy consumed at a rate of 1 kW over the course of an hour. One kilowatt-hour is equal to 3,600 kJ.

Capacitors and Dielectrics

Capacitors are devices used in circuits to store energy in the form of electric fields. They are most often composed of two oppositely charged parallel plates separated by a medium, generally air. This medium is referred to as the capacitor's **dielectric**. The dielectric material dictates the amount of energy in the electric field and, consequently, the amount of energy that can be stored by the capacitor. The measurable quality of a capacitor is known as its **capacitance**, or the amount of charge that it can store per volt of potential difference. This is given by the equation $C = \frac{Q}{V}$, with capacitance having units of farads or coulombs per volt. Physically, the capacitance depends on three things: the **area** of the parallel plates, the **separation distance** between them, and the **dielectric** material. For cases in which the separation distance is insignificant compared to the area, the capacitance can be found by the equation $C = \frac{\varepsilon A}{d}$, where ε is the permittivity of the dielectric material. Often, instead of being given the permittivity, we will be given the dielectric constant, κ, which is the ratio of the permittivities of the material and air, $\kappa = \frac{\varepsilon}{\varepsilon_{air}}$. This yields an obvious result of $\kappa_{air} = 1$.

The energy stored in a capacitor can be calculated in three different ways: $\boldsymbol{E} = \frac{CV^2}{2} = \frac{Q^2}{2C} = \frac{VQ}{2}$. Another quantity associated with capacitors is the electric field energy density, η. This energy density is found by $\eta = \frac{\varepsilon \boldsymbol{E}^2}{2}$.

Capacitors and Inductors in AC Circuits

Because of the constantly fluctuating nature of alternating current, capacitors and inductors both oppose immediate acceptance of the fluctuation. This opposition is referred to as **impedance** and is similar to resistance, also having units of ohms, but unlike resistance, impedance is a complex value, meaning that it may have an **imaginary component** as well as a **real component**. For ideal capacitors and inductors, impedance is purely imaginary, and for ideal resistors, impedance is purely real. It is only when combining the effects of these devices that the full expression for impedance, Z, is necessary: $Z = R + X_i$, where $i = \sqrt{(-1)}$. X is a quantity known as reactance. For capacitors, $X_c = \frac{1}{\omega C}$, where ω is the angular frequency of the current, and for inductors, $X_L = \omega L$.

RC Circuits

An RC circuit consists of a battery wired in series with a **resistor** and a **capacitor**. Since a capacitor in steady state allows no current flow, it makes no sense to analyze a steady-state RC circuit. Instead, we will look at an RC circuit that has only just been connected, with the capacitor uncharged. The battery supplies voltage V_B to the circuit, and since the capacitor's voltage is initially zero, the voltage across the resistor is initially V_B, giving an initial current of $I = \frac{V_B}{R}$. As current flows, the charge on the capacitor increases, which in turn creates an opposing voltage that

lowers the voltage drop across the resistor. Combining Ohm's Law with the KVL gives the voltage relation as $V_B = IR + \frac{Q}{C}$, where Q is the charge on the capacitor. Since the current is simply the transfer rate of the charge, this becomes a differential equation. Solving for charge and current yields the expressions $Q(t) = CV_B(1 - e^{-t/RC})$ and $I(t) = \left(\frac{V_B}{R}\right)e^{-t/RC}$. The factor RC in the exponent is referred to as the circuit's time constant. It is the amount of time required for the capacitor to charge up to 63.2% capacity.

If the battery is removed from the circuit after the capacitor is charged and the circuit is reconnected with just the resistor and capacitor, the capacitor will begin to drain at the same rate that it was charged. The current magnitude will follow the same equation as before, though it will be in the opposite direction. The new expression for the charge will be $Q(t) = CV_Be^{-t/RC}$.

Circuit Analysis

When resistors in a simple circuit are arranged in **series with a battery**, current must pass through each resistor consecutively in order to return to the battery. This immediately tells us that the current through each resistor is the same. By KVL, we know that the sum of the voltage drop across the resistors is equal to the voltage input by the battery, $V_B = IR_1 + IR_2 + \cdots + IR_n$. This may be restated as $V_B = I(R_1 + R_2 + \cdots + R_n)$. From this we can see that for resistors arranged in series, the equivalent resistance is the sum of the resistances, $R_{eq} = R_1 + R_2 + \cdots + Rn$.

When resistors in a simple circuit are arranged in parallel with a battery, the current need only pass through one of them to return to the battery. By KVL, we know that the voltage drop across each resistor is the same. Since the total current must equal the sum of the currents through the resistors, we may conclude from Ohm's Law that $I = \frac{V_B}{R_1} + \frac{V_B}{R_2} + \cdots + \frac{V_B}{R_n}$. We may restate this relation as $I = V_B\left(\frac{1}{R_1} + \frac{1}{R_2} + \cdots + \frac{1}{R_n}\right)$. Moving the resistance expression to the other side of the equation shows us that the equivalent resistance is $R_{eq} = \left(\frac{1}{R_1} + \frac{1}{R_2} + \cdots + \frac{1}{R_n}\right)^{-1}$ for resistors in parallel.

Capacitors have combination rules opposite to those of resistors. **Capacitors in series** have an equivalent value of $C_{eq} = \left(\frac{1}{C_1} + \frac{1}{C_2} + \cdots + \frac{1}{C_n}\right)^{-1}$, while capacitors in parallel have equivalence of $C_{eq} = C_1 + C_2 + \cdots + C_n$.

Inductors follow the same rules as resistors.

Review Video: Resistance of Electric Currents
Visit mometrix.com/academy and enter code: 668423

Measuring Devices

There are several devices that allow these circuit quantities to be measured to a great degree of accuracy. An **ammeter** is a device placed in series with a circuit to measure the current through that location. Ideally, an ammeter has as little internal resistance as possible to prevent altering the current it is trying to measure. A **voltmeter** measures the voltage or potential difference between two locations in a circuit. It has two leads that are connected in parallel with the circuit and consists of a very high resistance and an ammeter in series. This allows only a very small amount of current to be diverted through the voltmeter, but enough to determine the voltage by Ohm's Law. A **galvanometer** is the primary working component of an ammeter. It operates based on the idea that a wire in a magnetic field will experience a force proportional to the amount of current it is carrying. It converts the observed current into a dial reading. A **potentiometer** is a variable resistor, often controlled by a knob, that allows an operator to control the amount of voltage or current provided to a given circuit. They are commonly used in volume-control knobs. Potentiometers can also be called voltage dividers. Their use in circuit measurement is for finding voltages by comparing them to known voltages. A **multimeter** is a device that combines the functions of all the above devices into one. In addition to voltage, current, resistance and capacitance, they can typically measure inductance, frequency, and other quantities.

Power in AC Circuits

Unlike DC circuits, the power provided by an AC voltage source is not constant over time. Generally, an AC source will provide voltage in a sinusoidal pattern, $V(t) = V_{max}\sin(\omega t)$. Similarly, the current will be given by $I(t) = I_{max}\sin(\omega t)$. From our known equations for power, this yields a power of $P(t) = RI_{max}{}^2\sin^2(\omega t)$. However, if we wish to find the average power or the amount of energy transmission after a given period of time, we need to find some way to average voltage and current. The root-mean-square (rms) method, as the name suggests, takes the square root of the time average of the squared value. For sinusoidal functions such as the voltage and current here, the rms value is the maximum value divided by the square root of 2. For voltage and current, $V_{rms} = \frac{V_{max}}{\sqrt{2}}$, and $I_{rms} = \frac{I_{max}}{\sqrt{2}}$. In this way, the average power can be found as $P_{avg} = V_{rms}I_{rms}$, which can also be stated $P_{avg} = \frac{V_{max}I_{max}}{2}$. A DC source with supplied voltage V_B will provide the same power over time as an AC source if $V_B = V_{rms}$.

The Use of Ohm's Law and Kirchhoff's Laws

Circuit analysis is the process of determining the **current** or **voltage drop** across devices of interest in a circuit. Ohm's Law is useful in doing this since it definitively relates the current to the voltage drop for resistors, $V = IR$. Kirchhoff's voltage law (KVL) states that if you sum the voltage drops across all devices in any closed loop of a circuit, the sum will always be zero, $V_1 + V_2 + \cdots + V_n = 0$. This law is particularly useful if there are multiple closed-loop pathways in a circuit. Kirchhoff's current law (KCL) states that the amount of current entering a point must equal the amount of current leaving, $I_{in} = I_{out}$. This law may also be expanded to apply to the current entering and leaving a larger region of a circuit. In any given circuit analysis, it may be necessary to use all three of these laws.

Another important principle to remember in an ideal circuit is that any two points connected by only wire are at equal voltage. Only devices on the circuit may change the voltage. In actual practice, however, all wire has some amount of resistance. A battery that provides an EMF of V_B is only able to deliver a voltage to the circuit of $V = V_B - IR_B$, where R_B is the internal resistance of the battery. To express this concept in an ideal circuit, we would need to add a small resistor in series after the battery.

Review Video: ASP - Ohm's Law and Power
Visit mometrix.com/academy and enter code: 784016

Magnets and Magnetism

A **magnet** is a piece of metal, such as iron, steel, or magnetite (lodestone) that can affect another substance within its field of force that has like characteristics. Magnets can either attract or repel other substances. Magnets have two **poles**: north and south. Like poles repel and opposite poles (pairs of north and south) attract. The magnetic field is a set of invisible lines representing the paths of attraction and repulsion.

Magnetism can occur naturally, or ferromagnetic materials can be magnetized. Certain matter that is magnetized can retain its magnetic properties indefinitely and become a permanent magnet. Other matter can lose its magnetic properties. For example, an iron nail can be temporarily magnetized by stroking it repeatedly in the same direction using one pole of another magnet. Once magnetized, it can attract or repel other magnetically inclined materials, such as paper clips. Dropping the nail repeatedly will cause it to lose its magnetic properties.

Review Video: Magnets
Visit mometrix.com/academy and enter code: 570803

Magnetic Fields and Atomic Structure

The motions of subatomic structures (nuclei and electrons) produce a **magnetic field**. It is the direction of the spin and orbit that indicate the direction of the field. The strength of a magnetic field is known as the magnetic moment. As electrons spin and orbit a nucleus, they produce a magnetic field.

Pairs of electrons that spin and orbit in opposite directions cancel each other out, creating a **net magnetic field** of zero. Materials that have an unpaired electron are magnetic. Those with a weak attractive force are referred to as **paramagnetic materials**, while **ferromagnetic materials** have a strong attractive force. A **diamagnetic material** has electrons that are paired, and therefore does not typically have a magnetic moment. There are, however, some diamagnetic materials that have a weak magnetic field.

A magnetic field can be formed not only by a magnetic material, but also by electric current flowing through a wire. When a coiled wire is attached to the two ends of a battery, for example, an **electromagnet** can be formed by inserting a ferromagnetic material such as an iron bar within the coil. When electric current flows through the wire, the bar becomes a magnet. If there is no current, the magnetism is lost. A **magnetic domain** occurs when the magnetic fields of atoms are grouped and aligned. These groups form what can be thought of as miniature magnets within a material. This is what happens when an object like an iron nail is temporarily magnetized. Prior to magnetization, the organization of atoms and their various polarities are somewhat random with respect to where the north and south poles are pointing. After magnetization, a significant percentage of the poles are lined up in one direction, which is what causes the magnetic force exerted by the material.

Transverse and Longitudinal Waves

Transverse waves are waves whose oscillations are **perpendicular** to the direction of motion. A light wave is an example of a transverse wave. A group of light waves traveling in the same direction will be oscillating in several different planes. Light waves are said to be polarized when they are filtered such that only waves oscillating in a particular plane are allowed to pass, with the remainder being absorbed by the filter. If two such polarizing filters are employed successively and aligned to allow different planes of oscillation, they will block all light waves.

Longitudinal waves are waves that oscillate in the same direction as their primary motion. Their motion is restricted to a single axis, so they may not be polarized. A sound wave is an example of a longitudinal wave.

Velocity, Amplitude, Wavelength, and Frequency

The **velocity of a wave** is the rate at which it travels in a given medium. It is defined in the same way that velocity of physical objects is defined, a change in position divided by a change in time. A single wave may have a different velocity for every medium in which it travels. Some types of waves, such as light waves, do not require a medium.

Amplitude is one measure of a wave's strength. It is half the verticle distance between the highest and lowest points on the wave, the crest and trough, respectively. The vertical midpoint, halfway between the crest and trough, is sometimes called an equilibrium point, or a node. Amplitude is often denoted with an A.

The **wavelength** is the horizontal distance between successive crests or troughs, or the distance between the first and third of three successive nodes. Wavelength is generally denoted as λ.

Frequency is the number of crests or troughs that pass a particular point in a given period of time. It is the inverse of the period, the time required for the wave to cycle from one crest or trough to the next. Frequency, f, is generally measured in hertz, or cycles per second.

Velocity, wavelength, and frequency are not independent quantities. They are related by the expression $v = \lambda f$.

Intensity

Intensity is a physical quantity, equivalent to the flux through a given area over a period of time. It may also be defined as the energy density of a wave times its velocity. Intensity has units of watts per square meter. The intensity of light decreases as the distance from the light source increases. The inverse square law states that the intensity is inversely proportional to the square of the distance from the source. It is also directly proportional to the power of the light source. This is shown mathematically by the expression $I = \frac{CP}{r^2}$, where C is the proportionality constant. This may be better understood by imagining the light waves emanating from a source as an expanding sphere. As their distance from the source increases as r, the area over which they must divide themselves increases as $4\pi r^2$.

Standing Waves

A **standing wave** is the result of **interference** between two waves of the same frequency moving in opposite directions. These waves, although in constant motion, have certain points on the wave where the amplitude is zero, locations referred to as nodes. One example of a standing wave is a plucked guitar string. Since the string is attached at both ends, the fixed ends will be nodes. The primary tone will be that of the fundamental, or first harmonic, shown in the first figure below. It has a wavelength of twice the length of the string, L. The other three pictures below are those of the second through fourth harmonics. The nth harmonic has wavelength and frequency of $\lambda_n = \frac{2L}{n}$ and $f_n = \frac{nv}{2L}$, where v is wave velocity.

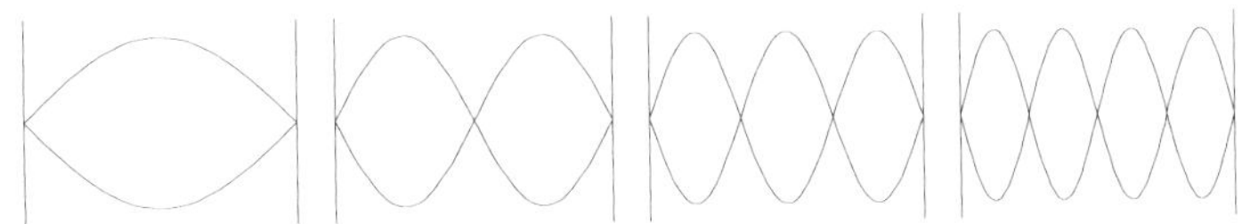

This same phenomenon occurs inside the tubes of wind instruments, though it is much more difficult to visualize. With a tube, however, there will be one or two open ends. Rather than a node, each open end will coincide with an antinode: that is, a crest or trough. For waves in a tube with two open ends, the wavelength and frequency calculations are the same as those for the plucked string. For the case with one open end, only the odd harmonics will be seen. The frequency of the nth harmonic becomes $f_n = \frac{nv}{4L}$, where n is odd.

Reflection, Transmission, and Absorption

When light waves make contact with matter, they are either reflected, transmitted, or absorbed. If the light is **reflected** from the surface of the matter, the **angle** at which it hits the surface will be the same as the angle at which it leaves. If the ray of light is perpendicular to the surface, it will be reflected back in the direction from which it came.

When light is **transmitted** from one medium to another, its direction may be **altered** upon entering the new medium. This is known as **refraction**. The degree to which the light is refracted depends on the speed at which light travels in each medium.

Light that is neither reflected nor transmitted will be **absorbed** by the surface and **stored as heat** energy. Because there are no ideal surfaces, most light and matter interaction will be a combination of two or even all three of these. Another result of imperfect surfaces is **scattering**, which occurs when waves are reflected in multiple directions. Rayleigh scattering is the specific case of a light wave being scattered by tiny particles that single out particular wavelengths. Dust particles in the atmosphere scatter primarily the blue wavelength of sunlight to give our sky a predominantly blue hue.

Review Video: Reflection, Transmission, and Absorption of Light
Visit mometrix.com/academy and enter code: 109410

Snell's Law

When light is transmitted from one medium to another, its direction may be altered upon entering the new medium. This is known as **refraction**. The degree to which the light is refracted depends on the index of refraction, n, for each medium. The **index of refraction** is a ratio of the speed of light in a vacuum to the speed of light in the medium in question, $n = \frac{c}{v_m}$. Since light can never travel faster than it does in a vacuum, the index of refraction is always greater than one. Snell's law gives the equation for determining the angle of refraction: $n_1 \sin(\theta_1) = n_2 \sin(\theta_2)$, where n is the index of refraction for each medium, and θ is the angle the light makes with the normal vector on each side of the interface between the two media.

We will examine a special case by trying to determine the angle of refraction for light traveling from a medium with $n_1 = 3$ to another medium with $n_2 = 1.5$. The light makes an angle $\theta_1 = 35°$ with the normal. Using Snell's law, we find that $\sin(\theta_2) = 1.15$. Since this is not mathematically possible, we conclude that the light cannot be refracted. This case is known as total internal reflection. When light travels from a more dense medium to a less dense medium, there is a minimum angle of incidence, beyond which all light will be reflected. This critical angle is $\theta_1 = \sin^{-1}\left(\frac{n_2}{n_1}\right)$. Fiber-optic cables make use of this phenomenon to ensure that the signal is fully reflected internally when it veers into the outer walls of the fiber.

Resonance and Natural Frequency

Every physical object has one or more **natural frequencies**, or frequencies at which it will naturally vibrate. The natural frequency is based on the object's dimensions, density, orientation, and other factors. If the object is acted on by a periodic force, it will vibrate at its natural frequency, regardless of the forcing frequency. If the excitation force is operating at the object's natural frequency, the object will experience **resonance**, in which the object receives all of the energy exerted by the excitation force. The amplitude of the vibration will increase rapidly and without bound until either the excitation force changes frequency or the natural frequency of the object is altered.

Diffraction and Dispersion

Diffraction occurs when a wave encounters a physical object. It includes phenomena such as bending, diverging, and other aperture effects. When light emerges from a single small slit, a rippling effect may be observed. The results of Young's double-slit experiment are due to diffraction as the light waves from these slits diverge. Similarly, light emerging from a circular aperture will project concentric light and dark rings due to diffraction. Diffraction grating is an arrangement of material whose reflective properties are intentionally varied at equally spaced intervals. Due to the arrangement, incident light is reflected in specific directions, known as diffraction orders, based on its wavelength.

Dispersion occurs when light consisting of multiple wavelengths enters a medium whose propagation behavior depends on the wavelength of transmitted light. This is what is observed when light passes through a prism, splitting it into its component colors.

Review Video: Diffraction of Light Waves
Visit mometrix.com/academy and enter code: 785494

Young's Double-Slit Experiment

Thomas Young's **double-slit experiment** visually demonstrated the interference between two sets of light waves. It consisted of shining light through two thin, closely spaced parallel slits and onto a screen. The interference between light waves from the two slits caused a pattern of alternately light and dark bands to appear on the screen, due to constructive and destructive interference, respectively. The dimensions of the experimental setup can be used to determine the wavelength of the light being projected onto the screen. This is given by the equation $\lambda = y\frac{d}{x}$, where y is the distance between the centers of two light bands, d is the distance between the slits, and x is the distance from the slits to the screen. Thin-film interference is caused when incident light is reflected both by a partially reflective thin layer on a surface and by the surface itself. This interference may be constructive or destructive.

Wave Superposition and Interference

The principle of **linear superposition** states that two or more waves occupying the same space create an effect equal to the sum of their individual amplitudes at that location. This is known as interference. If the resultant amplitude is larger than either individual amplitude, it is constructive interference. Similarly, if the interference reduces the effect, it is considered destructive.

Some special cases of interference are standing waves and beats, in which two waves having the same and nearly the same frequency, respectively, interfere with one another. Another concept related to interference is phase. If two waves with the same frequency are in phase, then they have perfectly constructive interference. The nodes in each wave will line up, as will the respective crests and troughs. If those same two waves are 180 degrees out of phase, they will experience perfectly destructive interference. The nodes will still line up, but each crest will be aligned with a trough, and vice versa. From this it can be seen that constructive interference results in a larger wave amplitude than destructive interference. If two identical waves are 180 degrees out of phase, the resultant wave will have zero amplitude. This effect is the design impetus for some noise-cancellation technology.

Doppler Effect

One common phenomenon of wave motion is the **Doppler effect**. It is a **disparity** between the emitted frequency and the observed frequency. It is the caused by **relative motion** between the

wave source and the **observer**. If the source and observer are both moving toward one another, the observed frequency is determined by the following equation: $f_o = f_e \frac{(v_w+v_o)}{(v_w-v_s)}$, where v_w is the speed of the wave. If the source or the observer is moving in the opposite direction, its sign must be reversed. The Doppler effect is most commonly observed when sound waves change pitch as an observer's relative motion to a train or emergency vehicle changes. The Doppler effect is also employed in the operation of speed-detecting radar guns. Microwaves are emitted at a known frequency and, after being reflected by the object in question, return at a different frequency, giving the object's speed.

Sound Waves

The **pitch of a sound** as it reaches one's ear is based on the frequency of the sound waves. A high-pitched sound has a higher frequency than a low-pitched sound. Like all waves, sound waves transmit energy. The rate at which this energy is transmitted is the sonic power. Loudness, or intensity of sound, is the sonic power received per unit area.

Beats occur when a pair of sound waves, whose frequencies differ only slightly, interfere with one another. This interference causes a periodic variation in sound intensity, whose frequency is equal to the difference between that of the two sound waves. This is noticeable when tuning two instruments to one another. As the two pitches get closer, the beat frequency will become smaller and smaller until it disappears entirely, indicating that the instruments are in tune.

Review Video: Sound
Visit mometrix.com/academy and enter code: 562378

Electromagnetic Spectrum

The **electromagnetic spectrum** is the range of all wavelengths and frequencies of known electromagnetic waves. Visible light occupies only a small portion of the electromagnetic spectrum. Some of the common classifications of electromagnetic waves are listed in the table below with their approximate frequency ranges.

Classification	Freq. (Hz)
Gamma Rays	$\sim 10^{19}$
X-Rays	$\sim 10^{17} - 10^{18}$
Ultraviolet	$\sim 10^{15} - 10^{16}$
Visible Light	$\sim 10^{14}$
Infra-red	$\sim 10^{11} - 10^{14}$
Microwaves	$\sim 10^{10} - 10^{11}$
Radio/TV	$\sim 10^{6} - 10^{9}$

Electromagnetic waves travel at the speed of light, $c = 3 \times 10^8$ m/s. To find the wavelength of any electromagnetic wave, simply divide c by the frequency. Visible light occupies a range of wavelengths from approximately 380 nm (violet) to 740 nm (red). The full spectrum of color can be found between these two wavelengths.

Review Video: Electromagnetic Spectrum
Visit mometrix.com/academy and enter code: 771761

Review Video: Light
Visit mometrix.com/academy and enter code: 900556

Real and Virtual Images

In optics, an **object's image** is what is seen when the object is viewed through a lens. The location of an object's image is related to the lens's **focal length** by the equation $\frac{1}{d_o} + \frac{1}{d_i} = \frac{1}{f}$, where f is the focal length, and d_o and d_i are the distance of the object and its image from the lens, respectively. A positive d_i indicates that the image is on the opposite side of the lens from the object. If the lens is a magnifying lens, the height of the object may be different from that of its image, and may even be inverted. The object's magnification, m, can be found as $m = \frac{-d_i}{d_o}$. The value for the magnification can then be used to relate the object's height to that of its image: $m = \frac{y_i}{y_o}$. Note that if the magnification is negative, then the image has been inverted.

Images may be either **real** or **virtual**. Real images are formed by light rays passing through the image location, while virtual images are only perceived by reverse extrapolating refracted light rays. Diverging lenses cannot create real images, only virtual ones. Real images are always on the opposite side of a converging lens from the object and are always inverted.

Thin Lenses

A **lens** is an optical device that **redirects light** to either converge or diverge in specific geometric patterns. Whether the lens converges or diverges is dependent on the lens being **convex** or **concave**, respectively. The particular angle of redirection is dictated by the lens's focal length. For a **converging lens**, this is the distance from the lens that parallel rays entering from the opposite side would intersect. For a **diverging lens**, it is the distance from the lens that parallel rays entering the lens would intersect if they were reverse extrapolated. However, the focal length of a diverging lens is always considered to be negative. A thin lens is a lens whose focal length is much greater than its thickness. By making this assumption, we can derive many helpful relations.

Concave Mirrors

Concave mirrors will create an image of an object in varying ways depending on the location of the object. The table below details the location, orientation, magnification, and nature of the image. The five object locations to be examined are between the mirror and the focal point (1), at the focal point (2), between the focal point and the center of curvature, or twice the focal point (3), at the center of curvature (4), and beyond the center of curvature (5).

Object	Image Location	Orientation	Magnification	Type
1	$d_i < 0$	upright	$m > 1$	virtual
2	none	none	none	none
3	$d_i > 2f$	inverted	$m < -1$	real
4	$d_i = 2f$	inverted	$m = -1$	real
5	$f < d_i < 2f$	inverted	$0 > m > -1$	real

Note in case 5 that the image may effectively be located at the focal point. This is the case for objects at extremely great, or near infinite, distances from the mirror. The magnification at these distances will be very small and a true infinite distance would result in a magnification of zero.

Plane Mirrors and Spherical Mirrors

Plane mirrors have very simple properties. They reflect only **virtual images**, they have no magnification, and the object's distance from the mirror is always equal to that of its image. Plane mirrors will also appear to reverse the directions left and right.

Spherical mirrors follow the same governing equations for finding image height, location, orientation, and magnification as do thin lenses; however, the sign convention for image location is reversed. A positive image location denotes that it is on the same side as the object. Spherical mirrors may be either **concave** or **convex**. Convex mirrors are by far the simpler of the two. They will always reflect virtual, upright images with magnification between zero and one. Concave mirrors have varying behavior based on the object location.

Simple Magnifier, the Microscope, and the Telescope

A simple magnifier, or commonly a **magnifying glass**, is a converging lens that creates an enlarged virtual image near the observer's eye. The object must be within a certain distance, about 25 cm or 10 inches, from the magnifier for it to operate properly. Otherwise, the image will be blurry.

A **microscope** is a magnifying device that is used to examine very small objects. It uses a series of lenses to capture light coming from the far side of the sample under examination. Often microscopes will have interchangeable magnification lenses mounted on a wheel, allowing the user to adjust the level of magnification by rotating in a different lens. Optical microscopes will generally be limited to a magnification of 1,500.

Telescopes are used to view very distant objects, most often celestial bodies. Telescopes use both lenses and mirrors to capture light from a distant source, focus it, and then magnify it. This creates a virtual image that is very much smaller than the object itself, and yet much larger than the object appears to the naked eye.

Prisms

Prisms are optical devices that alter the path or nature of light waves. Glass and plastic are the two most prevalent materials used to make prisms. There are three different types of prisms in common use. The most familiar of these is the dispersive prism, which splits a beam of light into its constituent wavelengths. For sunlight, this results in the full spectrum of color being displayed. These prisms are generally in the familiar triangular prism shape.

Polarizing prisms, as their name suggests, polarize light, but without significantly reducing the intensity, as a simple filter would. Waves that are oscillating in planes other than the desired plane are caused to rotate, so that they are oscillating in the desired plane. This type of prism is commonly used in cameras.

Reflective prisms are much less common than either of the others. They reflect light, often through the use of the total internal reflection phenomenon. Their primary use is in binoculars.

Heat Transfer

Heat transfer is the flow of thermal energy, which is measured by temperature. Heat will flow from warmer objects to cooler objects until an **equilibrium** is reached in which both objects are at the same temperature. Because the particles of warmer objects possess a higher kinetic energy than the particles of cooler objects, the particles of the warmer objects are vibrating more quickly and collide more often, transferring energy to the cooler objects in which the particles have less kinetic energy and are moving more slowly. Heat may be transferred by conduction, convection, or radiation. In **conduction**, heat is transferred by direct contact between two objects. In **convection**, heat is transferred by moving currents. In **radiation**, heat is transferred by electromagnetic waves.

Review Video: Heat Transfer at the Molecular Level
Visit mometrix.com/academy and enter code: 451646

Convection

Heat always flows from a region of higher temperature to a region of lower temperature. If two regions are at the same temperature, there is a thermal equilibrium between them and there will be no net heat transfer between them. Convection is a mode of heat transfer in which a surface in contact with a fluid experiences a heat flow. The heat rate for convection is given as $q = hA\Delta T$, where h is the convection coefficient, and q is the heat transferred per unit of time. The convection coefficient is dependent on a number of factors, including the configuration of the surface and the nature and velocity of the fluid. For complicated configurations, it often has to be determined experimentally.

Convection may be classified as either free or forced. In free convection, when a surface transfers heat to the surrounding air, the heated air becomes less dense and rises, allowing cooler air to descend and come into contact with the surface. Free convection may also be called natural convection. Forced convection in this example would involve forcibly cycling the air: for instance, with a fan. While this does generally require an additional input of work, the convection coefficient is always greater for forced convection.

Conduction

Conduction is a form of heat transfer that requires contact. Since heat is a measure of kinetic energy, most commonly vibration, at the atomic level, it may be transferred from one location to another or one object to another by contact. The rate at which heat is transferred is proportional to the material's thermal conductivity k, cross-sectional area A, and temperature gradient $\frac{\Delta T}{\Delta x}$:

$$q = kA\left(\frac{\Delta T}{\Delta x}\right)$$

If two ends of a rod are each held at a constant temperature, the heat transfer through the rod will be given as $q = k\mathrm{A}\left(\frac{T_H - T_L}{d}\right)$, where d is the length of the rod. The heat will flow from the hot end to the cold end. The thermal conductivity is generally given in units of $\frac{\mathrm{W}}{\mathrm{m\ K}}$. Metals are some of the best conductors, many having a thermal conductivity around 400 $\frac{\mathrm{W}}{\mathrm{m\ K}}$. The thermal conductivity of wood is very small, generally less than 0.5 $\frac{\mathrm{W}}{\mathrm{m\ K}}$. Diamond is extremely thermally conductive and may have a conductivity of over 2,000 $\frac{\mathrm{W}}{\mathrm{m\ K}}$. Although fluids also have thermal conductivity, they will tend to transfer heat primarily through convection.

Radiation

Radiation heat transfer occurs via electromagnetic radiation between two bodies. Unlike conduction and convection, radiation requires no medium in which to take place. Indeed, the heat we receive from the sun is entirely radiation since it must pass through a vacuum to reach us. Every body at a temperature above absolute zero emits heat radiation at a rate of $q = e\sigma AT^4$, where e is the surface emissivity and σ is the Stefan-Boltzmann constant. The net radiation heat-transfer rate for a body is given by $q = e\sigma A(T^4 - T_0^4)$, where T_0 is the temperature of the surroundings. Emissivity, which has a value between 0 and 1, is a measure of how well a surface absorbs and emits radiation. Dark-colored surfaces tend to have high emissivity, while shiny or reflective surfaces have low emissivity. In the radiation heat-rate equation, it is important to remember to use absolute temperature units, since the temperature value is being raised to a power.

Chemical, Electrical, Electromagnetic, Nuclear, and Thermal Energy

Different types of energy may be associated with systems:

- **Chemical energy** is the energy that is stored in chemical bonds and intermolecular forces.
- **Electrical energy** is the energy associated with the movement of electrons or ions through a material.
- **Electromagnetic energy** is the energy of electromagnetic waves of several frequencies including radio waves, microwaves, infrared light, visible light, ultraviolet light, x-rays, and gamma rays.
- **Nuclear energy** is the binding energy that is stored within an atom's nucleus.
- **Thermal energy** is the total internal kinetic energy of a system due to the random motions of the particles.

States of Matter

The four states of matter are solid, liquid, gas, and plasma. **Solids** have a definite shape and a definite volume. Because solid particles are held in fairly rigid positions, solids are the least compressible of the four states of matter. **Liquids** have definite volumes but no definite shapes. Because their particles are free to slip and slide over each other, liquids take the shape of their containers, but they still remain fairly incompressible by natural means. **Gases** have no definite shape or volume. Because gas particles are free to move, they move away from each other to fill their containers. Gases are compressible. **Plasmas** are high-temperature, ionized gases that exist only under very high temperatures at which electrons are stripped away from their atoms.

Review Video: States of Matter
Visit mometrix.com/academy and enter code: 742449

Review Video: Properties of Liquids
Visit mometrix.com/academy and enter code: 802024

Review Video: States of Matter [Advanced]
Visit mometrix.com/academy and enter code: 298130

The following table shows similarities and differences between solids, liquids, and gases:

	Solid	Liquid	Gas
Shape	Fixed shape	No fixed shape (assumes shape of container)	No fixed shape (assumes shape of container)
Volume	Fixed	Fixed	Changes to assume shape of container
Fluidity	Does not flow easily	Flows easily	Flows easily
Compressibility	Hard to compress	Hard to compress	Compresses

Six Different Types of Phase Change

A substance that is undergoing a change from a solid to a liquid is said to be melting. If this change occurs in the opposite direction, from liquid to solid, this change is called freezing. A liquid which is being converted to a gas is undergoing vaporization. The reverse of this process is known as condensation. Direct transitions from gas to solid and solid to gas are much less common in everyday life, but they can occur given the proper conditions. Solid to gas conversion is known as sublimation, while the reverse is called deposition.

Review Video: Chemical and Physical Properties of Matter
Visit mometrix.com/academy and enter code: 717349

Phase Diagram and Critical Point

A **phase diagram** is a graph or chart of pressure versus temperature that represents the solid, liquid, and gaseous phases of a substance and the transitions between these phases. Typically, **pressure** is located on the vertical axis, and temperature is located along the horizontal axis. The curves drawn on the graph represent points at which different phases are in an equilibrium state. These curves indicate at which pressure and temperature the phase changes of sublimation, melting, and boiling occur. Specifically, the curve between the liquid and gas phases indicates the pressures and temperatures at which the liquid and gas phases are in equilibrium. The curve between the solid and liquid phases indicates the temperatures and pressures at which the solid and liquid phases are in equilibrium. The open spaces on the graph represent the distinct phases solid, liquid, and gas. The point on the curve at which the graph splits is referred to as the **critical point.** At the critical point, the solid, liquid, and gas phases all exist in a state of equilibrium.

Lettered Regions of a Phase Diagram

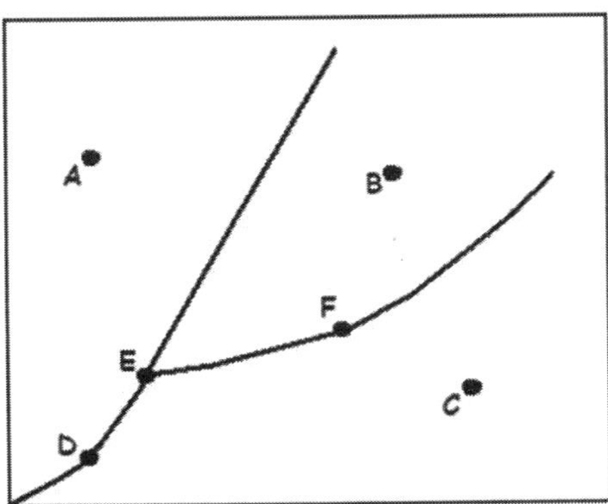

A—**Solid phase**: This is a region of high pressure and low temperature where the substance always exists as a solid.

B—**Liquid phase**: This is a region of pressure and temperature where the substance is in the liquid phase.

C—**Gas phase**: This is a region of pressure and temperature where the substance is in the gaseous phase.

D—**Sublimation point**: The portion of the curve that contains point D shows all the combinations of pressure and temperature at which the solid phase is in equilibrium with the gaseous phase.

E—**Critical point**: The point at which the solid, liquid, and gaseous phases are all in equilibrium.

F—**Boiling point**: The line that contains point F indicates all the combinations of pressure and temperature at which the liquid phase and gas phase are in equilibrium.

Laws of Thermodynamics

First Law

The **first law of thermodynamics** states that energy cannot be **created** or **destroyed**, but only **converted** from one form to another. It is generally applied as $Q = \Delta U + W$, where Q is the net heat energy added to a system, ΔU is the change in internal energy of the system, and W is the work done by the system. For any input of heat energy to a system, that energy must be either converted to internal energy through a temperature increase or expended in doing work. For a system that gives off heat, either the temperature of the system must decrease or work must be done on the system by its surroundings. By convention, work done by the system is positive while work done on the system is negative.

For instance, suppose a gas is compressed by a piston while the gas temperature remains constant. If we consider the gas to be the system, the work is negative, since the work is being performed on the gas. Since the temperature remains constant, $\Delta U = 0$. Thus, Q must be a negative quantity, indicating that heat is lost by the gas. Conversely, if the gas does positive work on the piston while remaining at a constant temperature, the gas must be receiving heat input from the surroundings.

Second Law

The **second law of thermodynamics** is primarily a statement of the natural tendency of all things toward disorder rather than order. It deals with a quantity called **entropy**, which is an inverse measure of the remaining useful energy in a system. If we take a system of a pot of hot water and an ice cube, the system entropy initially has a value of s_1. After the ice cube melts in the water and the system reaches an equilibrium temperature, the system has larger entropy value s_2, which is the maximum entropy for the system. The system cannot return to its initial state without work put into the system to refreeze the ice cube and reheat the water. If this is done and the system returns to a state with entropy s_1, then the entropy of the surroundings must at the same time increase by more than $s_2 - s_1$, since the net entropy from any process is always greater than zero. Reversible processes are those that may be accomplished in reverse without requiring additional work input. These processes do not exist in the real world, but can be useful for approximating some situations. All real processes are irreversible, meaning they require additional work input to accomplish in reverse. Another important concept is that of spontaneity, the ability of a process to occur without instigation. An ice cube located in an environment at a temperature above the freezing point will spontaneously melt. Although some processes can decrease system entropy at a cost to the entropy of the surroundings, all spontaneous processes involve an increase in system entropy.

Third and Zeroth Laws

The **third law of thermodynamics** regards the behavior of systems as they **approach absolute zero temperature**. Actually reaching a state of absolute zero is impossible. According to this law, all activity disappears as molecules slow to a standstill near absolute zero, and the system achieves a perfect crystal structure while the system entropy approaches its minimum value. For most systems, this would in fact be a value of zero entropy. Note that this does not violate the second law since causing a system to approach absolute zero would require an immense increase in the entropy of the surroundings, resulting in a positive net entropy. This law is used to determine the value of a material's standard entropy, which is its entropy at the standard temperature of 25 °C.

The **zeroth law of thermodynamics** deals with thermal equilibrium between two systems. It states that if two systems are both in thermal equilibrium with a third system, then they are in thermal equilibrium with each other. This may seem intuitive, but it is an important basis for the other thermodynamic laws.

Review Video: Laws of Thermodynamics
Visit mometrix.com/academy and enter code: 253607

Entropy

Entropy (S) is the amount of **disorder** or **randomness of a system**. According to the second law of thermodynamics, systems tend toward a state of greater entropy. The second law of thermodynamics can also be stated as $\Delta S > 0$. Processes with positive changes in entropy tend to be spontaneous. For example, melting is a process with a positive ΔS. When a solid changes into a liquid state, the substance becomes more disordered; therefore, entropy increases. Entropy also will increase in a reaction in which the number of moles of gases increases due to the amount of disorder increasing. Entropy increases when a solute dissolves into a solvent due to the increase in the number of particles. Entropy increases when a system is heated due to the particles moving faster and the amount of disorder increasing.

Spontaneous / Reversible Processes

Some chemical processes are **spontaneous**. According to the second law of thermodynamics, systems or processes always **tend to a state of greater entropy** or lower potential energy. Some exothermic chemical systems are spontaneous because they can increase their stability by reaching a lower potential energy. If processes or reactions have products at a lower potential energy, these processes tend to be spontaneous. Spontaneous reactions have only one direction as given by the second law of thermodynamics. Spontaneous processes go in the direction of greater entropy and lower potential energy. To be reversible, a reaction or process has to be able to go back and forth between two states. A spontaneous process is irreversible.

Concept of Change in Enthalpy

All chemical processes involve either the release or the absorption of heat. Enthalpy is this heat energy. **Enthalpy** is a state function that is equivalent to the amount of heat a system exchanges with its surroundings. For **exothermic processes**, which release heat, the change in enthalpy (ΔH) is negative because the final enthalpy is less than the initial enthalpy. For **endothermic processes**, which absorb heat, the change in enthalpy (ΔH) is positive because the final enthalpy is greater than the initial enthalpy.

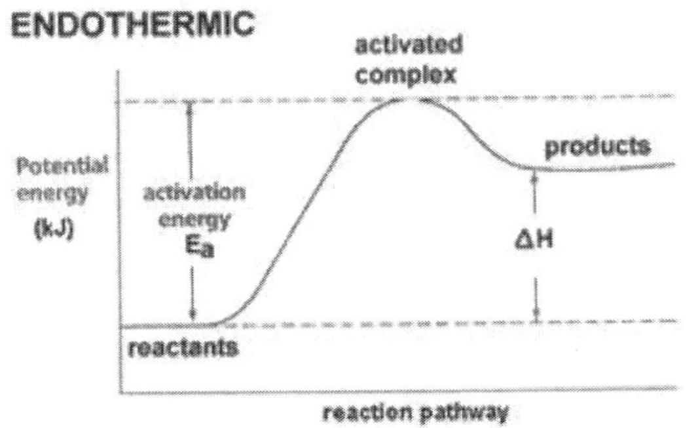

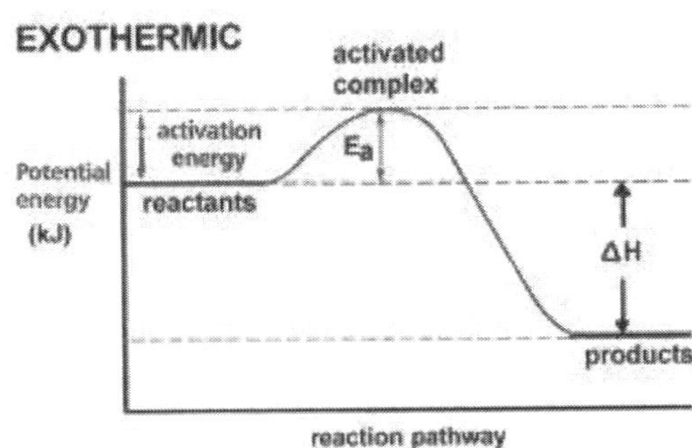

Review Video: Enthalpy
Visit mometrix.com/academy and enter code: 233315

Gibbs Energy

Gibbs energy (G), also known as Gibbs free energy, is the energy of the system that is available to do work. Gibbs energy determines the **spontaneity** of chemical and physical processes. Some processes are spontaneous because $\Delta H < 0$ or because $\Delta S > 0$. If one of the conditions is favorable but the other condition is not favorable, Gibbs energy can be used to determine if a process is spontaneous. Gibbs energy is given by $G = H - TS$. For processes that occur at constant temperature, $\Delta G = \Delta H - T\Delta S$. If ΔG is equal to zero, then the reaction is at equilibrium and neither the forward nor the reverse reaction is spontaneous. If ΔG is less than zero, then the forward reaction is spontaneous. If ΔG is greater than zero, then the reverse reaction is spontaneous.

Atomic Models and Theories

There have been many theories regarding the **structure** of atoms and their particles. Part of the challenge in developing an understanding of matter is that atoms and their particles are too small to be seen. It is believed that the first conceptualization of the atom was developed by **Democritus** in 400 B.C. Some of the more notable models are the solid sphere or billiard ball model postulated by **John Dalton**, the plum pudding or raisin bun model by **J.J. Thomson**, the planetary or nuclear model by **Ernest Rutherford**, the Bohr or orbit model by **Niels Bohr**, and the electron cloud or quantum mechanical model by **Louis de Broglie** and **Erwin Schrodinger**. Rutherford directed the alpha scattering experiment that discounted the plum pudding model. The shortcoming of the Bohr model was the belief that electrons orbited in fixed rather than changing ecliptic orbits.

Review Video: Atomic Models
Visit mometrix.com/academy and enter code: 434851

Review Video: John Dalton
Visit mometrix.com/academy and enter code: 565627

Thomson "Plum Pudding" Model

J.J. Thomson, the discoverer of the electron, suggested that the arrangement of protons and electrons within an atom could be approximated by dried fruit in a **plum pudding**. Thomson, whose discovery of the electron preceded that of the proton or neutron, hypothesized that an atom's electrons, the dried plums, were positioned uniformly inside the atom within a cloud of positive charge, the pudding. This model was later disproved.

Rutherford Scattering

Ernest Rutherford concluded from the work of Geiger and Marsden that the majority of the mass was concentrated in a minute, positively charged region, the **nucleus**, which was surrounded by **electrons**. When a positive alpha particle approached close enough to the nucleus, it was strongly repelled, enough so that it had the ability to rebound at high angles. The small nucleus size explained the small number of alpha particles that were repelled in this fashion. The scattering led to development of the **planetary model of the atom**, which was further developed by Niels Bohr into what is now known as the Bohr model.

Bohr Model

Niels Bohr postulated that the electrons orbiting the nucleus must occupy discrete orbits. These discrete orbits also corresponded to discrete levels of energy and angular momentum. Consequently, the only way that electrons could move between orbits was by making nearly instantaneous jumps between them. These jumps, known as **quantum leaps**, are associated with the absorption or emission of a quantum of energy, known as a photon. If the electron is jumping to a higher energy state, a photon must be absorbed. Similarly, if the electron is dropping to a lower energy state, a photon must be emitted.

Review Video: Structure of Atoms
Visit mometrix.com/academy and enter code: 905932

Basic Organization of Matter

An **element** is the most basic type of matter. It has unique properties and cannot be broken down into other elements. The smallest unit of an element is the **atom**. A chemical combination of two or more types of elements is called a compound. **Compounds** often have properties that are very different from those of their constituent elements. The smallest independent unit of an element or compound is known as a **molecule**. Most elements are found somewhere in nature in single-atom form, but a few elements only exist naturally in pairs. These are called diatomic elements, of which some of the most common are hydrogen, nitrogen, and oxygen. Elements and compounds are represented by chemical symbols, one or two letters, most often the first in the element name. More than one atom of the same element in a compound is represented with a subscript number designating how many atoms of that element are present. Water, for instance, contains two hydrogens and one oxygen. Thus, the chemical formula is H_2O. Methane contains one carbon and four hydrogens, so its formula is CH_4.

Review Video: Molecules
Visit mometrix.com/academy and enter code: 349910

Protons, Neutrons, and Electrons

The three major subatomic particles are the proton, neutron, and electron. The **proton**, which is located in the nucleus, has a relative charge of +1. The **neutron**, which is located in the nucleus, has a relative charge of 0. The **electron**, which is located outside the nucleus, has a relative charge of −1. The proton and neutron, which are essentially the same mass, are much more massive than the electron and make up the mass of the atom. The electron's mass is insignificant compared to the mass of the proton and neutron.

Review Video: Nuclear Charge
Visit mometrix.com/academy and enter code: 412575

Orbits and Orbitals

An **orbit** is a definite path, but an orbital is a region in space. The Bohr model described electrons as orbiting or following a definite path in space around the nucleus of an atom. But, according to **Heisenberg's uncertainty principle**, it is impossible to determine the location and the momentum of an electron simultaneously. Therefore, it is impossible to draw a definite path or orbit of an electron. An **orbital** as described by the quantum-mechanical model or the electron-cloud model is a region in space that is drawn in such a way as to indicate the probability of finding an electron at a specific location. The distance an orbital is located from the nucleus corresponds to the principal quantum number. The orbital shape corresponds to the subshell or azimuthal quantum number. The orbital orientation corresponds to the magnetic quantum number.

Quantum Numbers

The **principal quantum number** (n) describes an electron's shell or energy level and actually describes the size of the orbital. Electrons farther from the nucleus are at higher energy levels. The **subshell** or azimuthal quantum number (l) describes the electron's sublevel or subshell (*s, p, d,* or *f*) and specifies the shape of the orbital. Typical shapes include spherical, dumbbell, and clover leaf.

The **magnetic quantum number** (m_l) describes the orientation of the orbital in space. The spin or magnetic moment quantum number (m_s) describes the direction of the spin of the electron in the orbital.

Atomic Number and Mass Number

The **atomic number** of an element is the number of protons in the nucleus of an atom of that element. This is the number that identifies the type of an atom. For example, all oxygen atoms have eight protons, and all carbon atoms have six protons. Each element is identified by its specific atomic number.

The **mass number** is the number of protons and neutrons in the nucleus of an atom. Although the atomic number is the same for all atoms of a specific element, the mass number can vary due to the varying numbers of neutrons in various isotopes of the atom.

Isotopes

Isotopes are atoms of the same element that vary in their number of neutrons. Isotopes of the same element have the same number of protons and thus the same atomic number. But, because isotopes vary in the number of neutrons, they can be identified by their mass numbers. For example, two naturally occurring carbon isotopes are carbon-12 and carbon-13, which have mass numbers 12 and 13, respectively. The symbols $^{12}_{6}C$ and $^{13}_{6}C$ also represent the carbon isotopes. The general form of the symbol is $^{M}_{A}X$, where X represents the element symbol, M represents the mass number, and A represents the atomic number.

Average Atomic Mass

The **average atomic mass** is the weighted average of the masses of all the naturally occurring isotopes of an atom in comparison to the carbon-12 isotope. The unit for average atomic mass is the atomic mass unit (u). Atomic masses of isotopes are measured using a mass spectrometer by bombarding a gaseous sample of the isotope and measuring its relative deflections. Atomic masses can be calculated if the percent abundances and the atomic masses of the naturally occurring isotopes are known.

Cathode Ray Tube (CRT)

Electrons were discovered by Joseph John Thomson through scientific work with cathode ray tubes (CRTs). **Cathode rays** had been studied for many years, but it was Thomson who showed that cathode rays were **negatively charged particles**. Although Thomson could not determine an electron's charge or mass, he was able to determine the ratio of the charge to the mass. Thomson discovered that this ratio was constant regardless of the gas in the CRT. He was able to show that the cathode rays were actually streams of negatively charged particles by deflecting them with a positively charged plate.

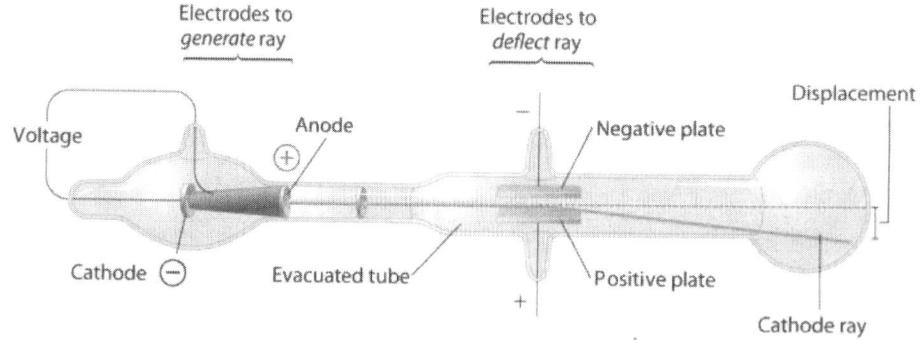

Gold Foil Experiment

After Thomson determined the ratio of the charge to the mass of an electron from studying cathode rays, he proposed the plum pudding model, in which he compared electrons to the raisins embedded in plum pudding. This model of the atom was disproved by the gold foil experiment. The gold foil experiment led to the discovery of the nucleus of an atom. Scientists at Rutherford's laboratory bombarded a thin gold foil with high-speed helium ions. Much to their surprise, some of the ions were reflected by the foil. The scientists concluded that the atom has a **hard central core**, which we now know to be the **nucleus**.

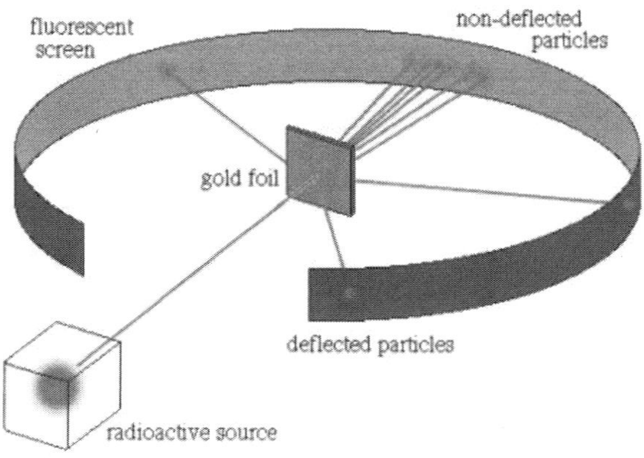

Problems that Rutherford's Model Had with Spectral Lines

Rutherford's model allowed for the electrons of an atom to be in an **infinite number of orbits** based on Newton's laws of motion. Rutherford believed that electrons could orbit the nucleus at any distance from the nucleus and that electrons could change velocity and direction at any moment. But, according to Rutherford's model, the electrons would lose energy and spiral into the nucleus. Unfortunately, if this was in fact true, then every atom would be **unstable**. Rutherford's model also does not correspond to the spectral lines emitted from gases at low pressure. The **spectral lines** are discrete bands of light at specific energy levels. These spectral lines indicate that electrons must be at specific distances from the nucleus. If electrons could be located at any distance from the nucleus, then these gases should emit continuous spectra instead of spectral lines.

Pure Substances

Pure substances are substances that cannot be further broken down into simpler substances and still retain their characteristics. Pure substances are categorized as either **elements** or **compounds**. Elements that consist of only one type of atom may be monatomic, diatomic, or polyatomic. For example, helium (He) and copper (Cu) are monatomic elements, and hydrogen (H_2) and oxygen (O_2) are diatomic elements. Phosphorus (P_4) and sulfur (S_8) are polyatomic elements. Compounds consist of molecules of more than one type of atom. For example, pure water (H_2O) is made up of molecules consisting of two atoms of hydrogen bonded to one atom of oxygen, and glucose ($C_6H_{12}O_6$) is made up of molecules of six carbon atoms and twelve hydrogen atoms bonded together with six oxygen atoms.

Mixtures

Mixtures can be classified as either homogeneous mixtures or heterogeneous mixtures. The molecules of **homogeneous mixtures** are distributed uniformly throughout the mixture, but the molecules of **heterogeneous mixtures** are not distributed uniformly throughout the mixture. Air is an example of a homogeneous mixture, and a pile of sand and rock is an example of a heterogeneous mixture. Solutions are homogeneous mixtures consisting of a **solute** (the substance that is dissolved) and a **solvent** (the substance doing the dissolving).

SUSPENSIONS

Suspensions are heterogeneous mixtures in which the particle size of the substance **suspended** is too large to be kept in suspension by Brownian motion. Once left undisturbed, suspensions will settle out to form layers. An example of a suspension is sand stirred into water. Left undisturbed, the sand will fall out of suspension and the water will form a layer on top of the sand.

MIXTURES WITH COMPOUNDS

Mixtures are similar to compounds in that they are produced when two or more substances are combined. However, there are some key differences as well. Compounds require a chemical combination of the constituent particles, while mixtures are simply the interspersion of particles. Unlike compounds, mixtures may be **separated** without a chemical change. A mixture retains the chemical properties of its constitutent particles, while a compound acquires a new set of properties. Given compounds can exist only in specific ratios, while mixtures may be any ratio of the involved substances.

CHEMICAL AND PHYSICAL PROPERTIES

Matter has both physical and chemical properties. **Physical properties** can be seen or observed without changing the identity or composition of matter. For example, the mass, volume, and density of a substance can be determined without permanently changing the sample. Other physical properties include color, boiling point, freezing point, solubility, odor, hardness, electrical conductivity, thermal conductivity, ductility, and malleability.

Chemical properties cannot be measured without changing the identity or composition of matter. Chemical properties describe how a substance reacts or changes to form a new substance. Examples of chemical properties include flammability, corrosivity, oxidation states, enthalpy of formation, and reactivity with other chemicals.

INTENSIVE AND EXTENSIVE PROPERTIES

Physical properties are categorized as either intensive or extensive. **Intensive properties** *do not* depend on the amount of matter or quantity of the sample. This means that intensive properties will not change if the sample size is increased or decreased. Intensive properties include color, hardness, melting point, boiling point, density, ductility, malleability, specific heat, temperature, concentration, and magnetization.

Extensive properties *do* depend on the amount of matter or quantity of the sample. Therefore, extensive properties do change if the sample size is increased or decreased. If the sample size is increased, the property increases. If the sample size is decreased, the property decreases. Extensive properties include volume, mass, weight, energy, entropy, number of moles, and electrical charge.

ATOMIC PROPERTIES OF NEUTRAL ATOMS, ANIONS, AND CATIONS

Neutral atoms have equal numbers of protons and electrons. **Cations** are positively-charged ions that are formed when atoms lose electrons in order to have a full outer shell of valence electrons. For example, the alkali metals sodium and potassium form the cations Na^+ and K^+, and the alkaline earth metals magnesium and calcium form the cations Mg^{2+} and Ca^{2+}.

Anions are negatively-charged ions that are formed when atoms gain electrons to fill their outer shell of valence electrons. For example, the halogens fluorine and chlorine form the anions F^- and Cl^-.

Chemical and Physical Changes

Physical changes do not produce new substances. The atoms or molecules may be rearranged, but no new substances are formed. **Phase changes** or changes of state such as melting, freezing, and sublimation are physical changes. For example, physical changes include the melting of ice, the boiling of water, sugar dissolving into water, and the crushing of a piece of chalk into a fine powder.

Chemical changes involve a **chemical reaction** and do produce new substances. When iron rusts, iron oxide is formed, indicating a chemical change. Other examples of chemical changes include baking a cake, burning wood, digesting food, and mixing an acid and a base.

Law of Conservation of Energy

The **law of conservation of energy** states that in a closed system, energy cannot be created or destroyed but only changed from one form to another. This is also known as the first law of thermodynamics. Another way to state this is that the **total energy in an isolated system is constant**. Energy comes in many forms that may be transformed from one kind to another, but in a closed system, the total amount of energy is conserved or remains constant. For example, potential energy can be converted to kinetic energy, thermal energy, radiant energy, or mechanical energy. In an isolated chemical reaction, there can be no energy created or destroyed. The energy simply changes forms.

Law of Conservation of Mass

The **law of conservation of mass** is also known as the **law of conservation of matter**. This basically means that in a closed system, the total mass of the products must equal the total mass of the reactants. This could also be stated that in a closed system, mass never changes. A consequence of this law is that matter is never created or destroyed during a typical chemical reaction. The atoms of the reactants are simply rearranged to form the products. The number and type of each specific atom involved in the reactants is identical to the number and type of atoms in the products. This is the key principle used when balancing chemical equations. In a balanced chemical equation, the number of moles of each element on the reactant side equals the number of moles of each element on the product side.

> **Review Video: How Do You Balance Chemical Equations?**
> Visit mometrix.com/academy and enter code: 341228

Conversion of Energy Within Chemical Systems

Chemical energy is the energy stored in molecules in the bonds between the atoms of those molecules and the energy associated with the intermolecular forces. This stored **potential energy** may be converted into **kinetic energy** and then into heat. During a chemical reaction, atoms may be rearranged and chemical bonds may be formed or broken accompanied by a corresponding absorption or release of energy, usually in the form of heat. According to the first law of thermodynamics, during these energy conversions, the **total amount of energy must be conserved**.

Bonds

Chemical bonds are the attractive forces that bind atoms together into molecules. Atoms form chemical bonds in an attempt to satisfy the octet rule. These bond types include covalent bonds, ionic bonds, and metallic bonds. **Covalent bonds** are formed from the sharing of electron pairs between two atoms in a molecule. **Ionic bonds** are formed from the transferring of electrons between one atom and another, which results in the formations of cations and anions. **Metallic bonding** results from the sharing of delocalized electrons among all of the atoms in a molecule.

IONIC BONDING

Ionic bonding results from the transfer of electrons between atoms. A **cation** or positive ion is formed when an atom loses one or more electrons. An **anion** or negative ion is formed when an atom gains one or more electrons. An ionic bond results from the electrostatic attraction between a cation and an anion. One example of a compound formed by ionic bonds is sodium chloride or NaCl. Sodium (Na) is an alkali metal and tends to form Na^+ ions. Chlorine (Cl) is a halogen and tends to form Cl^- ions. The Na^+ ion and the Cl^- ion are attracted to each other. This electrostatic attraction between these oppositely charged ions is what results in the ionic bond between them.

$$Na\cdot + Cl \longrightarrow [Na]^+[Cl]^-$$

electron transer from sodium to chlorine

Review Video: Ionic Bonds
Visit mometrix.com/academy and enter code: 116546

COVALENT BONDING

Covalent bonding results from the sharing of electrons between atoms. Atoms seek to fill their valence shell and will share electrons with another atom in order to have a full octet (except hydrogen and helium, which only hold two electrons in their valence shells). **Molecular compounds** have covalent bonds. **Organic compounds** such as proteins, carbohydrates, lipids, and nucleic acids are molecular compounds formed by covalent bonds. Methane (CH_4) is a molecular compound in which one carbon atom is covalently bonded to four hydrogen atoms as shown below.

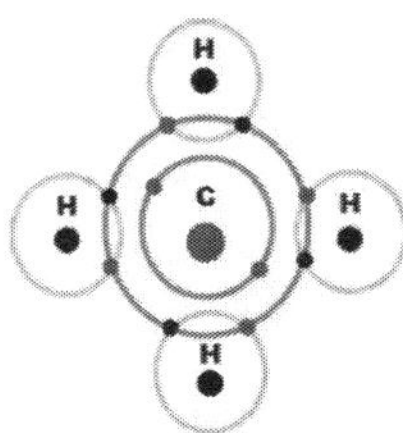

POLAR COVALENT BONDS, NONPOLAR COVALENT BONDS, AND HYBRIDIZATION

Polar covalent bonds result when electrons are shared unequally between atoms. **Nonpolar covalent bonds** result when electrons are shared equally between atoms. The unequal sharing of electrons is due to the differences in the electronegativities of the two atoms sharing the electrons. Partial charges develop due to this unequal sharing of electrons. The greater the difference in electronegativities between the two atoms, the stronger the dipole is. For example, the covalent bonds formed between the carbon atom and the two oxygen atoms in carbon dioxide are polar covalent bonds because the electronegativities of carbon and oxygen differ slightly. If the electronegativities are equal, then the covalent bonds are nonpolar. For example, the covalent double bond between two oxygen atoms is nonpolar because the oxygen atoms have the same electronegativities.

Review Video: Nonpolar Covalent Bonds
Visit mometrix.com/academy and enter code: 986465

Review Video: What are Covalent Bonds
Visit mometrix.com/academy and enter code: 482899

Metallic Bonding

Metallic bonding is a type of bonding between metals. Metallic bonds are similar to covalent bonds in that they are a type of sharing of electrons between atoms. However, in covalent bonding, the electrons are shared with only one other atom. In metallic bonding, the electrons are shared with all the surrounding atoms. These electrons are referred to as delocalized electrons. Metallic bonding is responsible for many of the characteristics in metals including conductivity, malleability, and ductility. An example of metallic bonding is the metallic bond between the copper atoms in a piece of copper wire.

Review Video: Metallic Bonds
Visit mometrix.com/academy and enter code: 230855

Groups and Periods in the Periodic Table

A **group** is a vertical column of the periodic table. Elements in the same group have the same number of **valence electrons**. For the representative elements, the number of valence electrons is equal to the group number. Because of their equal valence electrons, elements in the same groups have similar physical and chemical properties. A period is a horizontal row of the periodic table. Atomic number increases from left to right across a row. The **period** of an element corresponds to the **highest energy level** of the electrons in the atoms of that element. The energy level increases from top to bottom down a group.

Period \ Group	1 Hydrogen and alkali metals	2	3	4	5	6	7	8	9	10	11	12	13	14	15 Pnictogens	16 Chalcogens	17 Halogens	18 Noble gases
1	1 H Hydrogen																	2 He Helium
2	3 Li Lithium	4 Be Beryllium											5 B Boron	6 C Carbon	7 N Nitrogen	8 O Oxygen	9 F Fluorine	10 Ne Neon
3	11 Na Sodium	12 Mg Magnesium											13 Al Aluminium	14 Si Silicon	15 P Phosphorus	16 S Sulfur	17 Cl Chlorine	18 Ar Argon
4	19 K Potassium	20 Ca Calcium	21 Sc Scandium	22 Ti Titanium	23 V Vanadium	24 Cr Chromium	25 Mn Manganese	26 Fe Iron	27 Co Cobalt	28 Ni Nickel	29 Cu Copper	30 Zn Zinc	31 Ga Gallium	32 Ge Germanium	33 As Arsenic	34 Se Selenium	35 Br Bromine	36 Kr Krypton
5	37 Rb Rubidium	38 Sr Strontium	39 Y Yttrium	40 Zr Zirconium	41 Nb Niobium	42 Mo Molybdenum	43 Tc Technetium	44 Ru Ruthenium	45 Rh Rhodium	46 Pd Palladium	47 Ag Silver	48 Cd Cadmium	49 In Indium	50 Sn Tin	51 Sb Antimony	52 Te Tellurium	53 I Iodine	54 Xe Xenon
6	55 Cs Caesium	56 Ba Barium	Lanthanides 57-71	72 Hf Hafnium	73 Ta Tantalum	74 W Tungsten	75 Re Rhenium	76 Os Osmium	77 Ir Iridium	78 Pt Platinum	79 Au Gold	80 Hg Mercury	81 Tl Thallium	82 Pb Lead	83 Bi Bismuth	84 Po Polonium	85 At Astatine	86 Rn Radon
7	87 Fr Francium	88 Ra Radium	Actinides 89-103	104 Rf Rutherfordium	105 Db Dubnium	106 Sg Seaborgium	107 Bh Bohrium	108 Hs Hassium	109 Mt Meitnerium	110 Ds Darmstadtium	111 Rg Roentgenium	112 Cn Copernicium	113 Nh Nihonium	114 Fl Flerovium	115 Mc Moscovium	116 Lv Livermorium	117 Ts Tennessine	118 Og Oganesson

Lanthanides	57 La Lanthanum	58 Ce Cerium	59 Pr Praseodymium	60 Nd Neodymium	61 Pm Promethium	62 Sm Samarium	63 Eu Europium	64 Gd Gadolinium	65 Tb Terbium	66 Dy Dysprosium	67 Ho Holmium	68 Er Erbium	69 Tm Thulium	70 Yb Ytterbium	71 Lu Lutetium
Actinides	89 Ac Actinium	90 Th Thorium	91 Pa Protactinium	92 U Uranium	93 Np Neptunium	94 Pu Plutonium	95 Am Americium	96 Cm Curium	97 Bk Berkelium	98 Cf Californium	99 Es Einsteinium	100 Fm Fermium	101 Md Mendelevium	102 No Nobelium	103 Lr Lawrencium

Review Video: Periodic Table
Visit mometrix.com/academy and enter code: 154828

ATOMIC NUMBER AND ATOMIC MASS IN THE PERIODIC TABLE

The elements in the periodic table are arranged in order of **increasing atomic number** first left to right and then top to bottom across the periodic table. The **atomic number** represents the number of protons in the atoms of that element. Because of the increasing numbers of protons, the atomic mass typically also increases from left to right across a period and from top to bottom down a row. The **atomic mass** is a weighted average of all the naturally occurring isotopes of an element.

ATOMIC SYMBOLS

The **atomic symbol** for many elements is simply the first letter of the element name. For example, the atomic symbol for hydrogen is H, and the atomic symbol for carbon is C. The atomic symbol of other elements is the first two letters of the element name. For example, the atomic symbol for helium is He, and the atomic symbol for cobalt is Co. The atomic symbols of several elements are derived from Latin. For example, the atomic symbol for copper (Cu) is derived from *cuprum,* and the atomic symbol for iron (Fe) is derived from *ferrum.* The atomic symbol for tungsten (W) is derived from the German word *wolfram.*

ARRANGEMENT OF METALS, NONMETALS, AND METALLOIDS IN THE PERIODIC TABLE

The **metals** are located on the left side and center of the periodic table, and the **nonmetals** are located on the right side of the periodic table. The **metalloids** or **semimetals** form a zigzag line between the metals and nonmetals as shown below. Metals include the alkali metals such as lithium, sodium, and potassium and the alkaline earth metals such as beryllium, magnesium, and calcium. Metals also include the transition metals such as iron, copper, and nickel and the inner transition metals such as thorium, uranium, and plutonium. Nonmetals include the chalcogens such as oxygen and sulfur, the halogens such as fluorine and chlorine, and the noble gases such as helium and argon. Carbon, nitrogen, and phosphorus are also nonmetals. Metalloids or semimetals include boron, silicon, germanium, antimony, and polonium.

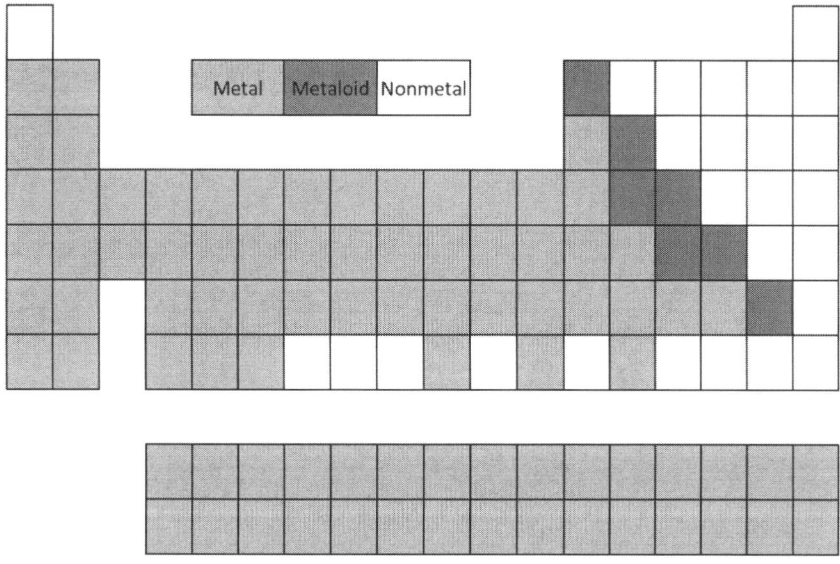

Review Video: Metals in the Periodic Table
Visit mometrix.com/academy and enter code: 506502

Arrangement of Transition Elements

The **transition elements** belong to one of two categories—transition metals or inner transition metals. The **transition metals** are located in the middle of the periodic table, and the inner transition metals are typically set off as two rows by themselves at the bottom of the periodic table. The transition metals correspond to the "*d* block" for orbital filling, and the inner transition metals correspond to the "*f* block" for orbital filling. Examples of transition metals include iron, copper, nickel, and zinc. The inner transition metals consist of the *lanthanide* or *rare-earth series*, which corresponds to the first row, and the *actinide series*, which corresponds to the second row of the inner transition metals. The *lanthanide series* includes lanthanum, cerium, and praseodymium. The *actinide series* includes actinium, uranium, and plutonium.

Types of Reactions

One way to organize chemical reactions is to sort them into two categories: **oxidation/reduction reactions** (also called redox reactions) and **metathesis reactions** (which include acid/base reactions). Oxidation/reduction reactions can involve the transfer of one or more electrons, or they can occur as a result of the transfer of oxygen, hydrogen, or halogen atoms. The species that loses electrons is oxidized and is referred to as the reducing agent. The species that gains electrons is reduced and is referred to as the oxidizing agent. The element undergoing oxidation experiences an increase in its oxidation number, while the element undergoing reduction experiences a decrease in its oxidation number. **Single replacement reactions** are types of oxidation/reduction reactions. In a single replacement reaction, electrons are transferred from one chemical species to another. The transfer of electrons results in changes in the nature and charge of the species.

Review Video: Chemical Reactions
Visit mometrix.com/academy and enter code: 579876

Review Video: Reaction Process
Visit mometrix.com/academy and enter code: 808039

Single Substitution, Displacement, and Replacement Reactions

Single substitution, **displacement**, or **replacement reactions** are when one reactant is displaced by another to form the final product ($A + BC \rightarrow AB + C$). Single substitution reactions can be cationic or anionic. When a piece of copper (Cu) is placed into a solution of silver nitrate ($AgNO_3$), the solution turns blue. The copper appears to be replaced with a silvery-white material. The equation is $2AgNO_3 + Cu \rightarrow Cu(NO_3)_2 + 2Ag$. When this reaction takes place, the copper dissolves and the silver in the silver nitrate solution precipitates (becomes a solid), resulting in copper nitrate and silver. Copper and silver have switched places in the nitrate.

Double displacement, **double replacement**, **substitution**, **metathesis**, or **ion exchange reactions** are when ions or bonds are exchanged by two compounds to form different compounds ($AC + BD \rightarrow AD + BC$). An example of this is that silver nitrate and sodium chloride form two different products (silver chloride and sodium nitrate) when they react. The formula for this reaction is $AgNO_3 + NaCl \rightarrow AgCl + NaNO_3$.

Review Video: Single-Replacement Reactions
Visit mometrix.com/academy and enter code: 442975

Combination and Decomposition Reactions

Combination, or **synthesis**, **reactions**: In a combination reaction, two or more reactants combine to form a single product ($A + B \rightarrow AB$). These reactions are also called synthesis or **addition reactions**. An example is burning hydrogen in air to produce water. The equation is $2H_2(g) + O_2(g) \rightarrow 2H_2O(l)$. Another example is when water and sulfur trioxide react to form sulfuric acid. The equation is $H_2O + SO_3 \rightarrow H_2SO_4$.

Decomposition (or desynthesis, decombination, or deconstruction) reactions: In a decomposition reaction, a reactant is broken down into two or more products ($AB \rightarrow A + B$). These reactions are also called analysis reactions. **Thermal decomposition** is caused by heat. **Electrolytic decomposition** is due to electricity. An example of this type of reaction is the decomposition of water into hydrogen and oxygen gas. The equation is $2H_2O \rightarrow 2H_2 + O_2$.

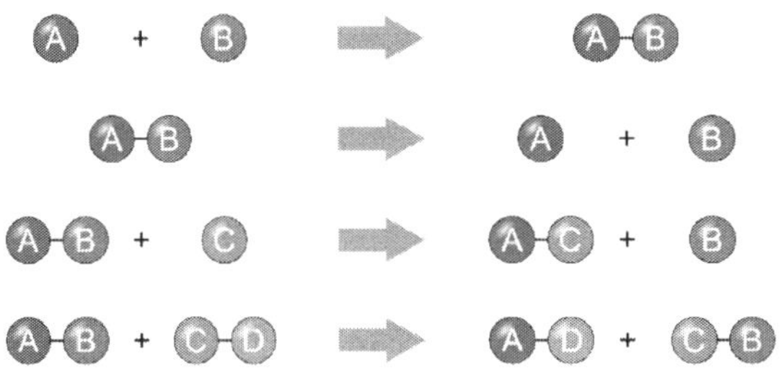

Acid/Base Reactions

In **acid/base reactions**, an **acid** is a compound that can donate a proton, while a **base** is a compound that can accept a proton. In these types of reactions, the acid and base react to form a salt and water. When the proton is donated, the base becomes water and the remaining ions form a salt. One method of determining whether a reaction is an oxidation/reduction or a metathesis reaction is that the oxidation number of atoms does not change during a metathesis reaction.

Isomerization and Neutralization Reactions

Isomerization, or **rearrangement**, is the process of forming a compound's isomer. Within a compound, bonds are reformed. The reactant and product have the same molecular formula, but different structural formulas and different properties ($A \rightarrow B$ or $A \rightarrow A'$). For example, butane (C_4H_{10}) is a hydrocarbon consisting of four carbon atoms in a straight chain. Heating it to 100° C or higher in the presence of a catalyst forms isobutane (methylpropane), which has a branched-chain structure. Boiling and freezing points are greatly different for butane and isobutane. A rearrangement reaction occurs within the molecule.

A **neutralization, acid-base**, or **proton transfer reaction** is when one compound acquires H^+ from another. These types of reactions are also usually double displacement reactions. The acid has an H^+ that is transferred to the base and neutralized to form a salt.

Chemical Kinetics

Chemical kinetics is the study of the **rates** or speeds of **chemical reactions** and the various factors that affect these rates or speeds. The rate or speed of a reaction is the change in concentration of the reactants or products per unit of time. Another way to state this is that chemical kinetics is the study of the rate of change of the concentrations of the reactants and products and the factors that affect that rate of change. The study of catalysts is part of chemical kinetics. Catalysts are substances that speed up the rate of reactions without being consumed. Examples of reactions that occur at different rates include the explosion of trinitrotoluene (TNT), which occurs at a very fast rate, compared to the burning of a log, which occurs at a much slower rate.

Give the Rate Law for this General Reaction: $aA + bB + cC \rightarrow$ Products. Define Each Letter.

The rate of a chemical reaction can be defined as the following:

$$\text{rate} = \frac{\text{change in concentration}}{\text{change in time}}$$

This is usually represented by a rate law. The rate law for the general reaction $aA + bB + cC \rightarrow$ Products is given by rate $= k[A]^x[B]^y[C]^z$, where k is the rate constant; [A], [B], and [C] represent the concentrations of the reactants; and x, y, and z represent the reaction orders. The exponents x, y, and z must be experimentally determined. They do not necessarily equal the coefficients from the balanced chemical equation.

Activation Energy

Activation energy is the minimum amount of energy that must be possessed by reactant atoms or molecules in order to react. This is due to the fact that it takes a certain amount of energy to break bonds or form bonds between atoms. Reactants lacking the activation energy required will not be able to perform the necessary breaking or forming of bonds regardless of how often they collide. Catalysts lower the activation energy of a reaction and therefore increase the rate of reaction.

Reaction Mechanism

Often, when studying specific reactions, only the net reactions are given. Realistically, reactions take place in a series of steps or elementary reactions as shown in the reaction mechanism.

Reaction mechanisms show how a reaction proceeds in a **series of steps**. Some steps are slow, and some are fast. Each step has its own reaction mechanism. The slowest step in the reaction mechanism coincides with the step with the greatest activation energy. This step is known as the rate-determining step.

Catalyst

A **catalyst** is a chemical that **accelerates** or speeds up a chemical reaction without being consumed or used up in the reaction. Although catalysts are not consumed or permanently changed during the process of the reaction, catalysts do participate in the elementary reaction of the reaction mechanisms. Catalysts cannot make an impossible reaction take place, but catalysts do greatly increase the rate of a reaction. Catalysts lower the **activation energy**. Because the activation energy is the minimum energy required for molecules to react, lowering the activation energy makes it possible for more of the reactant molecules to react.

Review Video: Catalysts
Visit mometrix.com/academy and enter code: 288189

Factors That Affect Reaction Rate

Factors that affect reaction rate include concentration, surface area, and temperature. Increasing the **concentration** of the reactants increases the number of collisions between those reactants and therefore increases the reaction rate. Increasing the **surface area of contact** between the reactants also increases the number of collisions and therefore increases the reaction rate. Finally, increasing the **temperature** of the reactants increases the number of collisions but more significantly also increases the kinetic energy of the reactants, which in turn increases the fraction of molecules meeting the activation energy requirement. With more molecules at the activation energy, more of the reactants are capable of completing the reaction.

Dilute and Concentrated

The terms **dilute** and **concentrated** have opposite meanings. In a solution, the **solute** is dissolved in the **solvent**. The more solute that is dissolved, the more concentrated is the solution. The less solute that is dissolved, the less concentrated and the more dilute is the solution. The terms are often associated with the preparation of a stock solution for a laboratory experiment. Stock solutions are typically ordered in a concentrated solution. To prepare for use in a chemistry lab, the stock solutions are diluted to the appropriate molarity by adding a specific amount of solvent such as water to a specific amount of stock solution.

Saturated, Unsaturated, and Supersaturated

The terms *saturated, unsaturated,* and *supersaturated* are associated with solutions. In a **solution**, a **solute** is added to a **solvent**. In a saturated solution, the solute is added to the solvent until no more solute is able to dissolve. The undissolved solute will settle down to the bottom of the beaker. A solution is considered unsaturated as long as more solute is able to go into solution under ordinary conditions. The solubility of solids in liquids typically increases as temperature increases. If the temperature of a solution is increased as the solute is being added, more solute than is normally possible may go into solution, forming a supersaturated solution.

Mixture, Solution, and Colloid

A **mixture** is made of two or more substances that are combined in various proportions. The exact proportion of the constituents is the defining characteristic of any mixture. There are two types of mixtures: homogeneous and heterogeneous. **Homogeneous** means that the mixture's composition and properties are uniform throughout. Conversely, **heterogeneous** means that the mixture's composition and properties are not uniform throughout.

A **solution** is a homogeneous mixture of substances that cannot be separated by filtration or centrifugation. Solutions are made by dissolving one or more solutes into a solvent. For example, in an aqueous glucose solution, glucose is the solute and water is the solvent. If there is more than one liquid present in the solution, then the most prevalent liquid is considered the solvent. The exact mechanism of dissolving varies depending on the mixture, but the result is always individual solute ions or molecules surrounded by solvent molecules. The proportion of solute to solvent for a particular solution is its **concentration**.

A **colloid** is a heterogeneous mixture in which small particles (<1 micrometer) are suspended, but not dissolved, in a liquid. As such, they can be separated by centrifugation. A commonplace example of a colloid is milk.

Review Video: Solutions
Visit mometrix.com/academy and enter code: 995937

Effects of Temperature, Surface Area, Agitation, and Pressure on the Dissolution Rate

Temperature, pressure, surface area, and agitation affect the **dissolution rate**. Increasing the **temperature** increases the kinetic energy of the molecules, which increases the number of collisions with the solute particles. Increasing the **surface area** of contact by stirring (agitation) or crushing a solid solute also increases the dissolution rate and helps prevent recrystallization. Increasing the **pressure** will increase the dissolution rate for gas solutes in liquid solvents because the added pressure will make it more difficult for the gas to escape. Increasing the pressure will have virtually no effect on the dissolution rate for solid solutes in liquid solvents under normal conditions.

Effect of Temperature and Pressure on Solubility

Temperature and pressure affect **solubility**. For gas solutes in liquid solvents, increasing the **temperature** increases the kinetic energy causing more gas particles to escape the surface of the liquid solvents and therefore decreasing the solubility of the solutes. For most solid solutes in liquid solvents, increasing the temperature increases the solubility, as shown in this solubility curve for selected salts. For gas solutes in liquid solvents, increasing the **pressure** increases the solubility.

Increasing the pressure of liquid or solid solutes in liquid solvents has virtually no effect under normal conditions.

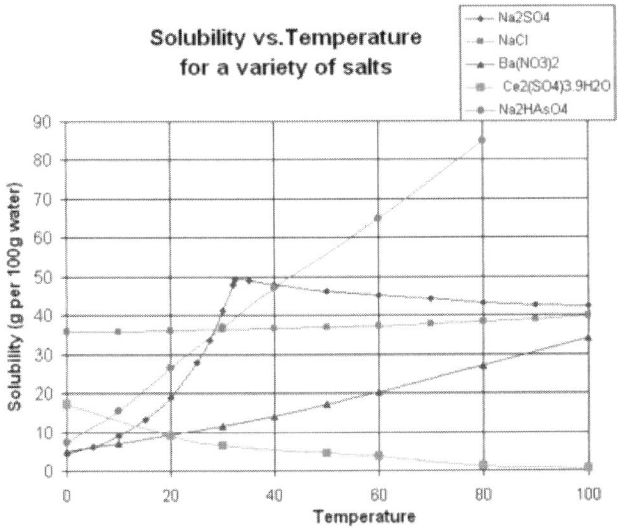

Differences Between Acids and Bases

There are several differences between **acids** and **bases**. Acidic solutions tend to taste sour, whereas basic solutions tend to taste bitter. Dilute bases tend to feel slippery, whereas dilute acids feel like water. Active metals such as magnesium and zinc react with acids to produce hydrogen gas, but active metals usually do not react with bases. Acids and bases form electrolytes in aqueous solutions and conduct electricity. Acids turn blue litmus red, but bases turn red litmus blue. Acidic solutions have a pH of less than 7, whereas basic solutions have a pH of greater than 7.

> **Review Video: Properties of Acids and Bases**
> Visit mometrix.com/academy and enter code: 645283

Arrhenius Acid and Base

Arrhenius acids are substances that produce hydrogen ions (H^+) when dissolved in water to form aqueous solutions. Arrhenius bases are substances that produce hydroxide ions (OH^-) when dissolved in water to form aqueous solutions. The **Arrhenius concept** is limited to acids and bases in aqueous solutions and cannot be applied to other solids, liquids, and gases. Examples of Arrhenius acids include hydrochloric acid (HCl) and sulfuric acid (H_2SO_4). Examples of Arrhenius bases include sodium hydroxide (NaOH) and magnesium hydroxide ($Mg(OH)_2$).

Brønsted–Lowry Acid and Base

The Brønsted–Lowry concept is based on the donation or the acceptance of a proton. According to the **Brønsted–Lowry concept**, an acid is a substance that donates one or more protons to another substance and a base is a substance that accepts a proton from another substance. The Brønsted–Lowry concept can be applied to substances other than aqueous solutions. This concept is much broader than the Arrhenius concept, which can only be applied to aqueous solutions. The Brønsted–Lowry concept states that a substance cannot act like an acid (donate its proton) unless another substance is available to act as a base (accept the donated proton). In this concept, water may act as either an acid or a base. Hydrochloric acid (HCl) is an example of a Brønsted–Lowry acid. Ammonia (NH_3) is an example of a Brønsted–Lowry base.

Lewis Acid and Base

A **Lewis acid** is any substance that can accept a pair of nonbonding electrons. A **Lewis base** is any substance that can donate a pair of nonbonding electrons. According to the **Lewis theory**, all cations such as Mg^{2+} and Cu^{2+} are Lewis acids. Trigonal planar molecules, which are exceptions to the octet rule such as BF_3, are Lewis acids. Molecules such as CO_2 that have multiple bonds between two atoms that differ in electronegativities are Lewis acids, also. According to the Lewis theory, all anions such as OH^- are Lewis bases. Other examples of Lewis bases include trigonal pyramidal molecules such as ammonia, NH_3, and nonmetal oxides such as carbon monoxide, CO. Some compounds such as water, H_2O, can be either Lewis acids or bases.

Neutralization Reaction

Neutralization is a reaction of an acid and a base that yields a salt and water. The general form of the reaction is:

$$\text{acid} + \text{base} \rightarrow \text{salt} + \text{water}$$

The salt is formed from the cation of the base and the anion of the acid. The water is formed from the cation of the acid and the anion of the base.

An example is the neutralization reaction of hydrochloric acid and sodium hydroxide to form sodium chloride and water:

$$HCl(aq) + NaOH(aq) \rightarrow NaCl(s) + H_2O(l)$$

Equivalence Point

The **equivalence point** is by definition the point in a titration at which the analyte is neutralized. When the acid–base indicator starts to change color, the equivalence point has been reached. At this point, equivalent amounts of acids and bases have reacted. Also, at this point, $[H^+] = [OH^-]$. On an acid–base titration curve, the slope of the curve increases dramatically at the equivalence point. For strong acids and bases, the equivalence point occurs at a pH of 7. The figures below show the equivalence points for a strong acid titrated with a strong base (a) and a strong base titrated with a strong acid (b).

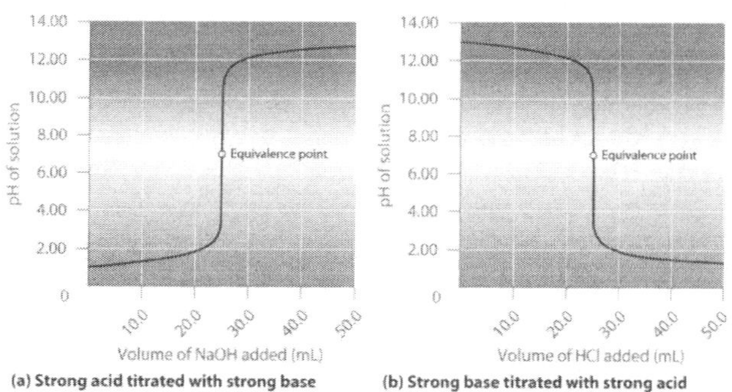

(a) Strong acid titrated with strong base (b) Strong base titrated with strong acid

Review Video: Titration
Visit mometrix.com/academy and enter code: 550131

Praxis Practice Test

English

1. Which of the following instructional techniques would be most appropriate for building and monitoring students' listening skills?

a. Read a story, poem, or other piece of literature to them each day before beginning class.
b. Give pop quizzes on the day's lessons at the end of class.
c. Preview concepts that will be introduced in class and then allow the students to answer recall-based questions verbally at the end of class.
d. Pay close attention to the students' answers on tests when they relate to classroom discussions.

2. Mrs. Baines' 6th-grade class is preparing for their "World Community" project in which each student selects a famous person from another country to research and report upon. The student will compile research into a written report and create a poster with interesting pictures and visual images related to that person. The students will also deliver a speech or series of quotations originally spoken by their research subject. Why would Mrs. Baines include this last portion of the project?

a. To help her students get ready for the play they will put on later in the year, practicing speaking another person's words with expression and interest.
b. To help students connect individual identity and oral expression while thinking about the world from another person's perspective.
c. To provide material for the listening recall and comprehension portions of the unit quizzes and tests.
d. To round out a project that is predominantly focused on reading and writing by adding a bit of speech into the requirements.

3. Which choice is most true regarding the relationship of listening skills to literacy development?

a. One of the last stages of literacy development is the honing of listening skills.
b. Once a student learns to read, it is unnecessary to practice listening comprehension.
c. Before students can become literate in any sense, they must be able to listen carefully to reading instruction.
d. Listening skills and comprehension are integral to literacy and should continue to be developed simultaneously with other literacy skills.

4. A 4th grade class will begin a unit next week in which students will be building oral language concepts through a variety of readings, projects and discussions. Which of the following genres would be most appropriate to use for reading text and class discussion?

a. Fiction
b. Folk tale
c. Biography
d. Science fiction

5. Which of the following activities is most helpful in developing general literacy skills of English language-learners or other students who are not yet reading fluently?

a. Solely focus on phonetics and building knowledge of sight words; without these skills, students will never be truly literate.
b. Assign partners or "buddies," allowing the language-learners to observe and learn from more literate classmates.
c. Allow students to participate verbally in class activities without grading or giving undue critique to reading or written work.
d. Set goals with each student during each assignment to allow them to feel a sense of accomplishment and gradually increase the level of challenge throughout the year.

6. Which of the following statements are most true regarding emergent readers?

a. Emergent readers are very well-suited for demonstrating fluent, expressive oral reading to their peers and are very confident serving as peer tutors. They show that they are ready for this role by appearing to 'emerge' from literacy instruction with confidence and excitement.
b. Emergent readers benefit from instruction across all aspects of literacy acquisition, including word identification, phonics, writing, listening, and speaking; they are still in the process of acquiring language skills in all forms and may be working at varied skill levels.
c. Emergent readers learn best when given the opportunity to listen and observe other students reading and speaking. Teachers should make efforts to ask the students to observe and listen as much as possible before attempting to read and write independently.
d. Emergent readers often display very high aptitudes in other disciplines, especially Social Studies and the Sciences. They have the innate ability to connect information from one class to the next.

7. Which student listed below exhibits signs of needing special instruction due to a learning disability or delay?

a. Jenna, a 6th-grade student who pauses to sound out long words with multiple syllables, slowing her oral reading.
b. Alina, whose thick accent makes her speech very difficult to understand when reading aloud or giving presentations.
c. Gavin, a 5th-grader who often does not remember concepts he has previously learned.
d. Billy, an 8th-grade student who frequently fails to turn in writing assignments and will sometimes skip over test questions that involve writing.

8. There are some students in Mr. Everly's class that do not speak aloud in class discussions on a regular basis. Class discussions tend to be dominated by a smaller group of more outspoken students. How should he address this circumstance?

a. No action is necessary.
b. Make a rule that each student must contribute at least once to class discussion before a student can speak a second time.
c. Verbally encourage the quieter students to speak during class time, telling them that their contributions are valuable.
d. Use group work to engage students in conversation, observing and encouraging quieter students in this context.

9. Which of the following choices is not a component of reading fluency?

a. Speed
b. Comprehension
c. Accuracy
d. Voice Modulation

10. If a student is reading a text aloud at an "instructional level," he or she should:

a. Find no more than one in five questions difficult to read.
b. Find no more than one in ten questions difficult to read.
c. Comprehend the majority, if not all, of what he reads.
d. Be able to instruct or teach other students to read and understand the text.

11. Aaron is chosen to read aloud in class today. His teacher finds it interesting that he struggles with words that have many graphemes, but few syllables. Which set of words did he misread?

a. Symphony, measure, chicken
b. Few, belt, halt
c. Auditorium, cacophony, friendliness
d. Hesitant, knowing, built

12. Which choice is the best way for a teacher to help students build their bank of sight words and vocabulary?

a. Using flash cards to drill and retain a large quantity of words.
b. Assign a wide variety of reading texts to introduce and familiarize students with words in different contexts.
c. Encourage parents to read with their children to help them learn new words and build motivation to read.
d. Provide each child with a dictionary and thesaurus to use during class work and homework and encourage them to explore word usage.

13. Mr. Blankenship, a 7th-grade language arts teacher, is planning class work related to comprehension of non-fiction writing. Which of the following skills should he introduce in order to help students build comprehension?

a. Text annotation
b. Rewriting text in your own words
c. Previewing and summarizing information
d. Making an outline

14. Brian is in 5th grade and says he hates to read. He has performed poorly on a consistent basis on classroom work and standardized testing, specifically with regard to reading comprehension. He has complained of disliking the texts he is given to read in class, saying that they are too easy, too hard, or simply boring. What might be a first step that a teacher should take in working to improve Brian's comprehension skills?

a. Deliver a reading comprehension assessment verbally, reading passages aloud to Brian and asking questions aloud. Analyze and monitor responses for comprehension.
b. Ask Brian to select something he likes to read from outside class and allow him to read it aloud, after which he answers selected oral comprehension questions.
c. Encourage Brian to read extensively, based on the belief that more practice yields better skill, which in turn builds motivation.
d. Establish a rewards system with Brian. Agree upon a point value for each completed comprehension lesson or class work. As Brian accumulates points, establish a larger reward that he can earn based on the points he gains.

15. Which of the following would be considered a *critical* or *inferential* comprehension skill?

a. Distinguishing between cause and effect
b. Understanding word meanings
c. Identifying literary techniques
d. Recalling events in a story

16. Which of the following is the best way to utilize the various levels of reading comprehension within a classroom to help *all* students build comprehension skills?

a. Use worksheets of varying difficulty to assign as class work.
b. Allow students who are stronger in reading comprehension to teach small lessons throughout the week.
c. Form groups that include students of varying abilities, and assign each person to lead discussion on an appropriate topic or question based upon ability level.
d. Assign partners or buddies, using a student who is stronger in comprehension to help one who is weaker complete class work.

17. Which of the following choices shows the best way to utilize technology in the writing process?

a. The student uses a personal voice recorder to record ideas in stream-of-consciousness. The student can then use the recording to transcribe thoughts into writing.
b. The student uses a word processor to begin writing from start to finish.
c. The student videotapes class discussions and views them in order to organize information regarding the topic.
d. The student uses an online graphic organizer to arrange the topic, main ideas, and supporting evidence into an outline, from which he can begin to write.

18. Which selection is most true regarding the use of journal writing in class?

a. Student journals should always contain very structured assignments. Without specific instructions about what to write, the journals will not likely show improvement.
b. Journals should never be graded to avoid the decrease of motivation. Students should always feel free to write whatever or however they feel at any given moment without fear of lower grades.
c. Student journals provide space in which students can express their feelings and thoughts. Teachers should provide parameters on content, conventions, and expectations to ensure that students are utilizing what they have learned about the writing process.
d. Parents and teachers can use journals as a resource to know more about the student. Teachers can use journal content to inform writing curriculum and instruction; parents can use their children's journals to gain insight about development.

19. Which of the following would *not* be used as instruction on writing conventions?

a. Practice correcting sentences with incorrect punctuation.
b. Re-writing work that is difficult to read due to word spacing and handwriting.
c. Brainstorming details to support the main concepts in an essay.
d. Checking spelling and using a dictionary and thesaurus to make sure that words are used correctly.

20. Students in a 7th-grade classroom arrive to see the following questions written on the board. Their teacher has graded the first writing assignment of the year. Which area of the writing process do you think she plans to address?

-What am I most interested in about this topic?

-How do I feel about this topic?

-What do I want to say about this topic?

-How can I say it so that my reader will understand what I mean?

a. Organization
b. Idea development
c. Persuasive writing
d. Revision

21. A 6th-grade class is beginning its first-ever independent research project, in which the teacher assigns points of intervention to scaffold student efforts. At what point should the teacher first meet with the student to help him or her with the inquiry process?

a. Choosing a topic
b. Gathering and selecting appropriate sources
c. Forming an outline
d. Writing a rough draft

Use the following information to answer questions 22 and 23:

> Mrs. Nelson teaches 6th- and 7th-graders in a middle school. A large part of the next month's studies will include learning about and applying study skills. The students will be applying various study skills to specific kinds of texts.

22. Mrs. Nelson's 7th-grade students have been reading about the SQ3R (survey, question, read/write, review) method of studying. This study plan allows the student to survey, preview information, formulate questions based on that preview, and then read in order to answer those questions. The student will then make notes in relation to these questions as well as other information in the text. Reviewing questions and notes is the final step of this ongoing process. To what kind of reading assignment should the students practice applying their new study method?

a. Poetry
b. A social studies textbook
c. Journal entries
d. A fiction story

23. The 6th-grade students in Mrs. Nelson's class are currently reading an adventure story, which they are enjoying very much. However, there are multiple plotlines developing simultaneously and the story contains many characters. Which study/analytical skill can Mrs. Nelson introduce to support the students?

a. Provide a "cheat sheet" containing synopses of each storyline and brief descriptions of the characters.
b. Show the movie of the same story shown in class.
c. Ask the students to pick characters and act out the story.
d. Create a story map with the students in class that contains major events in each plotline and brief descriptions of the characters as they read the story.

24. Which of the following describes the best way to incorporate research and individual inquiry into weekly class work?

a. Students visit the library or media center once a week to explore and check out books.
b. Students are asked to bring an article or essay from a newspaper, magazine, or academic website each week to share with the class.
c. Students complete a small section of a research project each week in class.
d. Whenever a question is posed during class discussion, a student can volunteer to research the answer in the library or online in the classroom.

25. A nationally-anticipated sporting event will be televised over the weekend, and Mr. Protos intends to incorporate this bit of the students' daily lives into his curriculum for teaching *viewing and representing*. This particular group of 8th-graders comprises Mr. Protos' Gifted and Talented English class and he would like to assign a bit of a challenge for them. Which assignment is the best blend of challenge and an already-existing event in the students' lives?

a. Hold an informal discussion on Monday regarding the meaning of "televised sports and our social development." Allow the students to contribute ideas about how this event has been embedded into their social consciousness.
b. Ask the students to journal about the sporting event as it happens, including predictions and reactions to its twists and turns. Discuss these real-time reactions in class on Monday.
c. Ask the students to watch the commercials on "mute" and keep a log of what they think the ads are representing. Discuss the accuracy of the students' assumptions and interpretations on Monday.
d. Assign a written report on the styles of athletes' dress, hair, and physical attributes and how these factors affect the viewing of—and engagement with—televised sports.

26. The graphic below is probably being used to teach which concept?

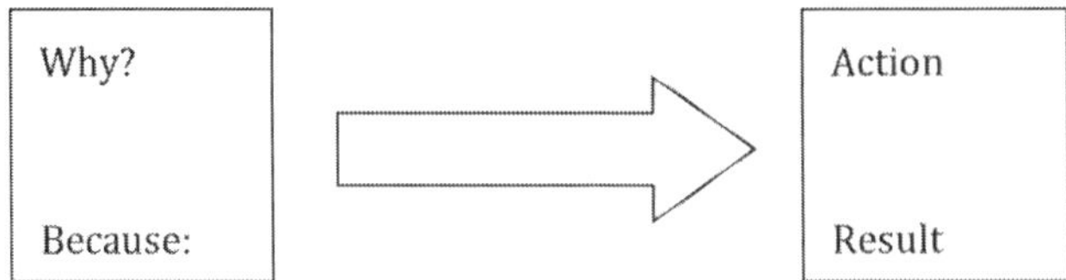

a. Character analysis
b. Cause and effect
c. Compare and contrast
d. Symbolism

27. Mr. Hawking is planning to show his students that it is possible to communicate ideas without actually speaking. How can he utilize the novel his students are reading in class to teach these concepts?

a. Have the students form groups and collaborate to adapt the novel into a play, which they can then act out for the class.
b. Play a game in which students draw simple pictures of characters, ideas, or events in the novel. The team that can correctly guess the largest number of 'pictograms' wins.
c. As a class, agree upon common bodily actions or hand gestures that represent certain aspects of everyday life. Practice using them each day to communicate without speaking.
d. Ask students to draw pictures and isolate new or interesting words to record in their journals and share with the class during "share time."

28. Which choice is the most accurate and appropriate for quickly assessing students' reading fluency and comprehension skills at any given point?

a. The teacher listens to each student read a short passage aloud and asks questions at the end to determine whether or not the student comprehends.
b. Use a reading scheme or set that includes readers (short books), worksheets, comprehension activities, and applications at the end of each month.
c. Assign worksheets that include both phonics work (to monitor fluency skills) and reading comprehension passages, followed by basic comprehension questions.
d. Lead a group or class discussion on the major concepts in any given unit of study, allowing students to vocalize what they feel confident with and address areas where extra instruction may be needed.

29. Which of the following assessments would be best for matching students to appropriately challenging books?

a. Ask the student to read aloud the vocabulary words listed on the back of the book to make sure that they can read most of them.
b. Choose reading books with suggested grade levels on the front cover.
c. Allow students to choose books that are "not too easy and not too hard."
d. Use the same grade-level book to help all students practice and achieve the same skills.

30. The following excerpt is an example of what kind of assessment?

> Date:
>
> Name:
>
> It took me __ minutes to read the first 10 pages of *The Trial of Dabney Moore.*
>
> 1. Describe the main character's personality in this book.
> 2. Why do you think Dabney chose to confess his crimes to the police?
> 3. If you were in Dabney's position, would you have acted in the same way? Why or why not?

a. Student response form
b. Cloze-style assessment
c. Fluency and articulation evaluation
d. Informal reading inventory

31. How can a teacher most effectively use assessment tools to communicate a student's progress to parents at conference time?

a. Utilize standardized test scores to break down each category of literacy development and discuss skill levels.
b. Show parents examples of the student's work across all aspects of his or her development and describe which areas are strongest and which areas need more work.
c. Give the parents an overview of the student's progress along with one or two specific areas upon which to work at improving at home.
d. Encourage students to be present in parent conferences to demonstrate reading skills and discuss plans for the coming term with both parents and teacher.

Mathematics

32. Ms. Grimes knows that her 4th-grade students will be taking standardized tests next month and hopes to prepare them well. She notices during practice testing that the students are struggling with money concepts, particularly the concept of making change. This is not a complete surprise to her, based upon the students' class work. What would be the best way to approach this scenario?

a. Review each question on the practice tests carefully and walk the students through the proper way to do each problem. Deliver the practice test again a few days later to determine if the students' skills have improved.
b. Use test questions and answers from last year's test to practice and memorize
c. Set up a miniature grocery store with real items and packages labeled with prices; allow the students to practice purchasing items at the "store" and making change. Monitor and review practice test questions.
d. Give more lessons on, and review about, adding and subtracting decimals in order to help the students solidify their procedural knowledge. Explain that money concepts are simply word problems that involve decimals.

33. Which answer choice is the most appropriate sequence for planning instructional units?

a. Imaginary numbers → Square roots
b. Rational numbers → Integers
c. Integers → Rational numbers
d. Real numbers → Square roots

34. Which number comes next in the sequence?

16, 24, 34, 46, 60

a. 72
b. 74
c. 76
d. 56

35. Given that x and y are integers $\neq 0$, which expression must yield a rational number?

a. $y\pi$
b. $\sqrt{xy}$
c. $\frac{x}{2y}$
d. $\frac{\sqrt{2}}{x}$

36. A child sells cups of lemonade for one quarter. Which linear function best models the profits of the lemonade stand?

a.

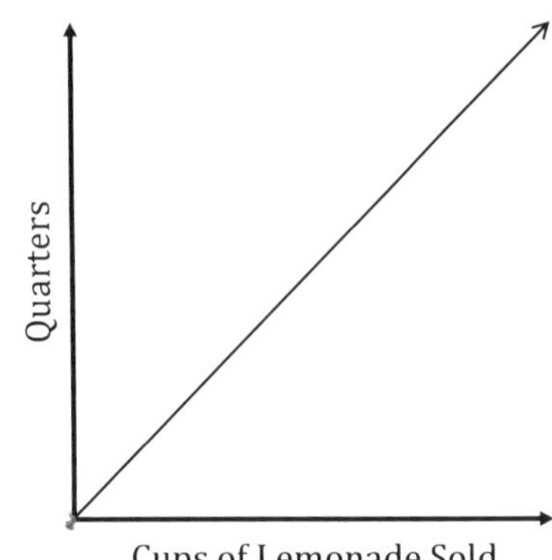

b.

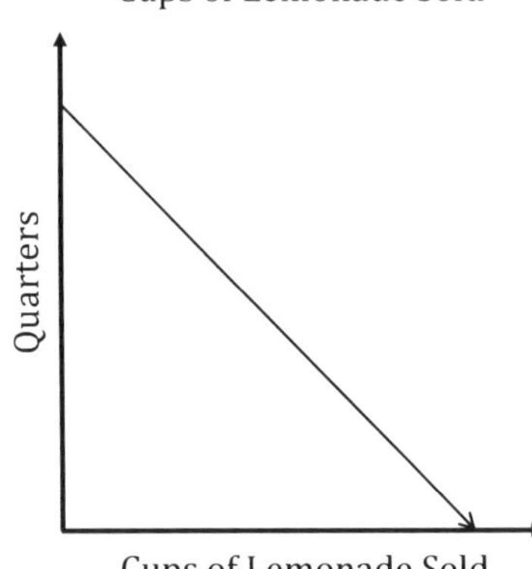

c.

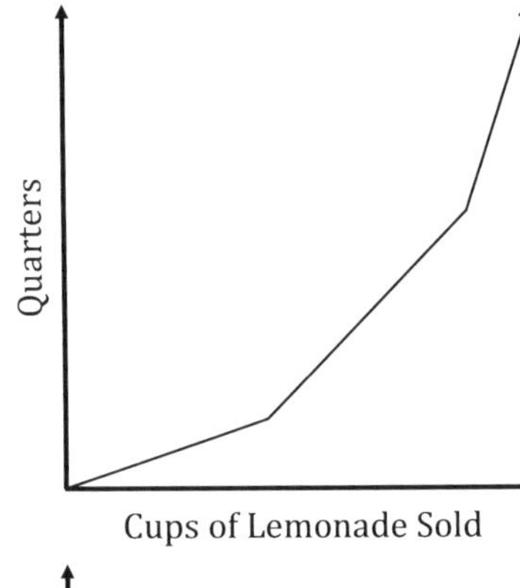

d.

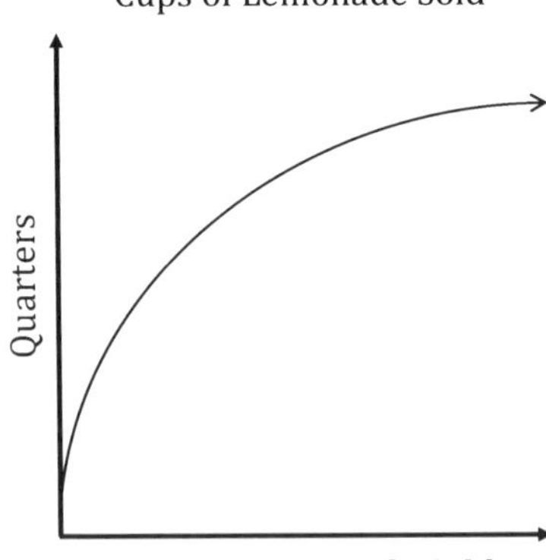

37. A family is considering building a wall from the back of their garage to their house. The two buildings already meet at one end and the resulting garden area would be in the shape of a right triangle. If the length of the wall is $\sqrt{369}$, and the long side of the garage is 12ft long, what is the area of the new garden in square feet?

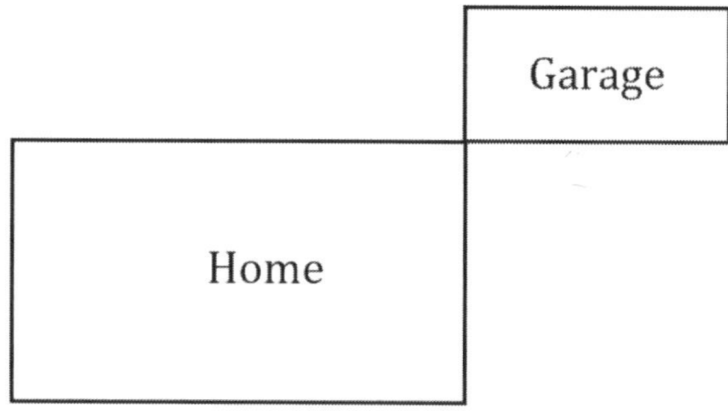

a. 120
b. 110
c. 100
d. 90

38. One gallon of paint covers 25 ft^2 of wall. The painter has painted 2/5 of the wall. If the paint costs $6.25 per gallon, the painter must spend at least how much more to finish the wall?

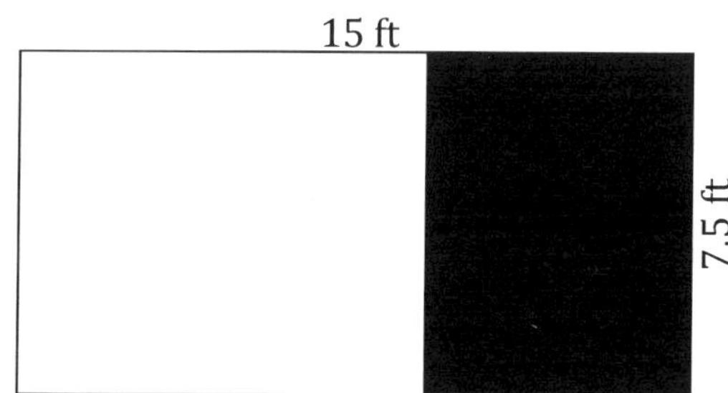

a. $18.75
b. $56.25
c. $12.50
d. $67.50

39. What other information is needed to determine that $\theta = 80°$?

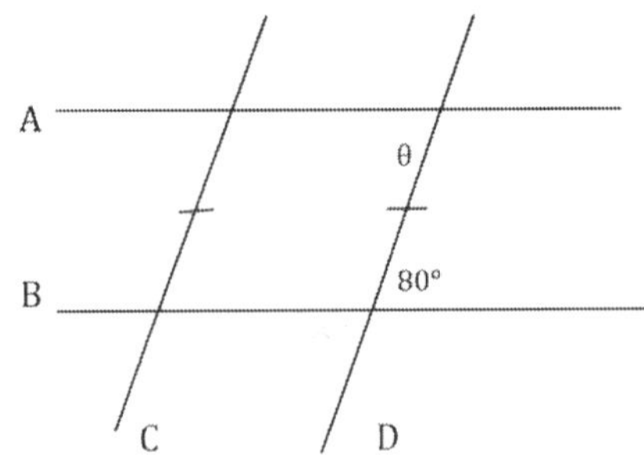

a. That line B is perpendicular to line D.
b. That line A is perpendicular to line C.
c. That lines C and D are parallel.
d. That lines A and B are parallel.

40. Given the right triangle below, where $\angle A = 60°$, which expression represents the length of side $\overline{BC}$?

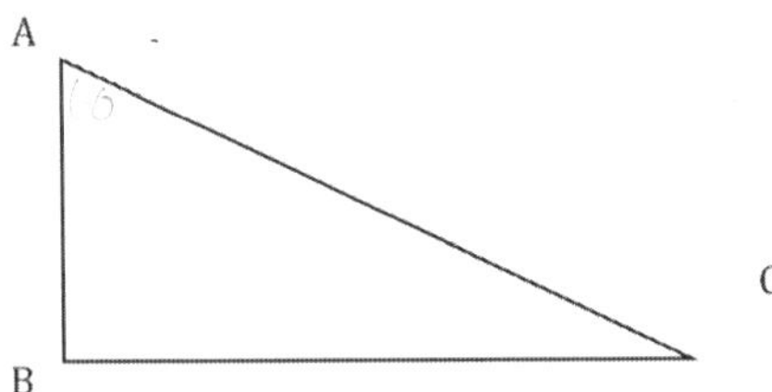

a. $\overline{AC} \sin 60$
b. $\overline{AC} \cos 60$
c. $\overline{AB} \sin 60$
d. $\overline{AB} \cos 30$

41. Ms. Byrne stresses the importance of daily math homework with her sixth- and seventh-grade students. She states that the consistent practice will help students solidify their understanding of mathematical principles. Ms. Byrne also reviews this homework on a daily basis to help her understand what the students understand and to guide her instruction. This practice is an example of:

a. Summative assessment
b. Diversity in assignments
c. Formative assessment
d. Standards set forth for middle-grade mathematics

42. Which of the following statements is false regarding teaching mathematics to English-language learners?

a. English-language learners often benefit from using manipulatives or other tangible tools to help them understand math concepts.
b. English-language learners typically find it much easier to participate in English-speaking mathematics classes, since they are usually less dependent on language than other subjects.
c. Teachers should place students into small groups or pairs when possible so that they feel comfortable asking questions and seeking further information needed to make progress.
d. It is helpful to include math vocabulary in instruction so that all students, especially English-language learners, understand what specific words mean when discussing math concepts.

43. By the end of what grade level should a student be able to use algebraic principles to analyze both proportional and non-proportional linear relationships?

a. 5th grade
b. 6th grade
c. 7th grade
d. 8th grade

44. Charlie recently took a standardized test. There were 65 people taking the test with Charlie; four of them earned higher scores than he did. Charlie falls into which score percentile?

a. 99th
b. 97th
c. 95th
d. 93rd

45. When planning a unit on linear equations, a teacher would most likely include discussion on which of the following topics?

a. Conjugating to remove irrational denominators
b. Slope of a straight line
c. Order of operations
d. Characteristics of the diagonals of various quadrilaterals

46. In a pack of 20 jelly beans, there are two licorice- and four cinnamon-flavored jelly beans. What is the probability of choosing a licorice jelly bean followed by a cinnamon jelly bean?

a. $\frac{2}{5}$
b. $\frac{8}{20}$
c. $\frac{2}{95}$
d. $\frac{1}{50}$

47. Which answer choice is a valid direct proof that the sum of two odd integers, $x + y$, is even?

a. Because they are odd, $x = 2a + 1$ and $y = 2b + 1$. The expression $x + y$ can then be written as $(2a + 1) + (2b + 1) = 2a + 2b + 2 = 2(a + b + 1)$. Because this final expression clearly has a factor of two, $x + y$ must be even.
b. Assume $y = 13$ and $x = 11$. $13 + 24 = 24$. 24 is even, therefore $x + y$ is even.
c. Let $x + y = z$, let $z = 2c$, $x = 2a + 1$, and $y = 2b + 1$. $2a + 1 + 2b + 1 = 2c$ which is the same as $2a + 2b = 2c - 2$, therefore $x + y$ is even.
d. If $x + y = z$, where z is even, then $x + y$ must be even.

48. A track runner recorded times for his sprint of 33, 27, 29, 30, and 34 seconds. Which expression represents the sample standard deviation of his recorded times?

a. $\frac{2.4^2+(-3.6)^2+(-1.6)^2+(-0.6)^2+3.4^2}{4}$
b. $\sqrt{\frac{2.4^2+(-3.6)^2+(-1.6)^2+(-0.6)^2+3.4^2}{4}}$
c. $\sqrt{\frac{2.4+(-3.6)+(-1.6)+(-0.6)+3.4}{5}}$
d. $\frac{2.4-3.6-1.6-0.6+3.4}{5}$

49. Which function would not contain an x-intercept?

a. $f(x) = (x+3)^2$
b. $f(x) = (x-6)^2 - 2x + 4$
c. $f(x) = x^2 + 3$
d. $f(x) = x^2 - 3x + 2$

50. ΔABC and ΔXYZ are similar. Which equation will give you the length of side $\overline{XZ}$?

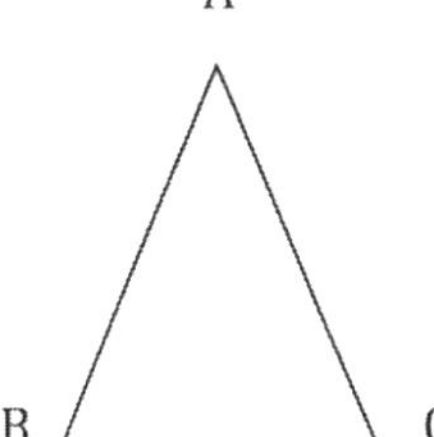

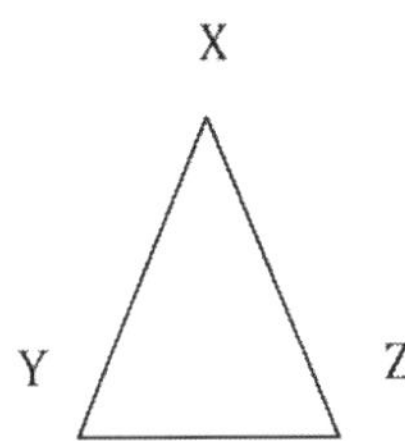

a. $\frac{\overline{AB}\times\overline{AC}}{\overline{BC}} = \overline{XZ}$
b. $\overline{AC}/\overline{BC} = \overline{XZ}$
c. $\overline{AC} \times \overline{YZ} = \overline{XZ}$
d. $\frac{\overline{YZ}\times\overline{AC}}{\overline{BC}} = \overline{XZ}$

51. A sheriff's office in a small town creates a chart of violent crimes in the area for the year of 2005. Based on the chart below, which prediction for 2006 seems the most appropriate?

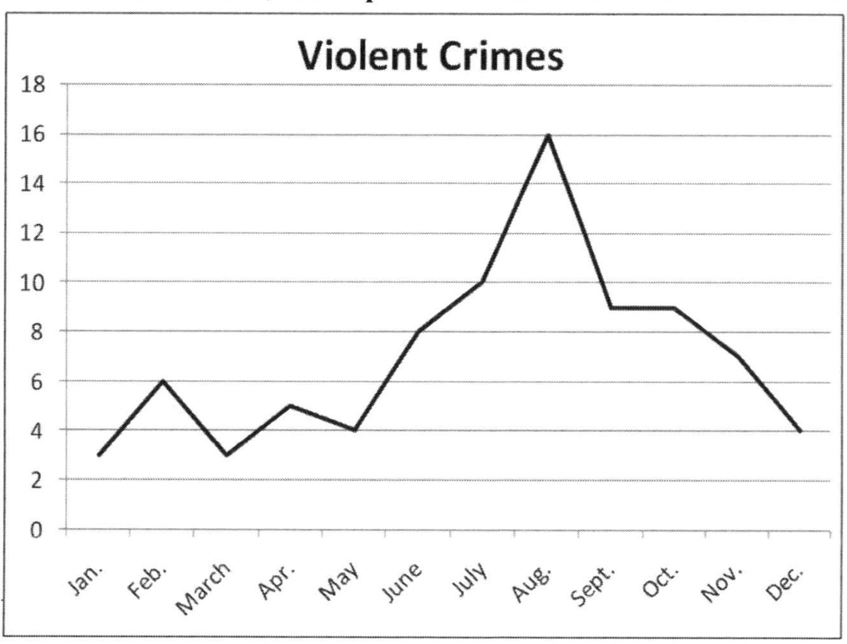

a. The winter months are likely to see a spike in violent crime rates.
b. Holiday months will likely see an increase in personal theft.
c. Violent crimes will be greatest when the weather is the warmest.
d. The number of violent crimes per month will continue to grow throughout the year.

52. When given the equation $8B + 11 = 43$, a student found $B = 6.75$. What mistake did the student most likely make?

a. When isolating the like terms, the student divided incorrectly by 8.
b. When isolating like terms, the student added instead of subtracting 11 from the right side.
c. The student used the wrong order of operations.
d. The student forgot to isolate like terms.

53. The expression $(2x + 3)(x - 2)$ can also be written as $2x^2 - x - 6$. Which of the following choices makes this transformation possible?

a. The distributive property
b. The commutative property
c. The associative property
d. The transformative property

54. Out of 60 contestants, Matt was the 37th person disqualified from the spelling bee. In which quartile did he place?

a. 1st
b. 2nd
c. 3rd
d. 4th

Social Studies

55. A teacher is planning a "Social Sciences Career Week." Parents of her students will visit in order to speak with the class about possibilities for career choices after graduation. Which of the following could be listed for Wednesday?

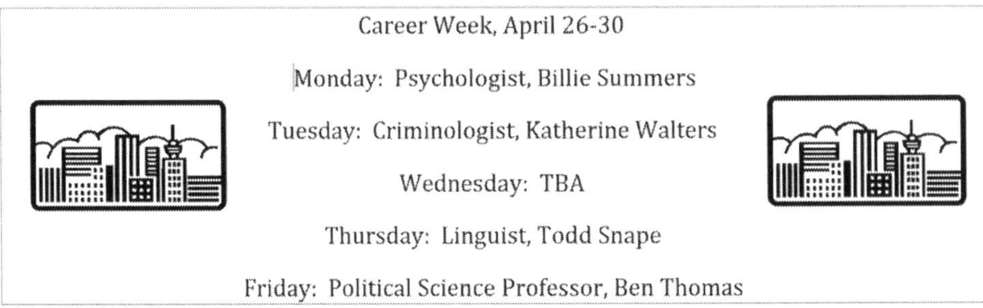

Career Week, April 26-30
Monday: Psychologist, Billie Summers
Tuesday: Criminologist, Katherine Walters
Wednesday: TBA
Thursday: Linguist, Todd Snape
Friday: Political Science Professor, Ben Thomas

a. Biologist, Maureen Benedict
b. Entymologist, James Frank
c. Anthropologist, Asher Vance
d. Physicist, Amy Van Buren

56. A 6th-grade English class will begin to read *Sadako and the Thousand Paper Cranes*, a novel about a young Japanese woman who refuses to give up hope while ill with leukemia, a result of an atom bomb that fell on her city. Which of the following choices would complement this novel most effectively?

a. Discussion of leukemia's effects on the body.
b. A visit to a museum to view photographs of the aftermath of Hiroshima and Nagasaki.
c. Selected text on Japanese culture and how it has been affected by the Second World War.
d. An origami lesson in which students can fold their own paper cranes just as the protagonist does.

57. Which skill should all students possess upon matriculating from elementary school into middle school?

a. The ability to identify different points of view related to a topic or event.
b. The ability to distinguish the difference between a primary and secondary source.
c. The ability to identify major eras in U.S. history, beginning with colonization.
d. The ability to identify bias in written material.

58. Which statement most closely illustrates the philosophy of integrated studies?

a. Teachers should be familiar with all academic disciplines and skills, rather than specializing in one area in-depth.
b. Each student must have equal access to any and all opportunities within the Texas public school system at large.
c. All aspects of Social Studies, and in fact other academic disciplines, are interrelated and evolve simultaneously in a complex manner.
d. Each skill set within the Social Studies discipline should be separately identified and taught as stand-alone sub-disciplines to increase clarity and understanding in all students.

59. Ms. Bailey's students have been studying the American Civil Rights Movement. Which country should she use for a parallel study to help students understand similarities and differences between cultures?

a. South Africa
b. England
c. Morocco
d. China

60. European explorers were responsible for the following changes in the lives of Native Americans, except:

a. The proliferation of horses and guns in the region.
b. The introduction of new diseases amongst the Native American population.
c. The strengthening of bonds between all Native American groups in response to European aggression.
d. The expansion of Christian mission work.

61. The concept of Manifest Destiny relates most closely to which era in American history?

a. Cold War
b. Civil Rights
c. Gilded Age
d. Westward Expansion

Use the map below to answer questions 62 and 63:

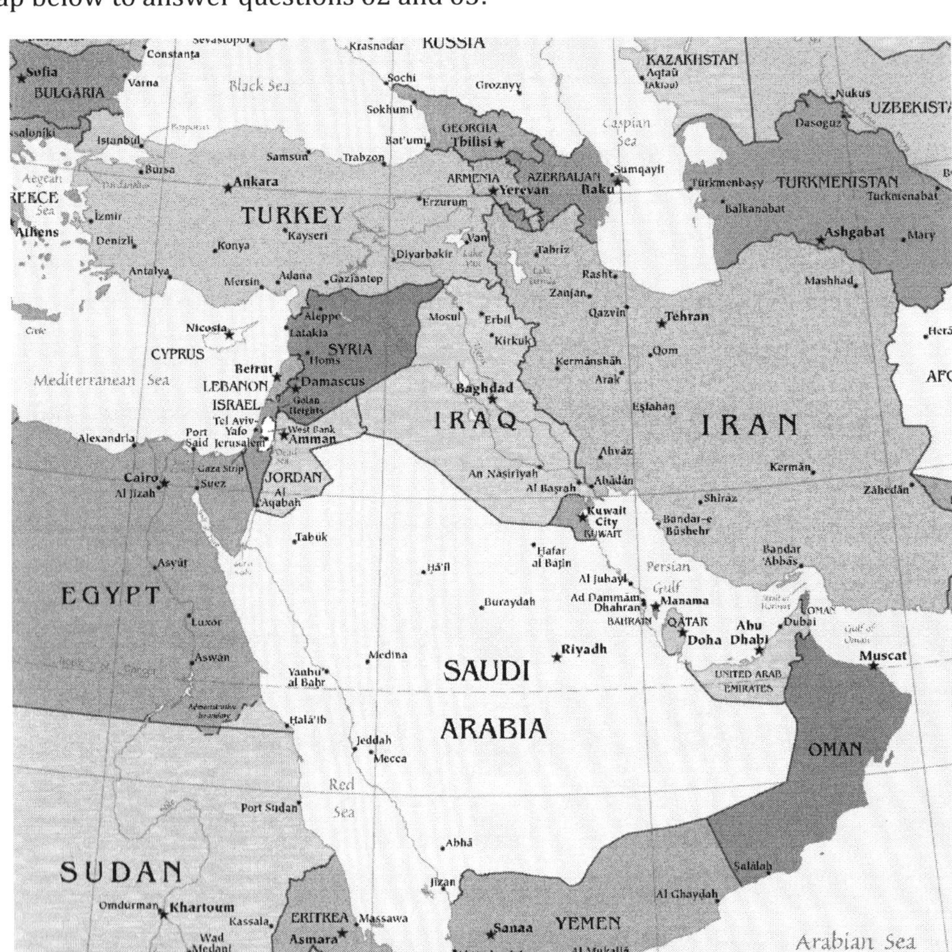

62. The map above depicts what area, specifically?

a. The place of origin for all major world religions.
b. The Holy Land
c. The Middle East
d. The Strait of Gibraltar

63. A group of 7th- and 8th-graders have elected to do research projects on the relationship and common interests between their state and the depicted region. What information could be added to this map to assist the students?

a. Commerce and Industry
b. Political divisions
c. Religious representations
d. An inset depicting the southwestern United States

Use the chart below to answer questions 64 and 65.

Area	April 1, 2000	April 1, 1990	State Rank as of April 1, 2000	State Rank as of April 1, 1990
Alabama	4,447,100	4,040,587	23	22
Alaska	626,932	550,043	48	49
Arizona	5,130,632	3,665,228	20	24
Arkansas	2,673,400	2,350,725	33	33
California	33,871,648	29,760,021	1	1
Colorado	4,301,261	3,294,394	24	26
Connecticut	3,405,565	3,287,116	29	27
Delaware	783,600	666,168	45	46
District of Columbia	572,059	606,900	(NA)	(NA)
Florida	15,982,378	12,937,926	4	4
Georgia	8,186,453	6,478,216	10	11
Hawaii	1,211,537	1,108,229	42	41
Idaho	1,293,953	1,006,749	39	42
Illinois	12,419,293	11,430,602	5	6
Indiana	6,080,485	5,544,159	14	14
Iowa	2,926,324	2,776,755	30	30
Kansas	2,688,418	2,477,574	32	32
Kentucky	4,041,769	3,685,296	25	23
Louisiana	4,468,976	4,219,973	22	21
Maine	1,274,923	1,227,928	40	38
Maryland	5,296,486	4,781,468	19	19
Massachusetts	6,349,097	6,016,425	13	13
Michigan	9,938,444	9,295,297	8	8
Minnesota	4,919,479	4,375,099	21	20
Mississippi	2,844,658	2,573,216	31	31
Missouri	5,595,211	5,117,073	17	15
Montana	902,195	799,065	44	44
Nebraska	1,711,263	1,578,385	38	36
Nevada	1,998,257	1,201,833	35	39
New Hampshire	1,235,786	1,109,252	41	40
New Jersey	8,414,350	7,730,188	9	9
New Mexico	1,819,046	1,515,069	36	37
New York	18,976,457	17,990,455	3	2
North Carolina	8,049,313	6,628,637	11	10
North Dakota	642,200	638,800	47	47
Ohio	11,353,140	10,847,115	7	7
Oklahoma	3,450,654	3,145,585	27	28
Oregon	3,421,399	2,842,321	28	29
Pennsylvania	12,281,054	11,881,643	6	5
Rhode Island	1,048,319	1,003,464	43	43
South Carolina	4,012,012	3,486,703	26	25
South Dakota	754,844	696,004	46	45
Tennessee	5,689,283	4,877,185	16	17
Texas	20,851,820	16,986,510	2	3
Utah	2,233,169	1,722,850	34	35
Vermont	608,827	562,758	49	48
Virginia	7,078,515	6,187,358	12	12
Washington	5,894,121	4,866,692	15	18
West Virginia	1,808,344	1,793,477	37	34
Wisconsin	5,363,675	4,891,769	18	16
Wyoming	493,782	453,588	50	50

64. Consider the chart above, listing states ranked by population data. Of those states whose populations increased during the last census, which state would show significant population decreases after the year 2005?

a. Missouri
b. Wyoming
c. New York
d. Louisiana

65. Which of the following would not be considered a primary reason for population migration?

a. Political or military conflict
b. Natural disaster
c. Unusually high birth rate
d. High numbers of skilled workers

66. The following illustration in the students' textbook is an example of what kind of industry?

a. Primary
b. Secondary
c. Tertiary
d. Healthcare

67. A downturn in economic activity, defined by a lowered Gross Domestic Product for two or more consecutive quarters, constitutes a:

a. Depression
b. Government Rescue Plan
c. Recession
d. Global Economic Crisis

68. During a report on the Industrial Revolution, Mary uses a poster to illustrate cause and effect relationships in the War of 1812. What could be added to make the organizer more informative?

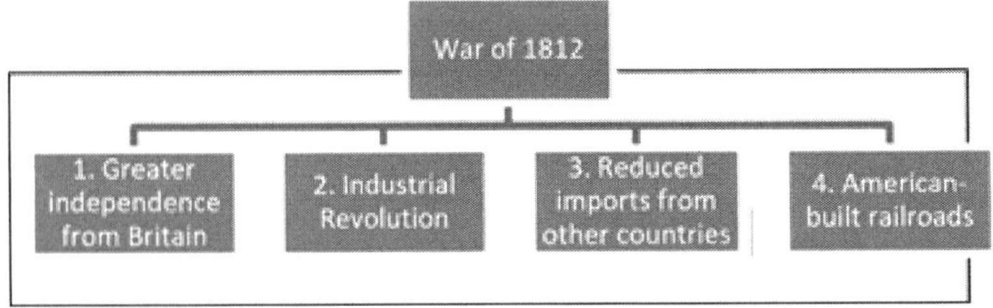

a. Placing boxes 1, 3 and 4 below box 2 and adding details to support
b. A third tier that provides details about boxes 1, 2 and 3
c. Handouts for each student to take home
d. Music, video or other multimedia to make the presentation more interesting

69. Which of the following choices best defines the concept of judicial review?

a. A quarterly journal containing articles and essays on current legal issues.
b. The process of reviewing evidence in a court case.
c. The court's power to decide if a law is constitutional.
d. The censoring of a judicial figure, specifically courtroom judges.

70. How could a teacher with 4th and 5th grade students put the concept of citizenship into a relevant context for her students?

a. Invite prominent citizens from the community to visit the class and speak about what citizenship means to the individual and the group.
b. Create a class "community" in which all students have jobs in the classroom and vote on issues important to the group.
c. Agree upon a class-wide service project through which students can help other in need.
d. Assign an essay topic requiring each student to write about "What Citizenship Means to Me."

71. In Government class, students are reading about and discussing controversy around immigration and naturalization laws. Which of the following Supreme Court decisions is ideal for illustrating the United States' long history of dialogue about citizenship?

a. Dred Scott v Sandford, 1857
b. Roe v Wade, 1973
c. Miranda v Arizona, 1963
d. Marbury *v Madison, 1803*

72. Which of the following is most true regarding the Electoral College?

a. The Electoral College requires that every voter's choice is directly represented in an election, thereby ensuring that the candidate with the largest popular vote wins the election.
b. The Electoral College greatly affects Presidential campaigning, since candidates often target their campaign stops and advertising to specific states depending on the number and scope of their Electoral votes.
c. The Electoral College consists of individuals appointed by the courts who are legally bound to vote for the candidates they represent.
d. The Electoral College educates young voters about the responsibilities of citizenship and participation in general elections.

Use the information below to answer questions 73 and 74

> My name is Amorosa. I am fourteen years old and I live near the Gulf Coast in South Texas. My father runs an oil refinery and my mother is a schoolteacher. I have two brothers, named Jorge and Emil—they are sixteen-year-old twins! After school, when there is no soccer practice, I love to spend time in the Art classroom. I love the paints, clays, fabrics, and other materials used to create beautiful things. Next year, my family and friends will celebrate my Quinceañera, a large party in honor of my 15th birthday. There will be music, food, a Court of Honor made up of my friends, and most importantly, a beautiful dress. In my city, there are talented women who design and make ball gowns that we will wear. When I celebrate my Quinceañera, I will help the dress designer create my dress.

73. Amorosa is an example of a student

a. who writes exceptionally well for a fourteen year old girl.
b. whose family maintains their cultural customs within a different national identity.
c. who exemplifies an artistic personality type that should be encouraged just as highly as are academic interests.
d. who is very focused on interpersonal relationships.

74. How could Amorosa's teacher encourage her to use her interests to build her understanding of various cultural influences and diversity?

a. Ask Amorosa to bring in pictures of all of the events surrounding the celebration to show her classmates.
b. Encourage Amorosa to research similar customs in other cultures present in Texas (e.g., Swiss, French, Native American) and compare and contrast them.
c. Require Amorosa to speak to her class about what her family's heritage means to her and how her culture has influenced the person she has become.
d. Allow Amorosa to use her artistic skills to teach so that she can work with children of all ages and backgrounds.

75. Which of the following choices details a benefit derived from widespread internet use paired with a corresponding negative consequence?

a. Greater access to information; decreased certainty regarding accuracy and validity of said information.
b. Social networking capacity; connectedness to friends and families.
c. Higher vulnerability to identity theft; increased opportunities for research and inquiry.
d. Higher rates of intellectual ability among children and teens; decrease in after-school jobs performed for compensation.

76. Based on its title, which essay demonstrates an important relationship between scientific discovery and social consciousness?

a. Stem Cell Research: A History
b. The Aeronautics Industry: Current Trends and Traits
c. From the Rotary Phone to the Instant Message: the Depersonalization of Modern Communication
d. The Magic of Penicillin: Freedom from Infectious Disease

Science

Use the information below to answer questions 77 - 79:

> Human dissections were performed as early as the third century BC and continued throughout historical eras. While the practice was controversial within some religious and political groups, early dissections and autopsies yielded much of the early knowledge regarding anatomy and biology. Animal dissection (vivisection) was introduced to the classroom in the 1920's. Medical students had utilized the practice previously; younger students now began to dissect fetal pigs, cats, frogs, and other small animals. Eventually, earthworms, crayfish, and starfish became more common candidates for dissection. Debate surrounding the practice of dissection intensified when Jennifer Graham, a high school student, sued her California school for not allowing her to complete an alternate project in lieu of dissecting a frog without lowering her grade. In the ensuing litigation, several states passed laws that allow students to choose whether or not they participate in animal dissection without risk of losing class credit.

77. Which of the following statements outlines an historical and fundamental basis for the ethics of animal vivisection (dissection) in a middle-school biology class?

a. Students should understand what they consume each day and how their food affects their bodies.
b. Dissection helps students determine whether or not they want to pursue scientific research related to investigation of bodily systems.
c. By participating in dissection, students receive a hands-on learning experience that deepens their understanding of anatomy, physiology, and life processes.
d. There is no ethical basis for the dissection of animals in classrooms. This practice harms both animal species and participating students.

78. If animal dissection is unavailable or unacceptable within a particular environment, what might be an appropriate alternative to provide students with similar instruction?

a. Large, colorful wall posters of relevant animals with detailed descriptions and anatomical labels.
b. Selected readings about the history and ethics of animal dissection.
c. Student participation in a CD-ROM, which contains a virtual dissection program.
d. Student-drawn diagrams of animals, complete with realistic colors, proportions, and labels.

79. Which of the following statements is true regarding a teacher's responsibilities in the classroom?

a. Teachers must communicate very clearly in the first days of each class that certain practices are required, and students must accept that they will sometimes be required to perform tasks with which they are uncomfortable in the name of scientific inquiry.
b. Teachers should avoid introducing controversial subjects in the classroom so that students do not become unduly upset or even traumatized; it is important to maintain a safe environment in which upsetting topics do not interfere with the learning process.
c. Teachers should clearly communicate classroom requirements but be mindful of the relevance and emotional nature of some aspects of scientific concepts. Teachers should create a safe space for students to discuss how concepts and practices affect their daily lives and use flexibility in designing lessons.
d. Teachers should strictly adhere to school policies and district and state laws; there has been a rise in litigation pertaining to school practices in recent years, and teachers should do whatever they can to avoid liability.

80. Mr. Harris' science classroom has been recently equipped with ten lab stations, which include a full supply of scientific tools, sinks, hot plates, and more. The students and teachers alike are looking forward to the hands-on activities that Mr. Harris will now be able to provide his young learners. What would be the best possible introductory unit in this scenario?

a. A hands-on demonstration of how the scientific method works in a scientific experiment and written follow-up work on each step in the process.
b. Lessons on various tools and parts of the lab, concentrating on how to use each item safely.
c. Several labs in which the students can witness visible chemical processes, increasing the students' excitement about the lab.
d. A discussion about the process leading up to the installation of the lab, including social science concepts regarding fundraising, interest, etc.

Use the chart below to answer questions 81 and 82:

Tool	Purpose
Beaker	Holding, stirring, mixing and heating liquids
Petri dish	Culture or grow cells
Meter stick	Measuring length
Graduated cylinder	Measuring volume
Bunsen burner	Heating, sterilizing, combustion
Spring Scale	Measuring objects
Balance	Measuring objects
Microscope	Viewing small objects
Compass	Determining direction based on earth's magnetic poles
Magnet	Multiple uses

81. The spring scale and the balance have similar purposes. What is the primary difference between them?

a. They measure the mass of an object using different mechanisms.
b. The balance is much safer and more appropriate for use by younger children because it does not use loaded springs.
c. They are two different names for the same piece of equipment.
d. Each item should be used during the appropriate season due to the effects of moisture in the atmosphere.

82. When heating chemicals within a beaker, which of the following is *not* an important safety precaution?

a. Do not fill the container to more than 1/3 - 1/2 full, to prevent overflow.
b. Always wear gloves and safety goggles.
c. Never point the beaker or tubing towards other people or yourself.
d. Never insert utensils into a mixing apparatus, to prevent explosions or release of dangerous toxins.

Use the diagram below to answer questions 83 and 84.

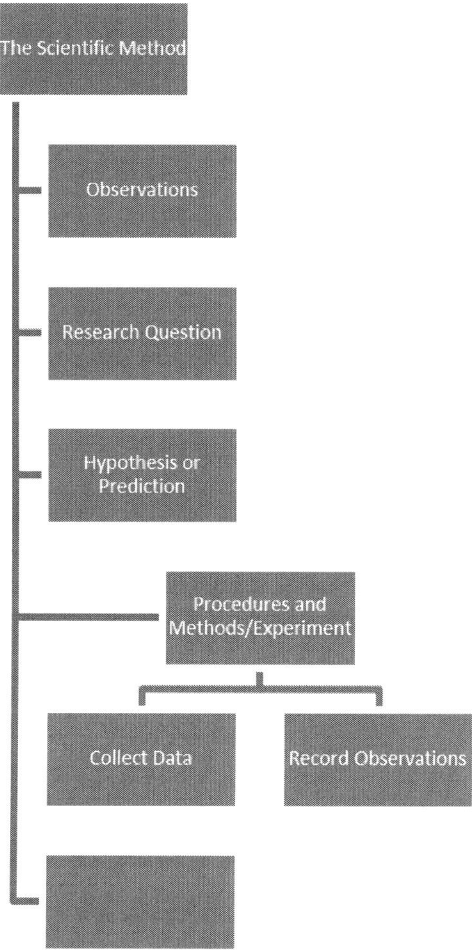

83. Which of the following steps should be added to make the process complete?

a. Publish information
b. Conclusion
c. Suggestions for further research
d. Create presentation

84. Which title probably refers to an experiment that could safely and accurately be carried out in a classroom context?

a. Low-fat vs. Low-carbohydrate: Which diet is more effective?
b. How Hybrid Cars Help our Environment
c. Which Apple Juice Brand Contains the Most Sugar?
d. Simple Machines and their Purposes

85. Which of the following scenarios best describes a lesson in which a teacher has utilized *anchored instruction* applied to space science?

a. Students work with solar system trading cards, matching parts of the solar system based upon characteristics and traits.
b. A teacher gives a lecture regarding the traits of each planet in our solar system, followed by group discussion.
c. Students do background reading on the size and scope of the solar system and use a scale-model of the system to answer questions about planet sizes and distance.
d. Students participate in an experiment that allows them to make their own miniature Black Holes in class, observing and recording behaviors.

86. Which of the following lessons would be the best set of examples illustrating the difference between scientific fact and theory?

a. Big Bang and Laws of Motion
b. Chaos theory and Evolution
c. Conservation of Mass/Elasticity and Carbon-14 Dating
d. Astronomical Wormholes and Black Holes

87. Which field of science is based on *a priori* evidence?

a. Natural science
b. Applied science
c. Formal science
d. General science

88. Science has evolved as a field of study for countless years. Which of the following individuals represents the earliest contributions to the field?

a. Archimedes
b. Galileo Galilei
c. Isaac Newton
d. Shen Kuo

Use the information below to answer questions 89-91:

Guidelines for Field Journals

1. Always record the date, place, and time spent observing.
2. Describe the weather, including temperature, cloud cover, condensation, and winds, as well as any foreign (not natural) influences on the environment.

89. A 7th-grade class is currently studying *biodiversity*. The class will be taking a field trip to help deepen their conceptual understanding of this concept. Students will also have a chance to practice working with and recording in their new field journals, which they will be using for the next few months. Where is the most likely destination for their field trip?

a. The zoo
b. The local pond
c. The water processing plant
d. The recycling center

90. What else could be added to these guidelines to help the students deepen their understanding of biodiversity?

a. Always bring binoculars, since some organisms can be difficult to see with the human eye.
b. Whenever possible, sketch or describe the connections and relationships between the living organisms in the environment.
c. Be very quiet, so as not to startle any living organisms you may be observing.
d. If necessary, take pictures or videos of interesting observations for later reference.

91. After their field trip, the students decide to work on a project together. Which of the following would be the best project, if its purpose were to protect biodiversity in its community?

a. Working together to improve the quality of food at the zoo.
b. Beginning a campaign to ban gas-motored boats from the pond.
c. Exploring water-treatment methods that are non-toxic.
d. Starting a recycling drive at school.

92. Ms. Burke plans to illustrate the difference between physical and chemical changes in substances. Which experiment can the students perform that will allow the students to observe a chemical change?

a. The students place an ice cube in a bowl and allow it to melt. They can then place the dish into the freezer, causing it to re-form into another shape.
b. A variety of objects, including metal nails, are left on the windowsill outside of the classroom for a period of time. Students observe and document the changes, including rust forming on the nails.
c. Students observe and record evaporation rates of water from various kinds of receptacles.
d. A food preparation area allows students to create their own snacks. While preparing the food, students observe the spreading of cream cheese on crackers, the melting of butter onto bread, and milk being added to cereals.

93. A teacher posts large, colored pictures of various items around her 4th-grade classroom, including a bicycle, an airplane, an electric scooter, a skateboard and a tractor. What might be her lesson for today?

a. Alternate modes of personal transportation in the absence of a car or truck
b. A discussion of which objects need to burn fuel, use electricity, or need other forms of power to move
c. The aerodynamic design and how it affects movement
d. Collection of data regarding students' experience with various vehicles and analysis of the data

94. A teacher provides her students with the checklist shown below for homework. What is the most likely purpose of the activity?

	Me	Parent 1	Parent 2
Eye color			
Ability to roll tongue			
Presence of widow's peak			
Hand dominance			
Presence of dimples			

a. To illustrate the purpose of taking medical history in the event of illness on a smaller, less negative scale.
b. To demonstrate how genetics plays a role in determining what traits are passed through generations.
c. To help students feel connected to parents during a tumultuous social period by identifying basic similarities.
d. To show the process of Darwin's theories of natural selection in humans.

95. The illustration below depicts the structures of glucose (top) and sucrose (bottom). The body converts which kind of sugar to energy?

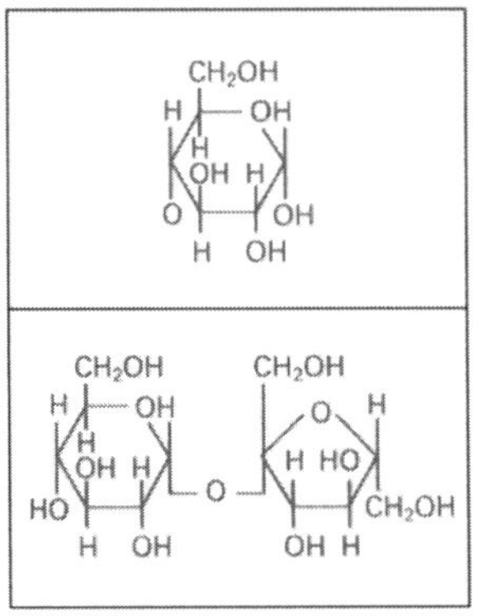

a. Sucrose
b. Fructose
c. Glucose
d. Dextrose

Use the diagram below to answer questions 96 and 97:

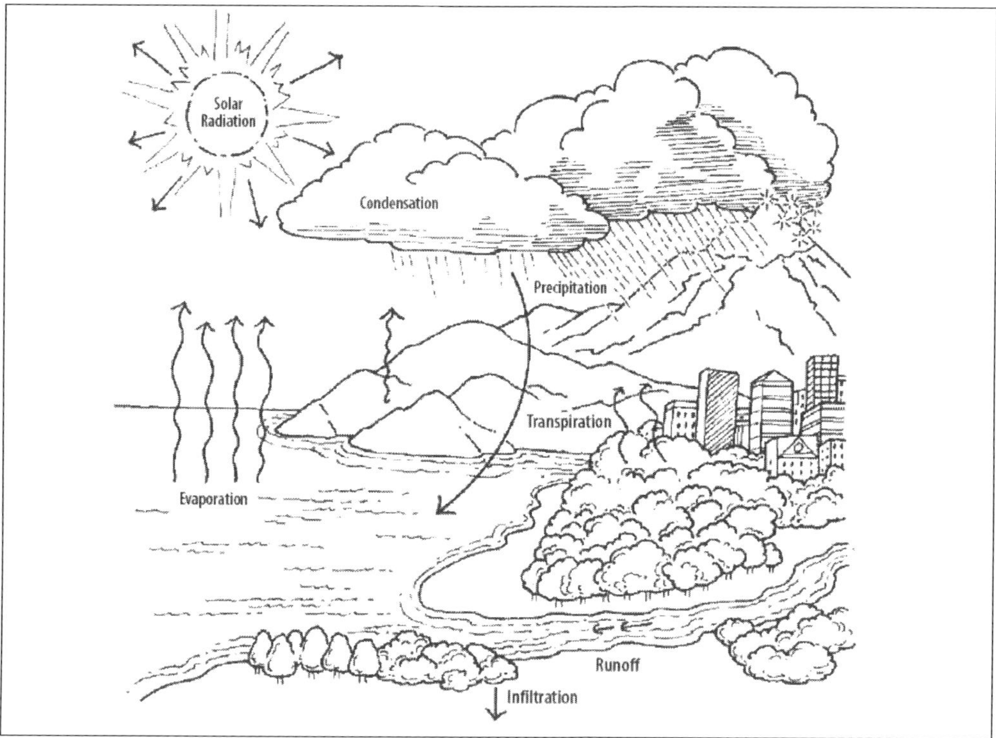

96. Which component of this diagram refers to the process by which vegetation and foliage release water vapor into the air?

a. Evaporation
b. Photosynthesis
c. Infiltration
d. Transpiration

97. Which step in the hydrologic cycle, if absent, would directly result in the effects of global warming?

a. Transpiration
b. Radiation
c. Condensation
d. Oceanic evaporation

98. The illustration below depicts the rock cycle. This cycle illustrates the fact that rocks are not unchanging entities; they undergo changes over time. Which of the following would not be considered a force driving the rock cycle?

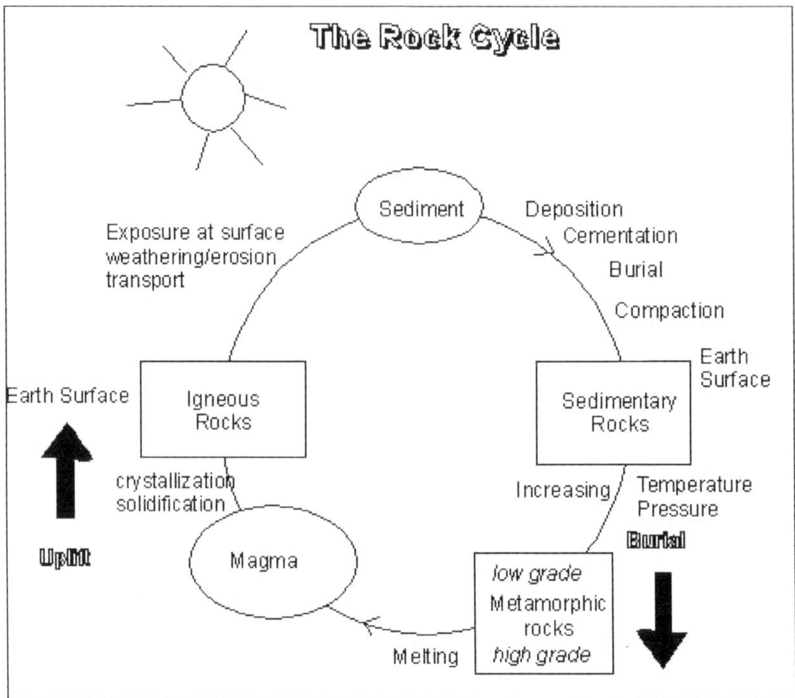

a. Plate tectonics
b. The water cycle
c. Global warming
d. Volcanic eruptions

99. The following topics are illustrative of what broader scientific concept?

Systems, order and organization
Evidence, models and explanation
Change, constancy and measurement
Evolution and equilibrium
Form and function

a. There are five major categories in teaching General Science that must be covered in their entireties.
b. There are unifying concepts that are common to all sciences.
c. In each branch of science, even specific topics such as systems can be broken down into component parts.
d. All scientific concepts can be theorized, evaluated, and proven using the scientific method of inquiry.

Pedagogy

100. The educator's code of ethics does not prohibit which of the following activities?

a. Interfering with the political rights of a colleague
b. Misrepresenting official district policies
c. Accepting gifts openly offered in appreciation of service
d. Revealing confidential student information without a lawful professional purpose or legal requirement

101. Which of the following statements best describes the type of education that the Individuals with Disabilities Education Act of 2004 (IDEA) requires for all students with identified emotional and learning disabilities?

a. A free and appropriate education, even in cases where the student has been suspended or expelled from school
b. An appropriate education, except in cases where the student's behavior causes him or her to be expelled from school
c. A free education that is conducted outside of the general education classroom
d. An appropriate education that must be paid for by the student's family

102. According to the Family Educational Rights and Privacy Act (FERPA), which of the following is true?

a. Students of any age can refuse to disclose educational records to their parents
b. Parents of children under 18 can inspect and request amendments to their children's educational records on demand
c. Teachers need written authorization from parents in order to disclose a student's educational record a school official with a legitimate educational interest
d. Written authorization from parents is required before a school releases a student's educational records to a school to which that student is transferring

103. Which of the following is typically the most effective way to state classroom rules?

a. Rules should be stated negatively (do not speak out of turn)
b. Rules should be stated positively (students will treat one another with respect)
c. Rules should be phrased politely (please don't chew gum)
d. Rules should use detailed and specific language to describe what is prohibited (don't hit, slap, kick, pinch, or shove other students)

104. In resolving behavior problems, a teacher should strive to be:

a. Consistent and judgmental
b. Consistent and objective
c. Patient and collaborative
d. Authoritative and judgmental

105. Which of the following strategies would foster students' intrinsic motivation to learn?

a. Helping students to develop a personal connection to and interest in the material they're learning
b. Emphasizing the rewards associated with academic success (recognition, a good job) and consequences associated with academic failure (shame, punishment by parents)
c. Both A and B
d. Neither A nor B

106. According to Jean Piaget's four-stage theory of cognitive development, the distinction between people at the concrete operational stage (approximately 7-12 years of age) and the formal operational stage (approximately 12-16 years of age) of development is that:

a. Unlike those at the concrete operational stage, those at the formal operational stage can think logically in concrete terms
b. Unlike those at the concrete operational stage, those at the formal operational stage are highly reliant on sensory and motor skills to learn
c. Those in the concrete operational stage are capable of abstract thought, while those at the formal operational stage can think only in concrete terms
d. Those in the concrete operational stage can think logically only with respect to concrete experiences, while those at the formal operational stage can reason in abstract and hypothetical terms

107. A teacher notes a significant gap between a student's intelligence as determined by IQ testing and the student's academic achievement. Which of the following might explain the student's poor performance relative to his or her potential?

a. The student has a learning disability such as dyslexia or dyscalculia
b. The student is distracted by a family problem such as homelessness or divorce
c. The student is an immigrant and is not proficient in the English language
d. All of the above

108. As students enter adolescence, their social lives will most likely take on which of the following characteristics?

a. Desire to spend most of their time with immediate family members
b. Membership in a small social group that has a shared set of values and interests
c. Marked rise in insecurity resulting from increased threats of violence
d. Decreased interest in ethnic and cultural identity

109. A teacher assigns his seventh grade students to research their families' cultural heritage by interviewing parents and grandparents. Which aspect of the students' social development would this project most directly facilitate?

a. Identity formation
b. Ability to interact cooperatively with peers
c. Leadership skills
d. Tolerance for other cultures

110. Ms. Andrews has recently learned that she will have a student in her fifth grade class whose family is currently living in a local homeless shelter. The teacher's most important responsibility to this student is to:

a. Ensure that she creates an accepting, non-judgmental classroom environment
b. Screen the new student to see if special education services are needed
c. Determine whether the student suffers from depression or anxiety disorder
d. Make sure that the student has adequate food and clothing

111. Mr. Gonzalez has noticed that one of his seventh grade students, Benji, has experienced a rapid decline in his academic performance over the past few weeks. Benji seems unusually sluggish on some days and abnormally restless on other days. He frequently arrives late to school, saying that he overslept. Which of the following is the most likely explanation for this change in Benji's behavior?

a. Benji has developed a learning disability, and should be screened for special education services
b. Benji's unpredictable behavior is normal for an adolescent and should not be cause for concern
c. Benji's behavior signals that he might be using illegal drugs
d. Benji is probably experiencing depression, and should be referred to the school counselor

112. A survey conducted by a local newspaper reports that most parents of middle school students think that bullying is very common among adolescent boys, but unlikely to occur among girls. What is the most likely explanation for this misconception?

a. The survey respondents were disproportionately male
b. The parents who were surveyed do not participate in school-related activities or monitor their children's social development closely
c. Parents are less likely to recognize bullying among girls because it is usually conducted through gossip and exclusion, rather than outright violence
d. The level of violence at the school is so high that parents didn't notice the bullying that occurs among girls

113. Each week, Mr. Jackson asks his seventh grade science students to write a brief research report about a different animal. While some of the students turn in detailed, high-quality reports based on Internet research, other students turn in well-written but simplistic reports based on print resources available in the school media center, which does not have Internet access. To address this disparity, Mr. Anderson should:

a. Tell the students who are turning in less detailed reports that they need to start using the Internet to conduct research, or he won't accept their reports
b. Ask the students who are using the Internet to stop using it, because it is unfair to the other students who are using the media center resources
c. Use a less rigorous grading scale for students who can't use the Internet
d. Provide students and their parents with a list of community resources like libraries that offer free Internet access and training

114. Students who are English Language Learners usually have which of the following traits in common?

a. A need for special education services
b. Normal to above-average intelligence
c. Above-average academic performance
d. Below-average academic aptitude due to their cultural background

115. Mrs. Li is a sixth grade general education teacher in an inclusion classroom where several students have learning disabilities in writing. To assess her students' reading comprehension skills, Mrs. Li asks them to write in their journals for 15 minutes each day after a period of sustained, silent reading. However, she's concerned that the learning disabled students will become frustrated with this timed writing assignment. How should Mrs. Li handle this dilemma?

a. She should ask the learning disabled students to write as much as they can during the 15 minute period, although they probably won't be able to completely convey their thoughts
b. She should let the learning disabled students continue to read during the writing period
c. She should take the learning disabled students to a quiet area and facilitate a 15 minute group reading discussion while the other students write
d. She should tell the students to start their journal entries during class, and finish them up for homework

116. Mr. Robinson, a fifth grade teacher, wants to improve his students' motivation by showing them that math and reading skills can be used to learn about important subjects like the environment, history, or multiculturalism. The best approach to achieve this objective would be to:

a. Ask students to conduct an independent research project on a topic of their choice
b. Have students practice math and reading skills in groups
c. Present a thematic unit that incorporates math and reading skills
d. Use curriculum-based methods to assess students' progress in math and reading

117. Ms. Frank conducts an assessment and discovers that most students in her fourth grade class are auditory learners, while a few are visual or kinesthetic learners. When teaching students a new concept, which of the following strategies would be most effective for the largest number of her students?

a. Having her students write an explanation of the new concept in their own words
b. Teaching the students a song that explains the new concept
c. Writing an explanation of the new concept on the chalkboard
d. Teaching the students to describe the concept using sign language

118. Of the practices listed below, which would be most likely to promote a productive classroom environment for middle-level students?

a. Providing opportunities for students to work cooperatively with peers
b. Frequently changing classroom routines to keep students engaged
c. Encouraging students to work independently to improve their ability to self-direct
d. Avoiding kinesthetic and active learning activities that overexcite students

119. Mr. Stratton has assigned his sixth grade social studies class to write a research report about a historical period that they have learned about in class during the year. To ensure that students understand what is expected of them and are able to complete the project on schedule, the best approach for Mr. Stratton to take would be to:

a. Take time to explain how to do the research and set several 'checkpoints' before projects are due
b. Pair students who have never completed a research project before with students who have
c. Hold after-school tutoring sessions to help students brainstorm ideas and conduct research
d. Send a note home to parents telling them about the project and the due date

120. Mrs. Frances wants to develop a theme-based unit that is interesting and relevant to her fifth grade students. Which of the following approaches would be most likely to help her achieve this goal?

a. Send a note to the students' parents asking them what theme their children should learn about
b. Review the success of theme-based units that were used by the students' teachers in previous years
c. Conduct an informal, open-ended survey to look for interests that the students share
d. Present three different theme ideas as ask the students to vote on the one that will be used in class

121. Ms. Fremont, a sixth grade language arts teacher, is planning a strategy to help students learn and practice note-taking skills. Which of the following approaches would be the best way to help students adopt this new skill?

a. Lecturing throughout the class period, and then collecting and grading students' notes at the end of class
b. Providing an outline of key words and points for students to fill in during the lecture, and gradually providing less and less detail in this outline until students are taking notes without assistance
c. Having students compare their notes with a partner's notes at the end of class
d. Providing students with audio-recorded lectures so they can practice taking notes at home

122. Mr. Swanson has implemented a token economy behavior management system for several disruptive students in his class. For each day that the students exhibit appropriate behavior, they earn a check mark, and if they have earned three check marks by the end of the week, they are allowed to play computer games for 30 minutes on Friday afternoon. So far, all of the students have earned enough check marks each week to get the reward, but each student is still disrupting class at least once per week. Which of the following strategies would probably be most effective for further reducing the students' disruptive behavior?

a. Taking away a check mark that the student has already earned if they engage in disruptive behavior
b. Explaining to the students that they have done a good job of improving their behavior, but that they can do even better; as a consequence, they now need to earn four check marks to get the reward, which is 45 minutes on the computer
c. Increasing the reward to one hour of computer time
d. Implementing a system where students start out with five check marks at the beginning of the week, and lose one check mark for each episode of disruptive behavior; students who still have five check marks at the end of the week earn 30 minutes of computer time

123. Ms. Carleton receives a phone call from one of her sixth grade students' parents. The parent is concerned that her daughter is performing poorly in language arts class, even though she has done well in this subject in the past. Ms. Carleton knows that this student has regularly failed to turn in homework assignments. How should Ms. Carleton respond to this parent's concerns?

a. She should tell the parent that her daughter clearly doesn't understand the course content, and needs a tutor
b. She should explain to the parent that her daughter isn't turning in homework assignments, and tell her to make sure that her daughter does so in the future
c. She should tell the parent that, unfortunately, the Federal Educational Right to Privacy Act (FERPA) prevents her from discussing her students' academic records without their permission
d. She should explain to the parent that her daughter has missed several homework assignments, and offer to tell the parent about future assignments so that she can ensure that her daughter completes them

124. Mr. Fields wants to design an assessment method for his sixth grade math class that will help his students learn from their assignments and motivate them to improve. Which of the following approaches is most likely to accomplish this objective?

a. Assigning ungraded homework problems and having weekly tests
b. Assigning nightly homework problems that are peer-graded in class the next day, and going over the answers after the assignment is graded
c. Assigning homework problems that are graded by the teacher and returned on the day before the unit test
d. Assigning nightly homework problems which are graded and returned with a correct answer key within three days

125. An eighth grade student is preparing a research paper for her language arts class, and she has used information from three books, one newspaper, and several websites created by the U.S government and non-profit organizations. For which of these resources should she include a citation in her bibliography?

a. Only the books
b. The books and the newspaper
c. The books, the newspaper, and the websites
d. The books, the newspaper, and the U.S. government websites only

126. A fifth grade teacher has a mainstreamed special education student in her class who has a behavioral disability. The student has become increasingly disruptive over the past few weeks. Which of the following steps should the teacher take first in attempting to resolve this situation?

a. The teacher should call the student's parents and ask them to speak with the student about her behavior
b. The teacher should send the student to the principal's office when the disruptive behavior occurs
c. The teacher should discuss the problem with the special education teacher
d. The teacher should isolate the student so that her class is not disrupted

127. A school district has established a help hotline for teachers to call when they have questions about using technology in the classroom, or when they encounter technical difficulties. A teacher has called the hotline for advice on how to create a slide show for his social studies class. A voice prompt asks the teacher to press one if he is calling with a question regarding software, two if he is calling with a question regarding hardware, three if he has a question about using the Internet, and four is he is calling with a question about audio-visual equipment. Which number should the teacher press to learn more about a slide show program?

a. 1
b. 2
c. 3
d. 4

128. Ellen, a seventh-grader, has been diagnosed with a serious illness and will be out of school for several months. Ellen's parents have asked her teachers to send her worksheets home to her in electronic form. All but which of the following could be used to send electronic copies of paper worksheets?

a. Copy machine
b. Scanner
c. Flash drive or disc
d. Email

129. A middle school art teacher has taken his class to the school's media center so that the students can use the Internet to research their favorite Renaissance artists. If students bookmark the websites that they find useful, which of the following statements is true?

a. The students can use those bookmarks to return to those websites on their home computer
b. The students can use those bookmarks to return to the same websites only if they are using a computer in the school's media center
c. The students can only use those bookmarks to return to the same websites if they also enable the computer's pop-up blocker
d. The students can only use those bookmarks to return to the websites they've selected if they're using that particular computer

130. Mr. Ferris has asked his eighth grade language arts students to submit their 500-word book reports in Microsoft Word format electronically via email. In terms of assessment, the main advantage of this method is that:

a. Mr. Ferris can grade the term papers more quickly and return them electronically so as not use up valuable class time while passing them out
b. Mr. Ferris can easily determine whether or not each student's report is the correct length
c. Mr. Ferris can use the change-tracking device in Microsoft Word to show the students how to improve their papers
d. Mr. Ferris can tabulate the number of specific grammatical errors the students have made in order to determine areas that he should focus on in class

131. Mrs. Thomas recently taught her fifth grade students a new math concept that they seemed to understand clearly. However, when she administered a unit test of the material, more than half of the students failed. Mrs. Thomas' first reaction should be to:

a. Give the students another chance to learn the material by re-teaching it the same way as she did the first time
b. Analyze the test and the results to determine whether the assessment was well-designed and fairly administered
c. Review the test results to discover exactly which aspect of the material the students had trouble with
d. Compare her students' test results with the performance of last year's fifth grade class on the same test to see if there is a discrepancy

Questions 132-135 refer to the following scenario:

> The administrators at a middle school are considering implementing a team-teaching model for sixth grade classes in the upcoming school year. The administrators, including the principal and vice-principal, have convened a staff meeting to discuss this possibility with the sixth grade teachers.

132. One of the sixth grade teachers, Mrs. Ling, favors the proposal and wants to convince her colleagues to support it as well. Which of the following arguments should she use to accurately and persuasively describe the advantages of team teaching for sixth grade students?

a. Team teaching reduces the student-teacher ratio, providing more individualized attention for students
b. Team teaching provides an effective "bridge" between the single-teacher model of elementary schools and the multiple-teacher model of high schools
c. Team teaching provides increased opportunities for interdisciplinary teaching
d. Team teaching allows students more opportunities to develop supportive relationships with teachers and fellow students

133. The teachers and administrators come to an agreement that they should implement a team-teaching model during the upcoming year. However, the vice-principal points out that they must determine how they will divide the students into the various teams. The principal suggests that they divide the students into teams on the basis of their academic ability, so that the higher-achieving students will not be held back by their peers. Mrs. Ling disagrees with this proposal, because she believes that this approach will cause students in the lower-achieving classes to feel stigmatized and fall further behind. What would be the best way for Mrs. Ling to persuade the administrators to agree with her views?

a. She should simply state how she feels about the ability grouping proposal and why she feels this way
b. She should tell the principal that she refuses to participate in the team-teaching plan if students are grouped by ability
c. She should affirm the principal's concerns, but explain why she feels that avoiding the stigmatizing effect of ability grouping is more important than providing enrichment opportunities for high-achieving students
d. She should not directly confront the principal, but instead resist implementing ability tracking in her own classes

134. In adjusting their lesson plans to accommodate the new team-teaching model, the teachers decide that it would be advantageous to create linkages between the various subjects that they teach. To do this, they want to create a thematic unit that will be taught jointly in math, science, social studies, and language arts classes. What is the best way for the teachers to develop the content of this unit?

a. Have each teacher create a curriculum map for the year, and compare these maps to find themes, content and skills that are similar
b. Design the thematic units first, and then have teachers adjust their lesson plans to accommodate them
c. Ask students to vote on themes that they would like to learn about, and then design the units around these themes
d. Select one teacher to design the thematic units and deliver them to the other teachers, who will find ways to fit the units into their lesson plans

135. At the end of the year, the teachers decide that they want to evaluate the effectiveness of the team-teaching model for their sixth grade students. Which of the following research strategies would provide them with the best assessment of the model?

a. The teachers should compare this group of students' performance on standardized tests in previous years with their performance in sixth grade at the end of the year
b. The teachers should compare the students' performance in classes that are part of the team teaching model (math, science, language arts, social studies) with their performance in classes that are not team-taught (health, physical education, art)
c. The teachers should compare their students' performance in sixth grade to the performance of sixth grade students at schools that do not use team teaching
d. The teachers should compare their sixth grade students' performance this year with the performance of sixth grade students in previous years where team teaching was not used; they should also consider the performance history of this particular group of sixth graders relative to previous groups

Questions 136-141 refer to the following scenario:

> During Mr. Aaron's 50 minute class period with his eighth grade language arts class of 30 students, he wants the students to read a short story and discuss their reactions to the story with their classmates. This exercise is intended to help the students develop their reading comprehension skills, as well as their communication skills and their ability to exchange opinions in a respectful manner with other students.

136. Given the learning objectives that Mr. Aaron has set for this lesson, what would be the best way to structure the discussion portion of the class?

a. Ask the students to write out their reactions, and then call on students and ask them to share these reactions with the class
b. Go over a list of rules for respectful discussion with the class, and then guide the discussion by calling on students to answer specific questions
c. Remind the students about rules for respectful discussion, and then provide the students with a list of questions that they discuss in small groups
d. Provide the students with a structured list of questions, and having the students discuss them in order as a class

137. Mr. Aaron notices that some of the students in his class seem to enjoy discussions and take a natural leadership role. Why might this be the case, and how could Mr. Aaron use this fact to enhance the discussion if he chose to use a small-group format?

a. These "natural leaders" probably have a high level of intrapersonal intelligence, and Mr. Aaron should be sure to put all of these student in the same discussion group so that they do not intimidate less outgoing students
b. The students are "natural leaders" because they have a great deal of interpersonal intelligence, and Mr. Aaron should spread these students throughout the groups so that they can help facilitate discussion
c. These "natural leaders" probably have a high level of interpersonal intelligence, and Mr. Aaron should be sure to put all of these student in the same discussion group so that they do not intimidate less outgoing students
d. The students are "natural leaders" because they have a great deal of intrapersonal intelligence, and Mr. Aaron should spread these students throughout the groups so that they can help facilitate discussion

138. Another language arts teacher at Mr. Aaron's school prefers not to use discussion in his classes, because he feels that is takes valuable time away from the study of reading and writing skills. In defending his practice of using discussion in his class, Mr. Aaron would be most likely to refer to which of these learning theories?

a. Hunter's theory of direct instruction
b. Piaget's theory of assimilation
c. Vygotsky's socio-cultural theory of learning
d. Gardner's theory of multiple intelligences

139. Mr. Aaron's discussion session goes well, and he decides to extend this idea and ask students to complete a group project in which they can perform a skit, create a poster, jointly write a book report, or create a collection or invention that relates to a book they're reading in class. The most effective way for Mr. Aaron to group the students would be to:

a. Allow students to choose their own groups, since they know with which other students they'll work best
b. Keep the same groups from the class discussion, since they seemed to work well
c. Create groups that are balanced in terms of the students' academic ability, so that no group will be at a particular disadvantage
d. Determine students' personal intelligence profiles (musical, interpersonal, mathematical, verbal, etc.) and assign students with similar strengths to the same group so that they can choose a project that fits their abilities

140. In designing the group project, Mr. Aaron wants to implement an assessment system that provides incentives for all students to contribute equally to the project and that is fair to students in cases where certain group members contribute more than others. Which of the following strategies would be most effective in helping him to achieve this objective?

a. Giving all students in the group the opportunity to confidentially rate the contributions of their fellow group members, and giving lower grades to students who are rated lower by the members of their group
b. Giving all students in the group the same grade so they'll be motivated to monitor one another's contributions and exercise teamwork skills
c. Asking students to submit a report detailing exactly what their contribution was to the project, and to provide a self-evaluation of the value of their own contribution
d. Grading the projects using a pass/fail system, since it is very difficult to equitably grade group projects

141. Ms. Schneider, a fifth grade teacher, has been assigned a paraprofessional who comes to her class three times a week to work with the mainstreamed special education students. For the past week, the paraprofessional has arrived late to the classroom and appeared distracted and disinterested in his duties. What should be the first step that Ms. Schneider takes to resolve the problem?

a. Ask the school principal to assign a different paraprofessional to her class
b. Send a note to the special education teacher explaining the problem
c. Take the paraprofessional aside and explain her concerns
d. Help the special education students write a letter to the paraprofessional explaining how his behavior is affecting their learning

142. Mrs. Alexander is preparing her seventh grade science class for the upcoming standardized achievement test, but the class has fallen behind. One day she receives a letter from one of her students' parents stating that she is a microbiology researcher and would be interested in coming to class to discuss some of the biology concepts that the students are learning. How should Mrs. Alexander respond to this request?

a. She should invite the student's parent to come speak to the class as soon as possible
b. She should tell the parent that she appreciates the suggestion, but her class has fallen behind and there is no time for the presentation
c. She should tell the parent that she can deliver a presentation after school hours so that students can attend if they chose to
d. She should explain the fact that the class has fallen behind in preparing for an upcoming standardized test, but that she would like to schedule a time for the parent's presentation after the test

143. The middle school teachers are in the middle of administering the test when the school's fire alarm is sounded. What should the teachers do?

a. The teachers should tell their students to continue taking the test, since it is probably just a drill
b. The teachers should ask the students to leave their tests at their desks and follow the usual fire evacuation procedures without discussing the test
c. The teachers should ask the students to follow the usual fire evacuation procedures, but take their tests with them
d. The teachers should immediately contact the administration for advice

144. While administering the test, a teacher notices that that a student has erased an answer so vigorously that she has torn her testing booklet. What should the teacher do?

a. Give the student a new test booklet with the same form number to use for the remainder of the test, and transcribe the student's responses from the torn booklet to the new booklet after the test
b. Simply ask the student to erase more carefully in the future
c. Give the new student a new test booklet with the same form number and ask her to immediately transfer her answers into the new booklet and continue the test
d. Give the student a new test booklet and ask her to continue using that test booklet, since two booklets can be scored as one

145. When the middle schools receive the test results later on, they see that the students' scores are reported in both raw and scaled form. The scaled scores will be most useful for:

a. Determining exactly how many questions students got right and wrong
b. Determining which types of questions students had the most trouble with
c. Comparing students' performance across different administrations of the same test
d. Predicting students' performance in the classroom and on future tests

146. In preparation for the upcoming school year, the test results shared with the teachers who will be working with the students the following year. How will this information be most useful to the students' new teachers?

a. It will determine which students should be placed in remedial classes
b. It will help the teachers plan their instruction based on the strengths and needs of the incoming students
c. It will help determine which students should repeat a grade
d. It will help the teachers decide whether or not they should use team teaching

147. After examining the assessment results for their incoming class of students, the teachers determine that about 35% of the students do not meet grade level standards for math. Which of the following approaches would be most likely to improve the overall performance of the class on future tests?

a. Having the underperforming students take math class three extra times per week, while reducing the number of math classes that students who exceeded the math standard take per week by three
b. Having all students take an extra three periods of math, while reducing science classes to only two times per week
c. Creating a compulsory after-school remediation program for the students who are behind in math
d. Finding creative ways to incorporate math instruction into other subject areas, and offering optional math tutoring during lunch and after school

148. In order to effectively lead a class discussion, what is the best thing for a teacher to do after posing a fairly complex question to the class?

a. Immediately call on a student to answer the question
b. Wait two minutes, and then call on a student to answer the question
c. Engage in another activity like writing on the board while waiting for the students to compose their answers
d. Tell students that if no one answers right away, she will call on a student

149. During a class discussion, a teacher has posed a question to her seventh grade art class, but no student has responded. What should she do?

a. Continue to wait until a student answers
b. Repeat the question
c. Rephrase the question
d. Tell the students the answer

150. Which of the following assessment methods is most likely to be used in a learner-centered middle school classroom?

a. A method that provides different alternatives for students to demonstrate their knowledge
b. A method that allows students to complete the assessment in groups
c. A structured method that allows students' mastery to be compared with that of other students
d. A multiple-choice test which students help to construct and grade

Answer Key and Explanations

English

1. C: Students will not typically arrive in the classroom with excellent listening skills; these skills must be introduced and honed as any others would be. Students often benefit from previewing material or pointing out what they should be listening *for*, since it will be virtually impossible for them to retain every piece of information proffered during class time. If the information is previewed, they are predisposed to listen carefully to important topics. When asked questions about the information, the teacher will be able to monitor how well they listened, as well as whether they understood what they heard. Choice A does involve listening skills, but does not provide direct instruction or a method of monitoring improvement; choices B and D monitor improvement but do not build skills.

2. B: As the students strive to understand individuals from around the world, the project would not be complete without attention to that individual's mode of oral expression. In reading about and repeating the research subject's own words, the students will have an opportunity, if guided appropriately, to learn about how a person's speech reflects their identity and thoughts. The students will assume the role of a person very different from themselves and be able to place themselves into another perspective via oral language.

3. D: Listening is a vital part of being literate and communicative. Students must often listen to understand instructions and content in class, as well as to make sense of the world around them. From an early age, students learn to listen in order to hear stories and other kinds of literature. This listening practice helps them prepare to learn in other ways, such as through reading and viewing. However, once other literacy skills start to develop, students still benefit from honing their listening skills. This practice helps them communicate more effectively and utilize every part of their senses to take in information. Literature and other texts can be appreciated through listening just as much as through reading.

4. B: Folk tales are stories that have been passed down orally through generations, and typically contain a kind of moral or lesson. Folk tales are most appropriate in this case because they are so influenced and bear a strong relationship to oral traditions across all cultures that could be present in the classroom. This genre provides many opportunities not only to read aloud, but to discuss the importance or oral language in learning lessons about culture and behavior.

5. D: Literacy skills include reading, writing, comprehending, expressing, communicating and a whole host of other concepts. Often, an individual student will possess varying abilities within each aspect of their literacy development. A teacher should take care not to approach this kind of student with an inflexible plan, or with the notion that certain skills (such as fluency) must be fully developed before others (such as comprehension). Setting small goals with the individual student allows him to take ownership over the process and work on various skill sets in tandem. All components of each student's literacy can improve simultaneously.

6. B: Emergent readers are students who are beginning to show signs of reading and writing independently, but still require quite a bit of scaffolding in their work. Often, these readers will show varied abilities within each of the components of literacy, perhaps working independently in one area while needing more help in another. Therefore, emergent readers benefit from specific instruction and exercises that address all the areas of literacy, rather than focusing on one skill at a time. In this way, all of their skills can evolve simultaneously and, ideally, more quickly.

7. C: Failing to remember previously-learned concepts is a red flag suggesting a learning disability. Note that the student is failing to remember concepts he has already *learned*, and not simply ideas that have been *introduced* once. If a student seems to know something one day and then does not know it the next, there may be a learning disability. The girls in the first two choices do not warrant special instruction; rather, they exhibit areas for improvement that can be worked on inside their normal classrooms, as part of daily instruction. Billy, in choice D, likely has some motivation or skill deficits in relation to writing that can be addressed in partnership with him, inside of daily lessons.

8. D: There will always be students who are quieter in class for a variety of reasons—they may be shy, be disinterested in the topics, or simply have trouble translating thoughts into verbal communication quickly enough. By reducing the number of contributors in the group, quieter students will have more time and freedom to speak aloud. Mr. Everly can then join the groups containing those students and observe them to ensure they are communicating appropriately and have a thorough-enough grasp of the material. If he is unsure about how the student is progressing, he can also engage him in conversation in the group without singling out that particular student.

9. B: Reading fluency refers to the speed, accuracy and appropriate intonation with which an individual reads. As a student is beginning to learn to read, he or she will be working primarily on sounding out words (phonetics), building recognition of words (sight words), and reading with speed and appropriate vocal modulation (emotion and pauses for punctuation). A fluent reader will read at a natural pace without making many mistakes. He or she will typically pause appropriately to communicate punctuation and modulate the voice with expression to add interest to the text. Comprehension (choice B) is typically thought of as a reading concept that evolves in tandem with fluency, but the former is not a component of the latter.

10. B: The term "instructional level" refers to the level at which a child can work on building reading fluency without the text being too easy or too difficult. If the child can read approximately 90% of the words without assistance, the text will be considered "instructional level." If the student needs less help, the teacher should move him to a more challenging-to-read piece or consider the text to be "independent level" reading. If the piece is too difficult, the level of difficulty should be lowered, or extra help should be provided in the areas of difficulty.

11. A: Graphemes are individual letters within a word, which can be distinguished from phonemes, or letter-sounds. The term syllable refers to a single unit of sound formed by a letter or combination of letters. The set of words in choice A holds words with more than a few letters, but only two to three syllables. Choice B consists of words with few graphemes and few syllables. Conversely, choice C holds words with both many graphemes and syllables. The final choice does not exhibit a pattern that is relevant to this question. This

12. B: Students build vocabulary and word knowledge through exposure and are more likely to remember words in context. The best way to help a student learn more words is through giving what they are learning a context for memory. Introducing a variety of reading material gives students more exposure to different kinds of words. Another way to introduce vocabulary is to encourage students to engage in conversation with adults; Students will be more likely to build sight words and vocabulary if they are not focused on learning words for the sake of learning them; rather, the words are retained easily if the student can remember how he or she learned it.

13. C: Non-fiction writing can cover a multitude of styles and content. The pieces Mr. Blankenship plans to introduce are not specified in the question, and could be anything from newspaper articles to biographies. Teaching students to preview the topic and information will help them attend to main ideas and important details. The summarizing step helps students put relevant ideas together and categorize information in their minds. Because non-fiction text is often more detailed than conceptual, choice B creates a three-step process that will help students understand and retain the ideas which they have read.

14. B: While test scores can tell a teacher that a student is struggling, they cannot diagnose *why* the student is struggling. The fact that Brian says he hates reading suggests that his confidence and motivation have been negatively affected. The teacher will have to assess Brian's reading skills, including fluency and comprehension, in order to determine where he needs extra help. The best way to get an older student to comply with this kind of assessment is to ask him to read something he likes. Brian's selection of text will give the teacher clues about his current reading level, as will his verbal reading of it. The comprehension questions will help the teacher know whether or not the problem is just comprehension, or an additional skill that is affecting his comprehension.

15. A: Critical, or inferential, comprehension refers to a student's ability to understand what is not explicitly stated in a text. This kind of comprehension can be more challenging for students because the ideas are implied and not written or explained within a text. In choices B, C and D, students can identify or answer questions, the answer to which can be agreed upon based on that what is written. In choice A, however, readers will have to make an inference or interpretation in order to use the skill. In order to distinguish cause and effect, the read must utilize that which is written in the text and interpret the material.

16. C: When a class contains students of varying abilities, using group work is a helpful model. Within a group, each student can contribute and learn in a relatively low-pressure environment. Often, when asked to speak in front of the entire class, some students will lack confidence. To avoid one student's dominance of the group, or conversely, another student failing to contribute, the teacher has assigned each student a specific discussion topic. In this way, each student gets a chance to lead and a chance to learn. Choice A relies on worksheets to provide instruction; choice B relies on the stronger students to teach instead of helping them to grow as well. Choice D is a less-thorough version of choice C.

17. D: Many students will rely too much on technology in the writing process, preventing them from making progress. The last choice uses a specific form of technology, an online program, to help the student organize ideas into an outline. This program keeps the student from skipping one of the most important aspects of learning to write: planning and organization. There are many tools that a student can use on a computer that will help him or her get ready to write. However, choice B shows how a computer or word processor can be used in an incorrect way. Choices A and C do not provide direct instruction on the writing process, but simply record ideas for the sake of retention.

18. C: Student journals can serve a variety of purposes if students are provided with the teacher's expectations. Journals are good examples of a student's writing progress throughout a given period of time. They also provide opportunities for students to express themselves through writing and drawing of many kinds. Students can also use journal assignments to practice specific writing skills. However, students should probably not be permitted to write freely without parameters, as this strategy would not always yield progress. Conversely, students will not feel motivated to write in journals if they are concerned about their grades.

19. C: There are six generally accepted traits of writing: ideas, word choice, sentence fluency, conventions, organization and voice. Writing conventions refer to aspects of writing that make the text easy to read. These conventions include spelling, punctuation, grammar, spacing and titles. Each choice in this question refers to some aspect of writing conventions except choice C. This choice refers to an aspect of the "ideas" trait, and working on supporting details and their relationship to main concepts would not fall under the writing conventions category.

20. B: The writing process typically contains six components, which include choices A, B, and D. Choice C is a style of writing that is related to the questions in the box. However, persuasive writing is not technically a part of the writing process; the writing process applies to all styles. In developing ideas, the student will decide what he wants to communicate about a given topic and how it should be communicated. This process precedes the organizational phase in that the student is focusing in on what is most important and eliminating information that is irrelevant to the topic.

21. A: While this answer may seem to be obvious, some teachers will make the mistake of allowing students to choose their own topics without help. However, a new researcher will likely need help choosing a topic that is appropriately narrow. Some students will choose topics from which they cannot possibly cover enough related information and produce a comprehensive report. Conversely, some students will choose an excessively narrow or obscure topic that will not provide enough material for research. There may also be topic choices that are not appropriate for a particular student based upon age or maturity level. The teacher would do well to meet with students and guide them in choosing topics that will suit first-time researchers as they learn this process.

22. B: The SQ3R method is very helpful when applied to a text that a student needs to read for informational purposes. By previewing and formulating questions, the student learns to turn his or her attention to salient ideas and details in the text. Reading with the goal of answering questions and confirming initial impressions about what is important in the text adds another layer to this process. By making notes and reviewing, the student can solidify important information in order to take a test or retain said information in memory for class discussions. The multi-layered study approach is best applied to a larger reading assignment in which the student will need to process the information multiple times, which is not usually necessary with poetry, journals, or stories.

23. D: Graphic organizers, story trees, and story maps are just a few tools students can use to "study" as they read. Rather than detail the events and characters for the students, Mrs. Nelson should have the students help her make a story map that includes the major events in each part of the story to help them remember. Characterizations can also be detailed, perhaps with a drawing or a picture of the person to aid in retention. By doing this, Mrs. Nelson is teaching the students to create organization for themselves in a way that can be used again and again as they learn.

24. B: In this scenario, every student will engage in individual inquiry each week. The assignment gives students some freedom to investigate what is interesting or important to them and share that information with their peers. In this way, students will be exercising the exact process of independent research each week on a small scale. Choice A gives too much freedom, since students may simply be checking out books that are fun to read, thereby circumventing the whole process of research. Choice C is one way to incorporate research, but could draw the project out for so long that the students do not grasp its purpose. Choice C provides opportunities for students to research answers, but does not prevent students from opting not to do the research.

25. C: In this choice, the students are directly engaging in media deconstruction, which refers to the process of analyzing media images and determining their intended meanings. This project directly relates to the *viewing and representing* portion of the curriculum and will directly affect students' ability to deconstruct modern-day images as well as academic and literary images. They will learn the difference between intended meaning and actual meaning and build their interpretive skills. Choice A may provide too much challenge and abstraction for 8th-graders. Choices B and D do not provide enough instruction to guide or build the students' skills and instead ask them to interpret and analyze without the benefit of guidance from the teacher. Choice C incorporates scaffolding and individual participation.

26. B: The words in the boxes suggest that the box on the left is the "cause" and the one on the right is the "effect." The arrow in the middle shows the relationship between the cause and the effect; the boxes and arrow can even be reversed if it is easier for students to discuss the effect first and the cause next. In choices A and D, the arrow would not apply to the concepts. Because choice C contains two ideas, it could be mistaken for the correct answer. However, there is little to no causation or causal relationship between the two ideas—they are two separate but equal analytical tools often used simultaneously.

27. B: Students are presented with countless visual symbols and images every day through media and in shared cultural exchanges. In teaching the students about viewing and representing, teachers can help them deconstruct these symbols and understand their meaning, as well as monitor what messages the students themselves are sending. Choice A would likely help students represent the novel in class, but might not be as informative if the students cannot speak. It may also be boring for other students to watch a wordless play made from an entire novel. Choice C would be a great activity for students to learn about representing information; however, this choice does not address the question prompt saying that Mr. Hawking will be utilizing the current class reading.

28. A: This choice provides the most direct route for assessing a student's reading fluency and comprehension. Having the student read aloud is the best way to monitor all aspects of fluency, including speed, accuracy, and vocal expression. In asking questions at the end, the teacher will not be relegated to correct or incorrect answers written upon a page. He or she will be able to hear the student's vocalization, which may reveal degrees of understanding not found in a worksheet.

29. A: It is important for students who are continuing to practice their reading skills to work at the appropriate level of challenge. Grade levels can be subjective when it comes to reading skills; i.e., not all 5th-grade texts contain the same material or skill levels. Students are not always best at choosing books that are challenging for them, sometimes opting for material that is too easy or too difficult. If the student can read the majority of the words in the book, but still find few new words to challenge them, the book is likely at an appropriate level of challenge.

30. A: A student response form measures two things: one, how fast a student will be able to read the story to himself and how well he will probably understand the text. In this kind of assessment, the teacher will be able to understand how a group of students might individually comprehend or move through a text ahead of time. This evaluation will allow the teacher to plan more effective lessons. Choice B refers to a kind of assessment in which a student will fill in blanks in a paragraph with words that make meaning out of what they have read. Choice C is not a commonly-used evaluation and choice D is a group-administered inventory.

31. B: Student development is holistic and covers a spectrum of skills that are all developing simultaneously, and at different rates. Literacy development is not a linear process, nor can it be completely illustrated by one specific test. While standardized tests are convenient for providing a snapshot of development, they may not be the best tool for describing such a complex process. However, providing examples such as writing samples or reading fluency assessments will give a parent an idea of what the student is doing in class. The teacher can then provide information about how the student is progressing compared to other students of the same age. Choices C and D focus more on giving students and parents responsibility for improving skills instead of communicating progress thus far.

Mathematics

32. C: Students often struggle with money, even though it is a familiar and real-world concept, because there are multiple aspects to consider. In order to do these problems accurately, students must be able to add and subtract decimals. However, they must also understand the practical applications of this concept in their lives. Choices A and B both use test material that will improve this skill without addressing the concept itself. Students need to understand how to make change in the "real world," as well as how to complete a word problem on a test. Choice C addresses the money on a conceptual level in a fun way, combined with monitoring test practice to make sure the students are translating this knowledge to this context. Choice D only addresses one aspect of this issue, without connecting the interrelated skills in a meaningful way.

33. C: Integers are defined as the set of natural numbers (including zero) and their negatives. You cannot define rational numbers without understanding integers. Rational numbers are defined as any number that can be expressed by a/b, when both a and b are integers, but b is not zero. Therefore, an appropriate order for lesson planning would be to discuss integers before rational numbers. Imaginary numbers arise as a necessity in the study of square roots and should therefore not be studied before them. Real numbers are typically introduced with the study of square roots.

34. C: The numbers in this sequence progress according to a pattern. Each progressing number can be expressed by the equation $x + 2 = n$, where $x =$ the difference between the previous two numbers and $n =$ the number added to the previous number to yield the progressing number. For instance, the difference in 24 and 16 is 8. By adding 2 to 8, you know that you must add 10 to 24 in order to yield 34. In the next part of the sequence, $x = 10$ and $n = 12$. $34 + 12 = 46$, the next number in the sequence.

35. C: A rational number is any number that can be expressed as a/b where a and b are both integers and $b \neq 0$. Both x and y are integers and do not equal zero. Any integer multiplied by 2 will yield another integer. Choice C expresses an equation in which an integer is divided by another integer, which yields a rational number.

36. A: The relationship between lemonade sold and the amount of quarters varies directly. As one variable increases, so does the other. The function in choice B suggests that the child loses quarters for every cup of lemonade sold. Choice C is inaccurate in that it neglects to include the cups of lemonade in its measurement. Quarters and dollars do not increase at the same rate. Choice D is not a linear function and suggests that there is a limit to how much money the child can earn, no matter how much lemonade is sold.

37. D: The area of the garden is based upon the formula $\frac{1}{2}bh$, in which b equals the base of the triangle and h equals the height of the triangle. However, only the length of the base is known. Because the problem includes a right triangle, the Pythagorean Theorem ($a^2 + b^2 = c^2$) can be used to derive the unknown length. The hypotenuse, C, is given as . $\sqrt{369}$ The value of A is 12. Therefore, $12^2 + b^2 = (\sqrt{369})^2$ and $b = 15$. By multiplying ½(12)(15), we find the correct answer, or 90 square feet.

38. A: The first step is to calculate the area left to paint. The total length is 15ft, so 2/5 the total length (the portion already painted) is 6 ft. Then, multiply 9 ft (the unpainted portion) by 7.5 ft (height of the wall). There are 67.5 ft^2 left to paint. The painter will need between two and three gallons to paint the rest of the wall, since two gallons would only cover 50 ft^2. Three gallons of paint costs $\frac{\$6.25}{\text{gal}} \times 3 = \$18.75$. Therefore, choice A lists the least amount the painter can spend.

39. D: Lines C and D are parallel, as indicated by the hash marks in the middle of either line. If choice D is correct, then transversal line D crosses two parallel lines and thus the corresponding angles that are created by this intersection are congruent. The given angle is a corresponding angle to θ and therefore congruent. By using geometric principles, one can determine that $\theta = 80°$.

40. A: The sine of $\angle A$ is the ratio of the length of the opposite side of the triangle to the length of the hypotenuse, or $\sin 60 = \overline{BC}/\overline{AC}$. To calculate the value of $\overline{BC}$, isolate that value in the expression. If one multiplies both sides of the equation by the length of the hypotenuse, $\overline{AC}$, one is left with the equation $\overline{AC} \sin 60 = \overline{BC}$.

41. C: Formative assessment refers to any kind of evaluation by a teacher that helps guide her instruction. In mathematics instruction, teachers need to know exactly what the students have mastered in order to teach them appropriately because so many principles must be taught consecutively and in appropriate order. Conversations, class work and homework are all examples of formative assessments. These practices help teachers know where students might need more help and where instruction should be focused.

42. B: There is a common misconception that English-language learners find it easier to learn math because this subject does not depend on a foreign language as much as it does on numbers. However, this assumption is based on the belief that all English-language learners use a common set of numbers, which is untrue for students that hail from various parts of the globe. Also, it is untrue that language does not play a major role in math instruction; in fact, it can be harder for some students to learn math because they are attempting to understand numeric principles without the benefit of a common language for explanation. Choices A, C and D are all beneficial techniques for instruction of English-language learners.

43. D: Students in 8th grade should be able to use basic algebraic concepts to analyze both proportional and non-proportional linear relationships. Remember that in a proportional relationship between x and y, the ratio between the two variables is constant. In a non-proportional relationship, the ratio is varied; in other words, the graph of the ratio between x and y will not be a straight line. Algebraic concepts are introduced in previous grades, but this standard is not expected to be used consistently until 8th grade.

44. D: The formula for percentile is $r = \frac{p}{100}(N + 1)$, where r is the rank in the total of all values of N. In this case the rank, r, equals 61 while the total number of values, N, is 65. Using these values for r and N:

$$61 = \frac{p}{100}(65 + 1)$$
$$\frac{61}{66} = \frac{p}{100}$$
$$92.\overline{42} = p$$

Thus, the closest correct answer is 93.

45. B: The gradient of a straight line refers to the slope of the line. This concept is vital to understanding linear equations. Choices A and C may be introduced during similar studies.

However, *all* linear equations will involve gradients. Choice D suggests that quadrilaterals may be related to linear equations; however, the two concepts are not directly related.

46. C: To find the probability of an event, divide the number of favorable outcomes by the total number of outcomes. When there are two events in which the first depends on the second, multiply the first ratio by the second ratio. In the first part of the problem, the probability of choosing a licorice jelly bean is two out of twenty possible outcomes, or $\frac{2}{20}$. Then, because one jelly bean has already been chosen, there are four cinnamon beans out of a total of 19, or $\frac{4}{19}$. By multiplying the two ratios and dividing by a common denominator, one arrives at the final probability of $\frac{2}{95}$.

47. A: A direct proof starts with a set of certainties and states a series of logical facts to prove a separate statement. Once $x + y$ is expressed in a valid format that clearly has a factor of two (as does $2(a + b + 1)$) it is certain that the sum of these two integers is even. Choice B contains a direct assumption, and is therefore incorrect. Choice C begins to make valid point but skips to the conclusion without clear explanation. Choice D makes no proof at all and simply restates the original information.

48. B: The first step in solving for the standard deviation is to find the mean of all the values. In this case, the mean is the average of all five recorded times. To calculate variance, calculate the average of the squared difference between the mean and each individual value. To find the standard deviation, take the square root of the variance. Choice B displays the appropriate formula, while all other choices contain gaps in the formula.

49. C: In order to solve for the x-intercept of a function, set the function equal to zero and solve for x. When this is done for $f(x) = x^2 + 3$, there will be an imaginary value for x, therefore there is no x-intercept. When given the function $(x) = x^2 + C$, the constant C moves the original graph up or down depending on its value. The parabola graphed from $f(x) = x^2$, usually touching the point (0, 0) is moved up to point (0, C), or in this case, (0, 3).

50. D: When two triangles are similar, the ratio of two sides of the first triangle is the same as the ratio of the same two sides on the second triangle. For these two triangles: $\overline{AC}/\overline{BC} = \overline{XZ}/\overline{YZ}$. In order to solve for the length of side $\overline{XZ}$, isolate it in that expression. Multiplying both sides of the previous equation by $\overline{YZ}$ yields $\frac{\overline{YZ}\times\overline{AC}}{\overline{BC}} = \overline{XZ}$.

51. C: If the rate of violent crimes per month is anything like it is the year before, it will be greatest in the summer months, as there is a spike in the data on the 2005 graph during the summer months. While there is some fluctuation up and down throughout the entire year, these months are well beyond the numbers of the other months and represent the only upward trend in the graph.

52. B: When learning to solve algebraic equations, it is necessary to treat the two sides of an equation equally. In order to isolate the variable, the first step is to subtract the constant from both sides. In this case, the constant is 11. By reworking the problem using the suggestion found in choice B, it is possible to arrive at the student's incorrect answer. The best method to solving this question is to use a trial and error method, determining which answer yields the incorrect answer.

53. A: The distributive property states that $a(b + c) = ab + ac$. Though the first half of the expression contains a constant and a variable, the distributive property still applies. It is possible that the associative or the commutative law can be applied when dealing with equations like this one, but the transformation is made possible by the law of distribution.

54. C: The quartile is found by separating any set of data into four equal parts. The most common way to determine quartile is to divide the total set in two, and then repeat that process with each half of the data. In this data, the set of 60 can be divided by four, creating divisions every 15 digits. The four quartiles are: 1-15, 16-30, 31-45, and 46-60. Because 37 falls within the third group, Matt was in the 3rd quartile.

Social Studies

55. C: The Social Sciences are many, and include multiple disciplines that are interconnected. Anthropology is the study of human beings and culture, and therefore this choice best falls into the category of Social Sciences. Choices A, C and D constitute scientific careers, but do not have obvious social links. Choice A focuses on biological studies, which involve humans but usually do not address social behaviors and trends. Choice B refers to the study of insects and choice C to the study of Physics. Neither choice addresses social developments of humans.

56. C: Ms. Fisher wants to support what the students are reading in English class, thereby integrating their studies. The integration of disciplines deepens students' understanding of the relationship between culture, history, science, and the individual. By studying parts of Japanese culture and the social ramifications of World War II, students will enjoy a richer experience while reading about one woman's true story. Their knowledge of history and social sciences will help them understand the main character fully and make educated judgments about the story.

57. A: By the 5th grade, students should have been exposed to the concept of point of view. They should understand that various individuals will possess different perspectives on the same topic or event; additionally, teachers should illustrate how the United States has evolved from the desire to embrace different points of view, generally speaking. Choice B refers to research and inquiry skills that are taught toward the beginning of the high school curriculum. Choice C is usually found in middle-school lessons. The final choice relies on the ability to understand different points of view, but is typically taught in middle-school, following the initial lessons mentioned in choice A.

58. C: Teachers should make every effort to illustrate for students that all Social Studies and other academic skills function together for deeper understanding.

59. A: The American Civil Rights movement arose to address the disproportionate lack of power of African Americans in the United States. Civil leaders of all backgrounds joined to fight for monetary, professional, cultural and voting rights for African Americans during the 1960's. The oppression inherent in the years leading up to the Civil Rights movement is much like the racial segregation in South Africa before 1994, called *apartheid*. Under this system, white citizens possessed far more power and wealth than their Black counterparts, who experienced similar disenfranchisement. By studying *apartheid*, students can gain a better understanding of important historical events and their effect on culture, as well as relationships between cultures across the globe.

60. C: As Europeans arrived, they brought many changes along with them. Guns and horses became much more prevalent in a short period of time. New diseases struck many Native Americans who had no immunity to the foreign illnesses. Europeans also brought with them many Christian missionaries who established missions and churches in the area. There were, however, a vast number of Native Americans living in separate groups of various sizes. Some groups and tribes joined forces to fight the Europeans, but others continued to fight amongst themselves, a continuation of struggles originating before the newcomers arrived.

61. D: Manifest Destiny refers to the belief that United States settlers could and had the right to expand into the western part of the country. This concept sometimes is believed to suggest that Americans had the divine or destined right to occupy all of North America. The term Manifest Destiny is commonly used as the historical term for the basis of expansion into the western territories in the late 1700's and early 1800's.

62. C: The area depicted by the map includes many countries considered to make up the Middle Eastern part of the world, which lies between Europe and Asia. Choice A is true for some major world religions, such as Islam, Christianity, and Judaism, yet there are other religions that have originated in other parts of the world, such as Buddhism and African traditional religions.

63. A: The Middle East region relies heavily on its export businesses, a large component of which is oil production. By adding information regarding commerce and industry, students can draw conclusions about similarities and connections between the two different places. While there are many facets to study of an entire global region, the primary similarity, or common interest, between their state and Middle Eastern states is in industry. Political and religious divisions are not common between the two entities, aside from the fact that they exist.

64. D: Louisiana's population increased during the last census. However, the year 2005 is significant, because Hurricane Katrina struck the coast of Louisiana during this time. As a result of this hurricane, many residents lost their homes, jobs, and even their lives. News media covered the mass exodus of Louisiana residents to neighboring states in order to find homes and work in the aftermath of the hurricane.

65. C: Populations will move or migrate for a variety of reasons, which are usually circumstances that significantly lower quality of life. The first two choices are obvious examples of negative scenarios leading residents to move to better locations. Choice D can be misleading in that it seems like a positive circumstance. However, high numbers of skilled workers can diminish the number of available jobs for all residents. The increased level of competition may result in population changes as people move away, searching for better jobs. High birth rates may eventually lead to large numbers of skilled workers, but usually do not bear direct correlation to migration rates.

66. C: Part of middle school economics study, includes the various kinds of industries. There are three generally accepted forms of industry in all economies: primary, secondary, and tertiary. Primary industry includes the harvesting of raw materials, including farming, mining, etc. Secondary industries process these materials. Tertiary businesses offer services to individuals, such as healthcare offices, drycleaners, restaurants, and so on. The dentist offers a service to patients or clients, thus making it a tertiary industry.

67. C: The terms *recession* and *depression* appeared in curricula more frequently as the national and international economies dipped in 2008 and 2009. All students are expected to understand how the United States' free enterprise system operates, as well as how other societies function economically. Identifying and defining periods of economic recession comprise a very relevant lesson in this discipline. There is no universal definition of an economic depression, although some economists suggest that this phenomenon yields a decline in GDP that exceeds 10% or lasts for several years.

68. A: Mary is describing the effects of the War of 1812 through this graphic organizer, which she has done accurately in this graph. However, the boxes on the bottom are somewhat vague, describing independence from Britain and industrial growth. By re-organizing her graph, Mary will demonstrate that the Industrial Revolution grew out of the War of 1812. Because industrial production grew, a new railroad system was built, production and refining was increased, and America relied less on foreign imports. All of these boxes are effects, or supporting details, of the War of 1812 and the Industrial Revolution.

69. C: Judicial review refers to a court's ability to determine if laws or trial decisions made by lower courts are constitutional or legal. This concept arises in instruction regarding the branches of government. The executive, judicial, and legislative branches are often discussed at their simplest levels, giving each branch a general purpose. However, when discussing checks and balances in government, students must understand how and why government is limited in order to maintain democracy and individual freedoms.

70. B: Being a citizen involves multiple responsibilities and exercising just as many freedoms with responsibility. Citizenship rests on the assumption that the individual will behave according to social rules and in a way that is best for the society as a whole. The best way to teach young students to be citizens is to allow them to actually *be* citizens. This scenario suggests that all students have jobs that contribute to their classroom in some way: sharpening pencils, watering plants, gathering papers, and various other tasks. The students also get practice identifying important issues and voting democratically upon them to come to a decision. While they may not vote on every single issue that arises, the teacher can guide students to participate in effective ways. With this practice, students will become accustomed to helping others and contributing to their community in a positive way.

71. A: In *Dred Scott v Sandford*, the slave Dred Scott attempted to gain his freedom based upon the fact that he had lived with his owners in abolitionist states during his lifetime. The Supreme Court denied his claim, stating that he was not a citizen of the United States and therefore could not bring suit in a federal court. This case illustrates the fact that this nation has been debating the concept of citizenship, and who can become a citizen, for centuries. Students will find their understanding of current events deepened by historical knowledge of laws and social belief systems.

72. B: The Electoral College consists of individuals who represent the popular vote. Each state is allotted a number of electoral voters based upon its representation in Congress. Once the general public has voted, the electoral voters cast their votes directly for President. States are given the freedom to choose electors according to their own specifications, and sometimes legally require the electors to vote for the candidates they support. Often, Presidential candidates will spend more time campaigning in states with larger numbers of electoral votes, or in states they believe will be crucial to winning the election. This process sometimes comes at the expense of states with smaller numbers, which do not hold early primaries, or are not deemed pivotal in the election process.

73. B: Amorosa writes about her family and about her anticipation of the *Quinceañera,* a traditional birthday celebration in Latin cultures. She describes her family members in detail, as well as that she is involved in soccer, school and art classes. Amorosa is a typical student in her interests and identification as part of a family unit. She clearly also identifies herself within her cultural heritage through her discussion of the *Quinceañera.* This is a celebration with a long history and specific customs that are shared by *Latina* girls and women, even within the United States.

74. B: Students are more motivated to inquire and learn new things when the topic at hand is relevant to their real lives. Since Amorosa is obviously looking forward to her *Quinceañera,* she may enjoy researching similar celebrations and customs inherent in other cultures. By relating this cultural research to an event, she is anticipating, her teacher will help her identify relevant similarities across many cultures. Amorosa will also have an opportunity to practice understanding contrasts between various events as well as cultures throughout the project that will aid her in deepening cultural awareness in the future.

75. A: With the proliferation of the World Wide Web, people of all ages and backgrounds have access to a vast repository of information. With this information, students can pursue interests and ideas from any place with an internet connection. Many internet websites have come about that are solely dedicated to assisting children in finding information. However, the internet also contains much information that is false or misleading, because there is very little oversight of its content. Therefore, teachers must educate students on how to determine what information they find online is reliable and can be trusted as accurate.

76. C: Scientific discovery is a hallmark of American culture. Some advances have benefits, and some of those also bring negative consequences. There are many discoveries in history that have greatly affected society and the way human beings think about their world. Communication devices have changed greatly over the years, from the telegraph to the telephone to communication over the internet. There has been much research in recent years focusing on the effect of communication technology and personal interactions. Because people can communicate through telephones, text messages, and the internet, it can be argued there is less face-to-face interaction between human beings in modern society. Thus, these technological advances may influence public consciousness by determining how and when we communicate with one another.

Science

77. C: Animal dissection is a controversial topic among science educators of young students. Some individuals feel that the practice is harmful to all involved. However, the historical basis for dissection aligns most closely with choice C, in that it is said to help students experience anatomy and scientific concepts in a tangible way. Regardless of a teacher's personal standpoint on animal dissection or use in the classroom, he must be educated in the historical foundations of scientific practices and be prepared to help students work through controversial issues.

78. C: The purpose of animal dissection in classrooms where this practice is used is to teach students about life processes, anatomy and physiology. Dissection is the most real way to illustrate these concepts because students can observe first-hand as they work. The CD-ROM program is mostly closely aligned with these goals of realism, since students will experience the same phenomena virtually.

79. C: Many scientific concepts can be troubling to students, as with adults, due to their emotional nature. For example, stem cell research, animal dissection, cloning, and other topics can create intense emotional divides within a classroom or school space. Teachers should be clear about what is required in each classroom, but take every measure to ensure that students can discuss their concerns without fear of judgment. Whenever possible, it is important to provide choices for students with legitimate objections to various assignments.

80. B: In a scientific lab, there are countless substances and tools that must be respected and used safely. Many chemicals and materials used in experiments can be very dangerous if not used properly and if students do not wear proper protective gear. Also, students should learn how to use sinks, hot plates, data collectors and other tools safely and efficiently. All of these lessons will allow students to interact properly with their environment and get the most out of their daily lessons and experiments.

81. A: Both the spring scale and the balance measure the size of an object. To use the balance, an object is placed on one side and is compared to another object of known mass. The balance technically compares the objects' weights; however, weight and mass are directly proportional. To use the spring scale, an object of unknown mass is hung on a hook and the observer can see how much the scale's needle is displaced by the hanging. The spring scale measures the force of gravity on an object's mass. While both tools measure mass, they do it using different mechanisms.

82. D: When heating chemicals or liquids in a beaker, there are many safety precautions that must be taken. Because most beakers are made of glass, gloves are important to prevent burns. Goggles will also prevent burning or irritation of the eyes from chemicals or hot liquids. There should be enough room within the beaker for reactions to take place without overflow, and the beaker should be pointed directly up to prevent spraying of substances onto lab participants. There will be times in which a stirring utensil is needed; as long as apparatus are comprised of the appropriate materials, insertion is safe.

83. B: The scientific method is the widely-used foundation of scientific research and inquiry. Students should be taught from the earliest stages how to initiate research and experimentation based on a question. The process then guides the inquirer to collect information that allows them, ultimately, to answer the initial question that was posed. Choices A, C and D are all possible outcomes of the initial inquiry, but cannot be accomplished without first making a conclusion.

84. C: In order to carry out an instructional experiment, students must be able to utilize the scientific methodology. In order to do this, they must be able to formulate predictions, collect data, and so on. The only choice that could be effectively tested within a classroom environment is that regarding sugar content in apple juice bottles. Students can test sugar levels in each bottle in order to confirm or contradict their hypotheses. Choice A would require outside research based on secondary sources, since students could not realistically conduct this experiment themselves. Both choices B and D are more likely topics that would be used for research writing or reports, and do not lend themselves to experimentation in the classroom.

85. C: The theory of anchored instruction involves a problem-based learning model. Students receive background knowledge through stories or other forms of learning and then use this information to complete various modules or activities. Within an anchored instruction-based lesson, all information necessary to solve problems or answer questions must be included in the format. In this way, students are learning something new by working independently within a procedural scaffold. In choice C, students read necessary background information and then use this, along with a scale-model, to answer questions about the solar system.

86. A: A scientific theory is a dynamic set of ideas that attempt to explain a scientific phenomenon. Scientific theories are not proven fact; scientific facts, or laws, are based in proof and concrete knowledge about our world and cannot be disproven. Choice A lists a theory, the Big Bang, which refers to a set of ideas about the origin of the universe. The laws of motion are proven facts that explain the behavior or objects in our environment. Choices B and D both list sets of theories without facts. Choice C shows two scientifically accepted facts, those of mass and electricity conservation and the process of carbon-14 dating of objects.

87. C: Formal sciences, such as mathematics, logics, and linguistics, employ what is deemed *a priori* evidence. This type of evidence is absent of experience and stems from observation and inherent knowledge. For example, we know that two objects added to one more object will yield three objects without formulating a hypothesis or experimenting. Natural sciences, such as social sciences, humanities, and natural studies, employ the scientific method of inquiry to gather information and knowledge. Applied sciences include those that apply scientific knowledge and progress to human needs, such as engineering and technology.

88. A: Archimedes, a Greek thinker, contributed to many fields of study during his lifetime (287-212 BC). He studied and wrote about mathematics and various sciences such as physics, engineering, and astronomy. His studies of geometry and mathematics, combined with his observations of the physical world, yielded many inventions and scientific discoveries that have spanned thousands of years. Galilei (1564-1642 AD) is often hailed as the 'father of modern science,' having made significant inroads in the fields of astronomy and physics. Newton (1643-1727 AD), while best known for his Laws of Motion, was a respected figure in many branches of scientific study. Kuo (1031-1085) was a Chinese scientist famous for his work in geology, geomorphology (land formations), zoology, botany, and cartography, simply to name a few.

89. B: Biodiversity refers to the wide diversity of living things on our planet, all of which are interconnected and affect one another. These living organisms can be studied within a particular biome, ecosystem, or the Earth as a whole. If students plan to visit a site and keep field journals, then they will need to observe a diverse group of organisms in their natural environment. The local pond contains a complete individual ecosystem, including water cycles, rock cycles, animals and life cycles. The zoo, in choice A, contains diverse animal life, but these animals are not living in their natural environment. Choices C and D would be informative field trips, but do not provide the life systems relevant to the topic of biodiversity.

90. B: One of the key concepts of biodiversity is the interconnectedness of living things. If students are visiting a natural environment, they will observe plants, animals, air and water phenomenon, as well as any non-natural environmental factors. In keeping a field journal, students will deepen their understanding of all these factors. Ideally, they will also start to note the relationships between living things and understand that none of them would survive without the others. Noting the relationships and effects organisms have upon one another will be an important part of keeping their journals.

91. B: Biodiversity deals with living organisms and their interconnections within an environment. We know that the local pond is the best environment in which to observe a contained ecosystem. Gas-powered boats leave harmful chemicals in the pond water, which will be absorbed into the ground and by animals living in and around the water. Those animals will be contaminated with those chemicals, as will plants growing from the groundwater. By eliminating these chemical contaminants, the protected pond environment will host healthy and thriving species for many years to come.

92. B: A physical change refers to one in which the substance being acted upon maintains its chemical composition. Thus, any change in which a substance melts, freezes, or evaporates is a physical change, as is one in which the substance simply changes its shape. A chemical change is one in which the substance changes in chemical substance. The only choice in which a new chemical entity is formed is that in which rust forms on a nail.

93. B: All of the items in the box are objects designed to be put in motion. Bikes and skateboards need energy created by the rider's motions in order to move, while the other vehicles require fuel or electricity in order to move as they should. Discussing the ways in which these real-life items can be put into motion deepens students' relevant knowledge about energy sources and movement. Choices A and D are possible activities that could be used in class. However, these discussions are a bit less relevant to direct instruction than the correct answer choice, B.

94. B: Genetics encompasses the concept of traits and how certain traits are passed from parents to offspring. The traits listed in the left-hand column are commonly studied in the field of genetics, as they are passed down based upon combinations of recessive and dominant genes. Choices A and C are not directly related to the chart. Choice D refers to the process by which organisms adapt to the environment. However, the traits listed in this chart are not vital to the survival of a species, making choice B a better fit.

95. C: The top portion of the illustration shows the molecular structure of glucose, which is used by the body for energy in completing tasks like walking, talking or writing. Sucrose, in the bottom picture, is made up of one glucose molecule and one fructose molecule. Fructose is a foreign sugar that is converted to fat by the body and not used for any benefit. Therefore, glucose is the sugar used for energy in the body; sucrose does contain glucose, but also contains fructose which converts to fat.

96. D: Transpiration is part of the hydrologic cycle, or water cycle. In this cycle, water is re-used repetitively in the environment because it naturally changes form from liquid to gas and back again. During transpiration, water that has been absorbed by plants from the ground is released into the air as a vapor. This vapor cannot be seen or detected by humans without specialized equipment.

97. D: Most of the evaporation in the atmosphere comes from the earth's oceans. When water from the oceans evaporates, the temperature in those large bodies of water is reduced. When the oceans are cooler on their surfaces, the planet's temperatures are cooler. Without the cooling that evaporation affords, the earth itself would grow warmer and warmer, contributing to the greenhouse effect and global warming phenomena.

98. C: In order to change the structure and form of rocks, intense or sustained changes must occur. Plate tectonics cause intense heat and pressure to modify rock structures. The water cycle can affect cooling and erosion that will also affect this cycle. Volcanic eruptions lead to melting and re-forming in a more effective way than would global warming, which is a much more gradual process.

99. B: The five major categories listed above show generally accepted common themes in all sciences. That is, each category above would be applicable to any science: psychology, sociology, physics, life sciences, aeronautics, geology and so on. There are hundreds of branches of science with specific means and ends. These five concepts, however, are common to all scientific purposes.

Pedagogy

100. C: educators may legally accept gifts that are offered openly by students, parents, supervisors, etc., provided these gifts are offered to recognize or express appreciation for the educator's service. Gifts that influence an educator's professional judgment are prohibited. The code prohibits educators from interfering with the political rights of their colleagues, deceiving others with regard to the policies of the school district or educational institution, and revealing confidential student information (unless the disclosure is for a lawful professional purpose or is required by law).

101. A: IDEA requires schools to provide learning disabled students with a free and appropriate education, even if the student has been suspended or expelled from school for disciplinary reasons. Since some students have disabilities that cause them to misbehave, refusing to educate them on this basis would constitute discrimination. Choice C is not correct because the IDEA requires learning disabled students to be educated in the least restrictive environment possible, so many students are taught wholly or partly in general education classrooms with non-disabled students.

Choice D is incorrect because schools are required to pay for accommodations for learning disabled students.

102. B: The FERPA stipulates that parents of children under 18 can inspect and request amendments to their children's educational records on demand (B). However, once students reach the age of majority, they become "eligible students." This means that this right is transferred to them and their permission is required to disclose their educational records to anyone, including their parents. Written permission from parents or the eligible student is not required in order to disclose records to a school official with a legitimate educational interest (C) or to a school to which the student is transferring (D).

103. B: effective rules are usually stated positively. Stating rules negatively, as in answer A or especially D, proscribe specific behaviors, but by definition "allow" all other behaviors not discussed. Further, it sends students the message that they are expected to misbehave, and makes positive reinforcement difficult. (It makes more sense to say, "Class, you can play for 15 minutes because you did an excellent job of working quietly today," than to say, "You did a good job of not yelling and bothering other students, so you may play outside"). While it may be appropriate to phrase rules politely (C), simply doing this does not have the same impact as stating them positively.

104. B: When resolving behavior problems, teachers should strive to be consistent and objective (B). Consistency is important because students will not feel that they are being singled out and treated differently than other students, and objectivity is key because practicing it will prevent the teacher's own biases from affecting his or her students. Together, objectivity and consistency will help the teacher run the classroom fairly and earn students' respect. A is incorrect because teachers should avoid reacting judgmentally to behavior. This can aggravate behavior problems with students who conclude that the teacher just "doesn't like" them or "doesn't understand" them. While patience and collaboration maybe useful in dealing with behavior problems, they are not as important as consistency and objectivity because being patient and/or collaborative alone does not provide a mode for directly addressing the behavior (i.e., one could be patient and collaborative but still inconsistent and ineffective at solving the behavior problem).

105. A: intrinsic motivation can be fostered by helping students to develop a personal connection to and interest in the material they're learning. Intrinsic motivation refers to a person's desire to do something (like a hobby) without any apparent material motivation and without any threat of punishment should the activity not be done. In contrast, answer B refers to extrinsic motivation. This type of motivation propels a person to do something not because they enjoy the activity for its own sake, but because they fear punishment or desire rewards produced by that activity.

106. D: According to Piaget's theory, the distinction between people at the concrete operational stage (approximately 7-12 years of age) and the formal operational stage (approximately 12-16 years of age) of development is that Those in the concrete operational stage can think logically only with respect to concrete experiences, while those at the formal operational stage can reason in abstract and hypothetical terms. Children at the sensorimotor stage (birth to 2 years old) rely on their sensory perception and motor skills to learn and understand the world around them, and children at the preoperational stage (3-7) think in a literal, symbolic manner.

107. D: When a student's academic performance is poorer than what is predicted by IQ testing, this is often a sign of a learning disability, and indicates that a student should be considered for placement in special education services. Such a discrepancy may also be explained by behavior problems associated with emotional disabilities such as oppositional defiant disorder, or temporary strains associated with family or personal problems. A third possibility is that the student is struggling because of limited English proficiency, and a plan is needed to improve English skills so that the student can succeed in all academic areas.

108. B: As students enter adolescence, their social lives will most likely revolve around membership in a small social group that has a shared set of values and interests. While students maintain interest in family, they will increasingly choose to spend more time with friends. While violence is likely to affect the lives of some students, physical insecurity is not a predominant characteristic of most adolescents. Adolescents also begin to show an increased interest in their ethnic or cultural heritage as part of the identity-formation process.

109. A: exploring their own cultural heritage would directly impact the identity formation process (developing a set of personal values and goals). While such a project may also teach students tolerance if the projects are shared with the class, the actual process of researching one's own background would facilitate identity formation more than tolerance.

110. A: the teacher's most important responsibility is to create an accepting, non-judgmental classroom environment. Since homeless students attending school face many obstacles ranging from transience to lack of appropriate clothing and hygiene tools, they will be more likely to continue attending if they are accepted by their teachers and peers. Since the student is living in a shelter, the relevant social service agency is responsible for ensuring that the student is fed and clothed. Teachers are also not responsible for diagnosing mental illnesses, although the teacher should inform the student's parent or caseworker know if she suspects a problem. While the teacher may want to screen the student for possible learning disabilities, she should not assume that poor academic performance is the result of a disability. Homelessness often results in prolonged absence from school and emotional problems that interfere with learning, and these factors may explain poor performance.

111. C: Benji's behavior signals that he might be using illegal drugs. Students who begin using drugs may suddenly become more sluggish or more restless than usual, and they may begin experiencing abnormal sleep patterns that interfere with school attendance. Choice A is incorrect because learning disabilities do not usually develop "overnight," unless they are caused by an accident or acute medical condition. Benji's symptoms also do not fit the symptoms of depression (D). Also, such rapid and detrimental changes are not normal, even for adolescents whose minds and bodies are changing rapidly (B).

112. C: While bullying among boys is usually displayed by obvious teasing and even violence, girls tend to use bullying tactics that are more discreet. For example, girls might spread false rumors about each other or exclude certain individuals from social activities. While parents and teachers are less likely to notice this type of bullying, it can be just a damaging to the victim's self esteem as violence.

113. D: the teacher should help the students who are not using the Internet find low-cost Internet access and training in their community. While teachers can require students to purchase certain low-cost school supplies like pencils and paper, they cannot expect that all students have the same knowledge or access to more expensive technologies like computers with word processing software and the Internet. It would also be counterproductive to prevent students who do have computer access from using it, because this would hold back their learning. The best solution to this problem would be to try to help all students gain access to the Internet.

114. B: students who are learning English as a second language typically have normal or above-average intelligence, although their academic performance may suffer because most assignments directly or indirectly require English language skills. Because English Language Learners are typically of normal intelligence, and because being an English Language Learner is not considered a disability, these students cannot be referred for special education services unless they have a true learning disability (A). Further, cultural background has no bearing on intelligence, so D is incorrect.

115. C: the best approach would be for Mrs. Li to take the learning disabled students to a quiet area and facilitate a 15 minute group reading discussion while the other students write. Since the objective of the writing assignment is actually to assess the students' reading comprehension, not their writing ability, this can be accomplished orally as well as in writing. Although giving students more time to complete the assignment would be appropriate if this were an assignment assessing writing ability, it would be unfair to ask students to complete extra homework due to their learning disability if there is another assessment method readily available.

116. C: Mr. Robinson can achieve this objective using a theme-based unit. Theme-based units allow students to explore a topic of interest from many different perspectives, and use their reading, math, writing and reasoning skills to learn more about the topic. For example, in a theme-based unit about weather, students might learn how to use number lines by reading a thermometer, read about the devastating effects of severe weather, and write about a time that the weather affected their lives.

117. B: Since most of the students in Ms. Frank's class are auditory learners, she would reach the majority of her students by teaching them a song about the new concept that they're learning. Auditory learners remember and comprehend concepts best using their sense of hearing.

118. A: of the practices described here, providing opportunities for students to work cooperatively with peers is most likely to promote a productive classroom environment for middle-level students. The classroom environment should be planned and structured, as opposed to frequently changed (B), and students should be encouraged to work cooperatively, rather than independently (C). In addition, kinesthetic and active learning activities can be very beneficial for middle-level students (D).

119. A: If Mr. Stratton's goal is to ensure that students understand what is expected of them and that they are are able to complete the project on schedule, the best approach for him to take would be to explain how to do the research and set several 'checkpoints' before the final product is due. By explaining the research process, Mr. Stratton ensures that all students understand what they're expected to do. Setting checkpoints, (for example, asking students to submit a brief description of their project one month before it is due and asking them to submit a rough draft one week before it is due), Mr. Stratton can make sure that all of his students are on track to complete the project as scheduled.

120. C: is the best answer here. If Mrs. Frances wants to develop a theme-based unit that is interesting and relevant to her fifth grade students, the best approach would be to conduct an informal, open-ended survey to look for interests that her students share. This approach would allow Mrs. Frances to find a topic that would interest the broadest range of students. While presenting several topics for students to vote upon (D) would also come close to achieving this goal, it is a less desirable alternative because it artificially narrows the choices available to students by predetermining the options.

121. B: in order to help students make the transition to note-taking, the best approach would be to provide an outline of key words and points for students to fill in during the lecture, and gradually provide less and less detail in this outline until students are taking notes without assistance. Although the other strategies mentioned also have advantages, this approach is the best because it includes both a method for teaching note-taking techniques (students start out with a template of what notes should look like) and an opportunity to practice the skill.

122. B: The most effective strategy for Mr. Swanson to use would be to explain to the students that they have done a good job of improving their behavior, but that they can do even better. As a consequence, they now need to earn four check marks to get the reward, which is 45 minutes on the computer. This strategy has several advantages over the other options presented here. Unlike A and D, this strategy maintains consistency with the previous plan, and it also increases the reward in proportion to the expected improvement in behavior. C would not be effective because it increases the reward without requiring a commensurate improvement in behavior.

123. D: Ms. Swanson should explain to the parent that her daughter has missed several homework assignments, and offer to tell the parent about future assignments so that she can ensure that her daughter completes them. This answer is better than answer B, because it lays out a clear plan for correcting the problem. Answer C is not correct because teachers are permitted to discuss students' academic records with the students' parents as long as those students are under the age of 18. Answer A is also incorrect because failure to turn in homework assignments does not necessarily indicate that a student doesn't understand the course content. Other causes of the problem should be eliminated before academic remediation is pursued.

124. B: Mr. Fields is most likely to achieve his objective by assigning nightly homework problems that are peer-graded in class the next day, and going over the answers after the assignment is graded. This method offers two advantages: first, students receive immediate feedback on their performance that they can begin to apply to future assignments and tests; second, students have the opportunity to find out why they arrived at wrong answers when the teacher goes over the problems. This makes assessment a positive experience that helps students perform better in the future, rather than making it a negative experience that de-motivates students by making them feel powerless to improve their performance.

125. C: All of the sources used by the student, including the books, the newspaper, and the websites should be cited in the bibliography. Citations should be included for all sources that are used in a research paper.

126. C: The teacher should first discuss the problem with the special education teacher, who may have additional insight on the problem based on information in the student's Individualized Education Plan (IEP). Adjustments to the IEP may be necessary if current strategies are ineffective. The student's parents should also be notified about the problem, but the special education teacher should be informed about any problems first. Punishing a student with a behavioral disability through isolation or any other method must be done after discussions with the special education teacher in order to be effective, and may actually constitute discrimination if not implemented appropriately.

127. A: The teacher should press one for software. Hardware refers to the physical parts of a computer, like the monitor and the keyboard. Software is a term that describes the programs that allow the computer user to perform various functions like typing a document or creating a slide show.

128. A: In order to send Ellen electronic copies of paper worksheets, a scanner and email, a disc or flash drive would probably be needed, but a copy machine would not be necessary. The teachers could scan the documents using a scanner and send them as an email attachment or save them to a disc. The disc could then be sent home and Ellen could download the documents and print them out, or Ellen could open and print the email attachment.

129. D: Bookmarks are saved on a particular computer, so the students would not be able to access those bookmarked websites from home or from other computers within the school's media center. Enabling the computer's pop-up blocker, which prevents additional windows from automatically opening when other websites are opened, would not be necessary in order for bookmarks to function.

130. C: Mr. Ferris can use the change-tracking device in Microsoft Word to show the students how to improve their papers. Answer D is not correct, because Mr. Ferris could still track grammatical errors if the reports were in paper form. Answers A and B are not correct because, although these are advantages, they are not as helpful for assessment purposes as answer C.

131. B: In order to identify and resolve the problem, Mrs. Thomas' first step should be to consider whether there may be a problem with the assessment itself. Perhaps the assessment did not directly test the material that was covered, or perhaps the students were not given adequate time to complete the assessment. Only if Mrs. Thomas finds no problems with the test itself should she analyze the results to find out exactly which aspects of the material the students struggled with.

132. B: Team teaching, which involves a group of students rotating between roughly 2-5 different teachers, is advantageous for middle school students because they are easily overwhelmed by the need to frequently change classes and teachers. The team-teaching model provides more consistency in terms of classmates and teachers, gradually easing students into the more complex model used in high schools (B). Team teaching is also advantageous because it allows teachers to more easily coordinate interdisciplinary lessons (C), and it helps breed familiarity and support between teacher and student members of the team as well (D). Although a 25:1 student teacher ratio is recommended for teams, the model itself does not inherently reduce the number of students assigned to teachers (A).

133. C: Mrs. Ling should affirm the principal's concerns, but explain why she feels that avoiding the stigmatizing effect of ability grouping is more important than providing enrichment opportunities for high-achieving students. This method would be more effective than simply stating her opinion (A), because it addresses the fact that both her own and the principal's opinions are based on important, but competing, values. In order to change the principal's mind, she must explain why she feels that the value she is advocating (avoiding stigmatization) is more important than the value advocated by the principal (providing unlimited learning opportunities for all students).

134. A: the best way to create effective thematic units would be to have each subject teacher create a curriculum map for the year, and compare these maps to find themes, content and skills that are similar. Designing the thematic units first, and then having teachers adjust their lesson plans to accommodate them (B) would not be effective because the units would be designed without reference to the learning objectives that the teachers have in place for their students that year. Having just one teacher design the units (D), or having students choose the units (C) would present a similar problem. It is crucial that thematic units be designed in response to a clearly outlined curriculum map that details what the students should learn and in what order. Otherwise, learning objectives may be overlooked or material may be presented in an illogical sequence that hampers learning.

135. D: In order to assess the effectiveness of the team-teaching model, the teachers should compare their sixth grade students' performance this year with the performance of students in previous years where team teaching was not used. This will eliminate the possibility of differences among schools that would be present if they compared their students to students in other schools (C). It would also rule out the possibility that performance typically increases in sixth grade relative to previous years, which would be present if they only compared the students' performance this year to their performance in previous year. They should also consider the performance history of this particular group of sixth graders relative to previous groups to rule out the possibility that this group of students' performance has been higher or lower overall.

136. C: The best way for Mr. Aaron to ensure that the discussion helps students achieve the learning objectives he has set forth would be to remind the students about rules for respectful discussion, and then provide the students with a list of questions that they discuss in small groups. By providing rules for the discussion, Mr. Aaron both instructs the students in the skill of respectful discussion and gives students the opportunity to practice it. By providing a list of questions and breaking the students into small groups, Mr. Aaron ensures that all students will have the opportunity to participate in the discussion, and provides the small groups with a guide so that they can stay on track without his immediate presence.

137. B: The students are "natural leaders" because they have a great deal of interpersonal intelligence, and Mr. Aaron should spread these students throughout the groups so that they can help facilitate discussion. Students that have exceptional interpersonal intelligence tend to be more outspoken and confident than their peers, but this does not mean that they are overbearing. To the contrary, they tend to be good at mediating and interacting with different types of people, and so it is likely that they would be effective discussion leaders.

138. C: Mr. Aaron would most likely appeal to Lev Vygotsky's socio-cultural theory of learning to explain the effectiveness of including discussion in his class sessions. Vygotsky argued that learning is a social process, and full intellectual development is not possible without social interaction with instructors (parents, teachers, etc.) and peers (collaborative learning). Mr. Aaron could point out that language arts students cannot learn to fully comprehend the texts they read without discussing their reading in a social setting.

139. D: Mr. Aaron should group the students by determining their personal intelligence profiles (musical, interpersonal, mathematical, verbal, etc.) and assigning students with similar strengths to the same groups so that they can choose a project that fits with their abilities. This method will ensure that all students can contribute effectively to the group and take pride in the group's work while showcasing their own talents.

140. A: Mr. Aaron should give all students in the group the opportunity to confidentially rate the contributions of their fellow group members, and give lower grades to students who are rated lower by the members of their group. This approach will give each student an incentive to contribute equally, because they can receive a lower grade if they do not contribute. This method would allow Mr. Aaron to grade fairly in cases where certain students fail to contribute.

141. C: Ms. Schneider should take the paraprofessional aside and explain her concerns. She should attempt to find out what is causing the behavior, and help the paraprofessional find a way to improve his performance. She should only begin approaching others regarding the problem after she has discussed the problem directly with the paraprofessional and given him a chance to improve his performance.

142. D: Mrs. Alexander should explain the fact that the class has fallen behind in preparing for an upcoming standardized test, but that she would like to schedule a time for the parent's presentation after the test. This way, all students will have the opportunity to hear the presentation, but the presentation will not detract from the students' ability to pass the standardized test.

143. B: The teachers should ask the students to leave their tests at their desks and follow the usual fire evacuation procedures without discussing the test. Students should always follow safety procedures, but if the test is to be resumed after the school building is cleared, it is important to ensure that students do not discuss the test or look at other students' tests.

144. A: The teacher should give the student a new test booklet with the same form number to use for the remainder of the test, and transcribe the student's responses from the torn booklet to the new booklet after the test. Asking the student to transcribe the answers during the test would affect her performance, but the answers must be transcribed because a torn booklet cannot be scored and two booklets cannot be scored together.

145. C: A scaled score is most useful for comparing students' performance across different administrations of the same test. (For example, comparing this year's sixth graders to last year's, or comparing the performance of students at different schools who took different versions of the same test. Raw scores simply indicate the number of questions a student answered correctly (A), and can only be used to compare students' performance on that specific version of the assessment.

146. B: This information will help the teachers plan their instruction based on the strengths and needs of the incoming students. Standardized test information should not be the sole basis on which students are given remedial instruction (A); their class performance should be strongly considered as well. D is incorrect because team teaching can be effective regardless of how well or poorly students perform on standardized tests, and C is incorrect because the decision to repeat a grade typically does not involve a student's future teachers, and should not be based solely on standardized test results.

147. D: The teachers' best option for improving students' overall performance on the test, including students who are not struggling with math, would be to find creative ways to incorporate math instruction into other subject areas, and to offer optional math tutoring during lunch and after school. This approach includes all students, so that students who are meeting the standard also have the opportunity to improve their performance. In addition, it does not detract from students' learning in other critical subject areas, or deprive students who are performing satisfactorily of math instruction.

148. C: The teacher can most effectively lead the discussion by engaging in another activity like writing on the board while waiting for the students to compose their answers. This action removes the pressure that the students feel and allows them time to remember the answer and compose their explanation. While waiting is important, two minutes (answer B) is probably too long, and calling on a student immediately will only make that student feel uncomfortable.

149. C: The teacher should try rephrasing the question before telling students the answer. Often, students fail to answer because they simply don't understand what information the teacher is looking for, rather than because they actually don't know the information. The teacher might try asking the question from a different angle, providing a hint, or using different terminology.

150. A: Learner-centered assessment provides alternatives that allow different students to be assessed differently. Although student participation in assessment creation (D) is also an important part of learner-centered assessment, a multiple choice test does not reflect the goals of learner-centered assessment because it does not provide an authentic assessment experience.

How to Overcome Test Anxiety

Just the thought of taking a test is enough to make most people a little nervous. A test is an important event that can have a long-term impact on your future, so it's important to take it seriously and it's natural to feel anxious about performing well. But just because anxiety is normal, that doesn't mean that it's helpful in test taking, or that you should simply accept it as part of your life. Anxiety can have a variety of effects. These effects can be mild, like making you feel slightly nervous, or severe, like blocking your ability to focus or remember even a simple detail.

If you experience test anxiety—whether severe or mild—it's important to know how to beat it. To discover this, first you need to understand what causes test anxiety.

Causes of Test Anxiety

While we often think of anxiety as an uncontrollable emotional state, it can actually be caused by simple, practical things. One of the most common causes of test anxiety is that a person does not feel adequately prepared for their test. This feeling can be the result of many different issues such as poor study habits or lack of organization, but the most common culprit is time management. Starting to study too late, failing to organize your study time to cover all of the material, or being distracted while you study will mean that you're not well prepared for the test. This may lead to cramming the night before, which will cause you to be physically and mentally exhausted for the test. Poor time management also contributes to feelings of stress, fear, and hopelessness as you realize you are not well prepared but don't know what to do about it.

Other times, test anxiety is not related to your preparation for the test but comes from unresolved fear. This may be a past failure on a test, or poor performance on tests in general. It may come from comparing yourself to others who seem to be performing better or from the stress of living up to expectations. Anxiety may be driven by fears of the future—how failure on this test would affect your educational and career goals. These fears are often completely irrational, but they can still negatively impact your test performance.

Review Video: 3 Reasons You Have Test Anxiety
Visit mometrix.com/academy and enter code: 428468

Elements of Test Anxiety

As mentioned earlier, test anxiety is considered to be an emotional state, but it has physical and mental components as well. Sometimes you may not even realize that you are suffering from test anxiety until you notice the physical symptoms. These can include trembling hands, rapid heartbeat, sweating, nausea, and tense muscles. Extreme anxiety may lead to fainting or vomiting. Obviously, any of these symptoms can have a negative impact on testing. It is important to recognize them as soon as they begin to occur so that you can address the problem before it damages your performance.

Review Video: 3 Ways to Tell You Have Test Anxiety
Visit mometrix.com/academy and enter code: 927847

The mental components of test anxiety include trouble focusing and inability to remember learned information. During a test, your mind is on high alert, which can help you recall information and stay focused for an extended period of time. However, anxiety interferes with your mind's natural processes, causing you to blank out, even on the questions you know well. The strain of testing during anxiety makes it difficult to stay focused, especially on a test that may take several hours. Extreme anxiety can take a huge mental toll, making it difficult not only to recall test information but even to understand the test questions or pull your thoughts together.

Review Video: How Test Anxiety Affects Memory
Visit mometrix.com/academy and enter code: 609003

Effects of Test Anxiety

Test anxiety is like a disease—if left untreated, it will get progressively worse. Anxiety leads to poor performance, and this reinforces the feelings of fear and failure, which in turn lead to poor performances on subsequent tests. It can grow from a mild nervousness to a crippling condition. If allowed to progress, test anxiety can have a big impact on your schooling, and consequently on your future.

Test anxiety can spread to other parts of your life. Anxiety on tests can become anxiety in any stressful situation, and blanking on a test can turn into panicking in a job situation. But fortunately, you don't have to let anxiety rule your testing and determine your grades. There are a number of relatively simple steps you can take to move past anxiety and function normally on a test and in the rest of life.

Review Video: How Test Anxiety Impacts Your Grades
Visit mometrix.com/academy and enter code: 939819

Physical Steps for Beating Test Anxiety

While test anxiety is a serious problem, the good news is that it can be overcome. It doesn't have to control your ability to think and remember information. While it may take time, you can begin taking steps today to beat anxiety.

Just as your first hint that you may be struggling with anxiety comes from the physical symptoms, the first step to treating it is also physical. Rest is crucial for having a clear, strong mind. If you are tired, it is much easier to give in to anxiety. But if you establish good sleep habits, your body and mind will be ready to perform optimally, without the strain of exhaustion. Additionally, sleeping well helps you to retain information better, so you're more likely to recall the answers when you see the test questions.

Getting good sleep means more than going to bed on time. It's important to allow your brain time to relax. Take study breaks from time to time so it doesn't get overworked, and don't study right before bed. Take time to rest your mind before trying to rest your body, or you may find it difficult to fall asleep.

Review Video: The Importance of Sleep for Your Brain
Visit mometrix.com/academy and enter code: 319338

Along with sleep, other aspects of physical health are important in preparing for a test. Good nutrition is vital for good brain function. Sugary foods and drinks may give a burst of energy but this burst is followed by a crash, both physically and emotionally. Instead, fuel your body with protein and vitamin-rich foods.

Also, drink plenty of water. Dehydration can lead to headaches and exhaustion, especially if your brain is already under stress from the rigors of the test. Particularly if your test is a long one, drink water during the breaks. And if possible, take an energy-boosting snack to eat between sections.

Review Video: How Diet Can Affect your Mood
Visit mometrix.com/academy and enter code: 624317

Along with sleep and diet, a third important part of physical health is exercise. Maintaining a steady workout schedule is helpful, but even taking 5-minute study breaks to walk can help get your blood pumping faster and clear your head. Exercise also releases endorphins, which contribute to a positive feeling and can help combat test anxiety.

When you nurture your physical health, you are also contributing to your mental health. If your body is healthy, your mind is much more likely to be healthy as well. So take time to rest, nourish your body with healthy food and water, and get moving as much as possible. Taking these physical steps will make you stronger and more able to take the mental steps necessary to overcome test anxiety.

Mental Steps for Beating Test Anxiety

Working on the mental side of test anxiety can be more challenging, but as with the physical side, there are clear steps you can take to overcome it. As mentioned earlier, test anxiety often stems from lack of preparation, so the obvious solution is to prepare for the test. Effective studying may be the most important weapon you have for beating test anxiety, but you can and should employ several other mental tools to combat fear.

First, boost your confidence by reminding yourself of past success—tests or projects that you aced. If you're putting as much effort into preparing for this test as you did for those, there's no reason you should expect to fail here. Work hard to prepare; then trust your preparation.

Second, surround yourself with encouraging people. It can be helpful to find a study group, but be sure that the people you're around will encourage a positive attitude. If you spend time with others who are anxious or cynical, this will only contribute to your own anxiety. Look for others who are motivated to study hard from a desire to succeed, not from a fear of failure.

Third, reward yourself. A test is physically and mentally tiring, even without anxiety, and it can be helpful to have something to look forward to. Plan an activity following the test, regardless of the outcome, such as going to a movie or getting ice cream.

When you are taking the test, if you find yourself beginning to feel anxious, remind yourself that you know the material. Visualize successfully completing the test. Then take a few deep, relaxing breaths and return to it. Work through the questions carefully but with confidence, knowing that you are capable of succeeding.

Developing a healthy mental approach to test taking will also aid in other areas of life. Test anxiety affects more than just the actual test—it can be damaging to your mental health and even contribute to depression. It's important to beat test anxiety before it becomes a problem for more than testing.

Review Video: Test Anxiety and Depression
Visit mometrix.com/academy and enter code: 904704

Study Strategy

Being prepared for the test is necessary to combat anxiety, but what does being prepared look like? You may study for hours on end and still not feel prepared. What you need is a strategy for test prep. The next few pages outline our recommended steps to help you plan out and conquer the challenge of preparation.

Step 1: Scope Out the Test

Learn everything you can about the format (multiple choice, essay, etc.) and what will be on the test. Gather any study materials, course outlines, or sample exams that may be available. Not only will this help you to prepare, but knowing what to expect can help to alleviate test anxiety.

Step 2: Map Out the Material

Look through the textbook or study guide and make note of how many chapters or sections it has. Then divide these over the time you have. For example, if a book has 15 chapters and you have five days to study, you need to cover three chapters each day. Even better, if you have the time, leave an extra day at the end for overall review after you have gone through the material in depth.

If time is limited, you may need to prioritize the material. Look through it and make note of which sections you think you already have a good grasp on, and which need review. While you are studying, skim quickly through the familiar sections and take more time on the challenging parts. Write out your plan so you don't get lost as you go. Having a written plan also helps you feel more in control of the study, so anxiety is less likely to arise from feeling overwhelmed at the amount to cover.

Step 3: Gather Your Tools

Decide what study method works best for you. Do you prefer to highlight in the book as you study and then go back over the highlighted portions? Or do you type out notes of the important information? Or is it helpful to make flashcards that you can carry with you? Assemble the pens, index cards, highlighters, post-it notes, and any other materials you may need so you won't be distracted by getting up to find things while you study.

If you're having a hard time retaining the information or organizing your notes, experiment with different methods. For example, try color-coding by subject with colored pens, highlighters, or post-it notes. If you learn better by hearing, try recording yourself reading your notes so you can listen while in the car, working out, or simply sitting at your desk. Ask a friend to quiz you from your flashcards, or try teaching someone the material to solidify it in your mind.

Step 4: Create Your Environment

It's important to avoid distractions while you study. This includes both the obvious distractions like visitors and the subtle distractions like an uncomfortable chair (or a too-comfortable couch that makes you want to fall asleep). Set up the best study environment possible: good lighting and a comfortable work area. If background music helps you focus, you may want to turn it on, but otherwise keep the room quiet. If you are using a computer to take notes, be sure you don't have any other windows open, especially applications like social media, games, or anything else that could distract you. Silence your phone and turn off notifications. Be sure to keep water close by so you stay hydrated while you study (but avoid unhealthy drinks and snacks).

Also, take into account the best time of day to study. Are you freshest first thing in the morning? Try to set aside some time then to work through the material. Is your mind clearer in the afternoon or evening? Schedule your study session then. Another method is to study at the same time of day that you will take the test, so that your brain gets used to working on the material at that time and will be ready to focus at test time.

STEP 5: STUDY!

Once you have done all the study preparation, it's time to settle into the actual studying. Sit down, take a few moments to settle your mind so you can focus, and begin to follow your study plan. Don't give in to distractions or let yourself procrastinate. This is your time to prepare so you'll be ready to fearlessly approach the test. Make the most of the time and stay focused.

Of course, you don't want to burn out. If you study too long you may find that you're not retaining the information very well. Take regular study breaks. For example, taking five minutes out of every hour to walk briskly, breathing deeply and swinging your arms, can help your mind stay fresh.

As you get to the end of each chapter or section, it's a good idea to do a quick review. Remind yourself of what you learned and work on any difficult parts. When you feel that you've mastered the material, move on to the next part. At the end of your study session, briefly skim through your notes again.

But while review is helpful, cramming last minute is NOT. If at all possible, work ahead so that you won't need to fit all your study into the last day. Cramming overloads your brain with more information than it can process and retain, and your tired mind may struggle to recall even previously learned information when it is overwhelmed with last-minute study. Also, the urgent nature of cramming and the stress placed on your brain contribute to anxiety. You'll be more likely to go to the test feeling unprepared and having trouble thinking clearly.

So don't cram, and don't stay up late before the test, even just to review your notes at a leisurely pace. Your brain needs rest more than it needs to go over the information again. In fact, plan to finish your studies by noon or early afternoon the day before the test. Give your brain the rest of the day to relax or focus on other things, and get a good night's sleep. Then you will be fresh for the test and better able to recall what you've studied.

STEP 6: TAKE A PRACTICE TEST

Many courses offer sample tests, either online or in the study materials. This is an excellent resource to check whether you have mastered the material, as well as to prepare for the test format and environment.

Check the test format ahead of time: the number of questions, the type (multiple choice, free response, etc.), and the time limit. Then create a plan for working through them. For example, if you have 30 minutes to take a 60-question test, your limit is 30 seconds per question. Spend less time on the questions you know well so that you can take more time on the difficult ones.

If you have time to take several practice tests, take the first one open book, with no time limit. Work through the questions at your own pace and make sure you fully understand them. Gradually work up to taking a test under test conditions: sit at a desk with all study materials put away and set a timer. Pace yourself to make sure you finish the test with time to spare and go back to check your answers if you have time.

After each test, check your answers. On the questions you missed, be sure you understand why you missed them. Did you misread the question (tests can use tricky wording)? Did you forget the information? Or was it something you hadn't learned? Go back and study any shaky areas that the practice tests reveal.

Taking these tests not only helps with your grade, but also aids in combating test anxiety. If you're already used to the test conditions, you're less likely to worry about it, and working through tests until you're scoring well gives you a confidence boost. Go through the practice tests until you feel comfortable, and then you can go into the test knowing that you're ready for it.

Test Tips

On test day, you should be confident, knowing that you've prepared well and are ready to answer the questions. But aside from preparation, there are several test day strategies you can employ to maximize your performance.

First, as stated before, get a good night's sleep the night before the test (and for several nights before that, if possible). Go into the test with a fresh, alert mind rather than staying up late to study.

Try not to change too much about your normal routine on the day of the test. It's important to eat a nutritious breakfast, but if you normally don't eat breakfast at all, consider eating just a protein bar. If you're a coffee drinker, go ahead and have your normal coffee. Just make sure you time it so that the caffeine doesn't wear off right in the middle of your test. Avoid sugary beverages, and drink enough water to stay hydrated but not so much that you need a restroom break 10 minutes into the test. If your test isn't first thing in the morning, consider going for a walk or doing a light workout before the test to get your blood flowing.

Allow yourself enough time to get ready, and leave for the test with plenty of time to spare so you won't have the anxiety of scrambling to arrive in time. Another reason to be early is to select a good seat. It's helpful to sit away from doors and windows, which can be distracting. Find a good seat, get out your supplies, and settle your mind before the test begins.

When the test begins, start by going over the instructions carefully, even if you already know what to expect. Make sure you avoid any careless mistakes by following the directions.

Then begin working through the questions, pacing yourself as you've practiced. If you're not sure on an answer, don't spend too much time on it, and don't let it shake your confidence. Either skip it and come back later, or eliminate as many wrong answers as possible and guess among the remaining ones. Don't dwell on these questions as you continue—put them out of your mind and focus on what lies ahead.

Be sure to read all of the answer choices, even if you're sure the first one is the right answer. Sometimes you'll find a better one if you keep reading. But don't second-guess yourself if you do immediately know the answer. Your gut instinct is usually right. Don't let test anxiety rob you of the information you know.

If you have time at the end of the test (and if the test format allows), go back and review your answers. Be cautious about changing any, since your first instinct tends to be correct, but make sure you didn't misread any of the questions or accidentally mark the wrong answer choice. Look over any you skipped and make an educated guess.

At the end, leave the test feeling confident. You've done your best, so don't waste time worrying about your performance or wishing you could change anything. Instead, celebrate the successful completion of this test. And finally, use this test to learn how to deal with anxiety even better next time.

Review Video: 5 Tips to Beat Test Anxiety
Visit mometrix.com/academy and enter code: 570656

Important Qualification

Not all anxiety is created equal. If your test anxiety is causing major issues in your life beyond the classroom or testing center, or if you are experiencing troubling physical symptoms related to your anxiety, it may be a sign of a serious physiological or psychological condition. If this sounds like your situation, we strongly encourage you to seek professional help.

How to Overcome Your Fear of Math

Not again. You're sitting in math class, look down at your test, and immediately start to panic. Your stomach is in knots, your heart is racing, and you break out in a cold sweat. You're staring at the paper, but everything looks like it's written in a foreign language. Even though you studied, you're blanking out on how to begin solving these problems.

Does this sound familiar? If so, then you're not alone! You may be like millions of other people who experience math anxiety. Anxiety about performing well in math is a common experience for students of all ages. In this article, we'll discuss what math anxiety is, common misconceptions about learning math, and tips and strategies for overcoming math anxiety.

What Is Math Anxiety?

Psychologist Mark H. Ashcraft explains math anxiety as a feeling of tension, apprehension, or fear that interferes with math performance. Having math anxiety negatively impacts people's beliefs about themselves and what they can achieve. It hinders achievement within the math classroom and affects the successful application of mathematics in the real world.

Symptoms and Signs of Math Anxiety

To overcome math anxiety, you must recognize its symptoms. Becoming aware of the signs of math anxiety is the first step in addressing and resolving these fears.

Negative Self-Talk

If you have math anxiety, you've most likely said at least one of these statements to yourself:

- "I hate math."
- "I'm not good at math."
- "I'm not a math person."

The way we speak to ourselves and think about ourselves matters. Our thoughts become our words, our words become our actions, and our actions become our habits. Thinking negatively about math creates a self-fulfilling prophecy. In other words, if you take an idea as a fact, then it will come true because your behaviors will align to match it.

Avoidance

Some people who are fearful or anxious about math will tend to avoid it altogether. Avoidance can manifest in the following ways:

- Lack of engagement with math content
- Not completing homework and other assignments
- Not asking for help when needed
- Skipping class
- Avoiding math-related courses and activities

Avoidance is one of the most harmful impacts of math anxiety. If you steer clear of math at all costs, then you can't set yourself up for the success you deserve.

Lack of Motivation

Students with math anxiety may experience a lack of motivation. They may struggle to find the incentive to get engaged with what they view as a frightening subject. These students are often overwhelmed, making it difficult for them to complete or even start math assignments.

Procrastination

Another symptom of math anxiety is procrastination. Students may voluntarily delay or postpone their classwork and assignments, even if they know there will be a negative consequence for doing so. Additionally, they may choose to wait until the last minute to start projects and homework, even when they know they need more time to put forth their best effort.

Physiological Reactions

Many people with a fear of math experience physiological side effects. These may include an increase in heart rate, sweatiness, shakiness, nausea, and irregular breathing. These symptoms make it difficult to focus on the math content, causing the student even more stress and fear.

Strong Emotional Responses

Math anxiety also affects people on an emotional level. Responding to math content with strong emotions such as panic, anger, or despair can be a sign of math anxiety.

Low Test Scores and Performance

Low achievement can be both a symptom and a cause of math anxiety. When someone does not take the steps needed to perform well on tests and assessments, they are less likely to pass. The more they perform poorly, the more they accept this poor performance as a fact that can't be changed.

Feeling Alone

People who experience math anxiety feel like they are the only ones struggling, even if the math they are working on is challenging to many people. Feeling isolated in what they perceive as failure can trigger tension or nervousness.

Feeling of Permanency

Math anxiety can feel very permanent. You may assume that you are naturally bad at math and always will be. Viewing math as a natural ability rather than a skill that can be learned causes people to believe that nothing will help them improve. They take their current math abilities as fact and assume that they can't be changed. As a result, they give up, stop trying to improve, and avoid engaging with math altogether.

Lack of Confidence

People with low self-confidence in math tend to feel awkward and incompetent when asked to solve a math problem. They don't feel comfortable taking chances or risks when problem-solving because they second-guess themselves and assume they are incorrect. They don't trust in their ability to learn the content and solve problems correctly.

Panic

A general sense of unexplained panic is also a sign of math anxiety. You may feel a sudden sense of fear that triggers physical reactions, even when there is no apparent reason for such a response.

CAUSES OF MATH ANXIETY

Math anxiety can start at a young age and may have one or more underlying causes. Common causes of math anxiety include the following:

THE ATTITUDE OF PARENTS OR GUARDIANS

Parents often put pressure on their children to perform well in school. Although their intentions are usually good, this pressure can lead to anxiety, especially if the student is struggling with a subject or class.

Perhaps your parents or others in your life hold negative predispositions about math based on their own experiences. For instance, if your mother once claimed she was not good at math, then you might have incorrectly interpreted this as a predisposed trait that was passed down to you.

TEACHER INFLUENCE

Students often pick up on their teachers' attitudes about the content being taught. If a teacher is happy and excited about math, students are more likely to mirror these emotions. However, if a teacher lacks enthusiasm or genuine interest, then students are more inclined to disengage.

Teachers have a responsibility to cultivate a welcoming classroom culture that is accepting of mistakes. When teachers blame students for not understanding a concept, they create a hostile classroom environment where mistakes are not tolerated. This tension increases student stress and anxiety, creating conditions that are not conducive to inquiry and learning. Instead, when teachers normalize mistakes as a natural part of the problem-solving process, they give their students the freedom to explore and grapple with the math content. In such an environment, students feel comfortable taking chances because they are not afraid of being wrong.

Students need teachers that can help when they're having problems understanding difficult concepts. In doing so, educators may need to change how they teach the content. Since different people have unique learning styles, it's the job of the teacher to adapt to the needs of each student. Additionally, teachers should encourage students to explore alternate problem-solving strategies, even if it's not the preferred method of the educator.

FEAR OF BEING WRONG

Embarrassing situations can be traumatic, especially for young children and adolescents. These experiences can stay with people through their adult lives. Those with math anxiety may experience a fear of being wrong, especially in front of a group of peers. This fear can be paralyzing, interfering with the student's concentration and ability to focus on the problem at hand.

TIMED ASSESSMENTS

Timed assessments can help improve math fluency, but they often create unnecessary pressure for students to complete an unrealistic number of problems within a specified timeframe. Many studies have shown that timed assessments often result in increased levels of anxiety, reducing a student's overall competence and ability to problem-solve.

Debunking Math Myths

There are lots of myths about math that are related to the causes and development of math-related anxiety. Although these myths have been proven to be false, many people take them as fact. Let's go over a few of the most common myths about learning math.

MYTH: MEN ARE BETTER AT MATH THAN WOMEN

Math has a reputation for being a male-dominant subject, but this doesn't mean that men are inherently better at math than women. Many famous mathematical discoveries have been made by women. Katherine Johnson, Dame Mary Lucy Cartwright, and Marjorie Lee Brown are just a few of the many famous women mathematicians. Expecting to be good or bad at math because of your gender sets you up for stress and confusion. Math is a skill that can be learned, just like cooking or riding a bike.

MYTH: THERE IS ONLY ONE GOOD WAY TO SOLVE MATH PROBLEMS

There are many ways to get the correct answer when it comes to math. No two people have the same brain, so everyone takes a slightly different approach to problem-solving. Moreover, there isn't one way of problem-solving that's superior to another. Your way of working through a problem might differ from someone else's, and that is okay. Math can be a highly individualized process, so the best method for you should be the one that makes you feel the most comfortable and makes the most sense to you.

MYTH: MATH REQUIRES A GOOD MEMORY

For many years, mathematics was taught through memorization. However, learning in such a way hinders the development of critical thinking and conceptual understanding. These skill sets are much more valuable than basic memorization. For instance, you might be great at memorizing mathematical formulas, but if you don't understand what they mean, then you can't apply them to different scenarios in the real world. When a student is working from memory, they are limited in the strategies available to them to problem-solve. In other words, they assume there is only one correct way to do the math, which is the method they memorized. Having a variety of problem-solving options can help students figure out which method works best for them. Additionally, it provides students with a better understanding of how and why certain mathematical strategies work. While memorization can be helpful in some instances, it is not an absolute requirement for mathematicians.

MYTH: MATH IS NOT CREATIVE

Math requires imagination and intuition. Contrary to popular belief, it is a highly creative field. Mathematical creativity can help in developing new ways to think about and solve problems. Many people incorrectly assume that all things are either creative or analytical. However, this black-and-white view is limiting because the field of mathematics involves both creativity and logic.

MYTH: MATH ISN'T SUPPOSED TO BE FUN

Whoever told you that math isn't supposed to be fun is a liar. There are tons of math-based activities and games that foster friendly competition and engagement. Math is often best learned through play, and lots of mobile apps and computer games exemplify this.

Additionally, math can be an exceptionally collaborative and social experience. Studying or working through problems with a friend often makes the process a lot more fun. The excitement and satisfaction of solving a difficult problem with others is quite rewarding. Math can be fun if you look for ways to make it more collaborative and enjoyable.

Myth: Not Everyone Is Capable of Learning Math

There's no such thing as a "math person." Although many people think that you're either good at math or you're not, this is simply not true. Everyone is capable of learning and applying mathematics. However, not everyone learns the same way. Since each person has a different learning style, the trick is to find the strategies and learning tools that work best for you. Some people learn best through hands-on experiences, and others find success through the use of visual aids. Others are auditory learners and learn best by hearing and listening. When people are overwhelmed or feel that math is too hard, it's often because they haven't found the learning strategy that works best for them.

Myth: Good Mathematicians Work Quickly and Never Make Mistakes

There is no prize for finishing first in math. It's not a race, and speed isn't a measure of your ability. Good mathematicians take their time to ensure their work is accurate. As you gain more experience and practice, you will naturally become faster and more confident.

Additionally, everyone makes mistakes, including good mathematicians. Mistakes are a normal part of the problem-solving process, and they're not a bad thing. The important thing is that we take the time to learn from our mistakes, understand where our misconceptions are, and move forward.

Myth: You Don't Need Math in the Real World

Our day-to-day lives are so infused with mathematical concepts that we often don't even realize when we're using math in the real world. In fact, most people tend to underestimate how much we do math in our everyday lives. It's involved in an enormous variety of daily activities such as shopping, baking, finances, and gardening, as well as in many careers, including architecture, nursing, design, and sales.

Tips and Strategies for Overcoming Math Anxiety

If your anxiety is getting in the way of your level of mathematical engagement, then there are lots of steps you can take. Check out the strategies below to start building confidence in math today.

Focus on Understanding, Not Memorization

Don't drive yourself crazy trying to memorize every single formula or mathematical process. Instead, shift your attention to understanding concepts. Those who prioritize memorization over conceptual understanding tend to have lower achievement levels in math. Students who memorize may be able to complete some math, but they don't understand the process well enough to apply it to different situations. Memorization comes with time and practice, but it won't help alleviate math anxiety. On the other hand, conceptual understanding will give you the building blocks of knowledge you need to build up your confidence.

Replace Negative Self-Talk with Positive Self-Talk

Start to notice how you think about yourself. Whenever you catch yourself thinking something negative, try replacing that thought with a positive affirmation. Instead of continuing the negative thought, pause to reframe the situation. For ideas on how to get started, take a look at the table below:

Instead of thinking...	Try thinking...
"I can't do this math." "I'm not a math person."	"I'm up for the challenge, and I'm training my brain in math."
"This problem is too hard."	"This problem is hard, so this might take some time and effort. I know I can do this."
"I give up."	"What strategies can help me solve this problem?"
"I made a mistake, so I'm not good at this."	"Everyone makes mistakes. Mistakes help me to grow and understand."
"I'll never be smart enough."	"I can figure this out, and I am smart enough."

Practice Mindfulness

Practicing mindfulness and focusing on your breathing can help alleviate some of the physical symptoms of math anxiety. By taking deep breaths, you can remind your nervous system that you are not in immediate danger. Doing so will reduce your heart rate and help with any irregular breathing or shakiness. Taking the edge off of the physiological effects of anxiety will clear your mind, allowing your brain to focus its energy on problem-solving.

Do Some Math Every Day

Think about learning math as if you were learning a foreign language. If you don't use it, you lose it. If you don't practice your math skills regularly, you'll have a harder time achieving comprehension and fluency. Set some amount of time aside each day, even if it's just for a few minutes, to practice. It might take some discipline to build a habit around this, but doing so will help increase your mathematical self-assurance.

Use All of Your Resources

Everyone has a different learning style, and there are plenty of resources out there to support all learners. When you get stuck on a math problem, think about the tools you have access to, and use them when applicable. Such resources may include flashcards, graphic organizers, study guides, interactive notebooks, and peer study groups. All of these are great tools to accommodate your individual learning style. Finding the tools and resources that work for your learning style will give you the confidence you need to succeed.

Realize That You Aren't Alone

Remind yourself that lots of other people struggle with math anxiety, including teachers, nurses, and even successful mathematicians. You aren't the only one who panics when faced with a new or challenging problem. It's probably much more common than you think. Realizing that you aren't alone in your experience can help put some distance between yourself and the emotions you feel about math. It also helps to normalize the anxiety and shift your perspective.

Ask Questions

If there's a concept you don't understand and you've tried everything you can, then it's okay to ask for help! You can always ask your teacher or professor for help. If you're not learning math in a traditional classroom, you may want to join a study group, work with a tutor, or talk to your friends. More often than not, you aren't the only one of your peers who needs clarity on a mathematical concept. Seeking understanding is a great way to increase self-confidence in math.

Remember That There's More Than One Way To Solve A Problem

Since everyone learns differently, it's best to focus on understanding a math problem with an approach that makes sense to you. If the way it's being taught is confusing to you, don't give up. Instead, work to understand the problem using a different technique. There's almost always more than one problem-solving method when it comes to math. Don't get stressed if one of them doesn't make sense to you. Instead, shift your focus to what does make sense. Chances are high that you know more than you think you do.

Visualization

Visualization is the process of creating images in your mind's eye. Picture yourself as a successful, confident mathematician. Think about how you would feel and how you would behave. What would your work area look like? How would you organize your belongings? The more you focus on something, the more likely you are to achieve it. Visualizing teaches your brain that you can achieve whatever it is that you want. Thinking about success in mathematics will lead to acting like a successful mathematician. This, in turn, leads to actual success.

Focus on the Easiest Problems First

To increase your confidence when working on a math test or assignment, try solving the easiest problems first. Doing so will remind you that you are successful in math and that you do have what it takes. This process will increase your belief in yourself, giving you the confidence you need to tackle more complex problems.

Find a Support Group

A study buddy, tutor, or peer group can go a long way in decreasing math-related anxiety. Such support systems offer lots of benefits, including a safe place to ask questions, additional practice with mathematical concepts, and an understanding of other problem-solving explanations that may work better for you. Equipping yourself with a support group is one of the fastest ways to eliminate math anxiety.

Reward Yourself for Working Hard

Recognize the amount of effort you're putting in to overcome your math anxiety. It's not an easy task, so you deserve acknowledgement. Surround yourself with people who will provide you with the positive reinforcement you deserve.

Remember, You Can Do This!

Conquering a fear of math can be challenging, but there are lots of strategies that can help you out. Your own beliefs about your mathematical capabilities can limit your potential. Working toward a growth mindset can have a tremendous impact on decreasing math-related anxiety and building confidence. By knowing the symptoms of math anxiety and recognizing common misconceptions about learning math, you can develop a plan to address your fear of math. Utilizing the strategies discussed can help you overcome this anxiety and build the confidence you need to succeed.

Thank You

We at Mometrix would like to extend our heartfelt thanks to you, our friend and patron, for allowing us to play a part in your journey. It is a privilege to serve people from all walks of life who are unified in their commitment to building the best future they can for themselves.

The preparation you devote to these important testing milestones may be the most valuable educational opportunity you have for making a real difference in your life. We encourage you to put your heart into it—that feeling of succeeding, overcoming, and yes, conquering will be well worth the hours you've invested.

We want to hear your story, your struggles and your successes, and if you see any opportunities for us to improve our materials so we can help others even more effectively in the future, please share that with us as well. **The team at Mometrix would be absolutely thrilled to hear from you!** So please, send us an email (support@mometrix.com) and let's stay in touch.

If you'd like some additional help, check out these other resources we offer for your exam:
http://MometrixFlashcards.com/PraxisII

Additional Bonus Material

Due to our efforts to try to keep this book to a manageable length, we've created a link that will give you access to all of your additional bonus material.

Please visit http://www.mometrix.com/bonus948/priipaca4-8 to access the information.